THE TYPE V CITY

ROGER FULLINGTON SERIES IN ARCHITECTURE

THE TYPE V CITY

CODIFYING MATERIAL INEQUITY IN URBAN AMERICA

Jeana Ripple

University of Texas Press *Austin*

Publication of this book was made possible in part by support from Roger Fullington and a challenge grant from the National Endowment for the Humanities.

Printed in the United States of America
First edition, 2025

♾ The paper used in this book meets the minimum requirements of ANSI/NISO Z39.48-1992 (R1997) (Permanence of Paper).

Library of Congress Cataloging-in-Publication Data

Names: Ripple, Jeana, author.
Title: The type V city : codifying material inequity in urban America / Jeana Ripple.
Description: First edition. | Austin : University of Texas Press, 2025. | Includes bibliographical references and index.
Identifiers: LCCN 2024033902 (print) | LCCN 2024033903 (ebook)
ISBN 978-1-4773-3162-0 (hardcover)
ISBN 978-1-4773-3163-7 (pdf)
ISBN 978-1-4773-3164-4 (epub)
Subjects: LCSH: Building laws—United States—History. | Building laws—Social aspects—United States. | Building laws—Political aspects—United States—History. | Building laws—Environmental aspects—United States. | Building laws—Economic aspects—United States. | City planning and redevelopment law—United States—History. | Wooden-frame buildings—United States—History—Case studies. | Construction industry—Standards—Social aspects—United States. | Standards, Engineering—Social aspects—United States. | LCGFT: Case studies.
Classification: LCC KF5701 .R57 2025 (print) | LCC KF5701 (ebook) | DDC 343.7307/869—dc23/eng/20240731
LC record available at https://lccn.loc.gov/2024033902
LC ebook record available at https://lccn.loc.gov/2024033903

doi:10.7560/331620

To Chris

CONTENTS

ILLUSTRATIONS

PLATES

FIGURES

TABLES

ACRONYMS

ACS	American Community Survey
AFLCIO	American Federation of Labor and Congress of Industrial Organizations
AIA	American Institute of Architects
ANSI	American National Standards Institute
ASHRAE	American Society of Heating, Refrigerating, and Air-Conditioning Engineers
AWPA	American Wood Protection Association
BLL	Blood lead levels
BOCA	Building Officials and Code Administration
CBA	Community benefit agreement
CCA	Chromated copper arsenate
CDC	Centers for Disease Control
CPS	Current Population Survey, US Census
EEOC	Equal Employment Opportunity Commission
EPA	Environmental Protection Agency
ESG	Environmental, Social, Governance
FEMA	Federal Emergency Management Agency
FHA	Federal Housing Administration
GRESB	Global Real Estate Sustainability Benchmark
HOLC	Home Owners Loan Corporation
HUD	Department of Housing and Urban Development
IBC	International Building Codes
ICC	International Code Council
IRC	International Residential Code
LEED	Leadership in Energy and Environmental Design
NAAHB	National Association of American Home Builders
NFIP	National Flood Insurance Program
NGO	Nongovernmental organization
NIST	National Institute of Standards and Technology
OSB	Oriented Strand Board
PCP	Pentachlorophenol
RAPIDS	Registered Apprenticeship Partners Information Management Data System
SBC	Standard Building Code
SEC	US Securities and Exchange Commission
SVI	Social Vulnerability Index
UBC	Uniform Building Code
USGBC	United States Green Building Council

THE TYPE V CITY

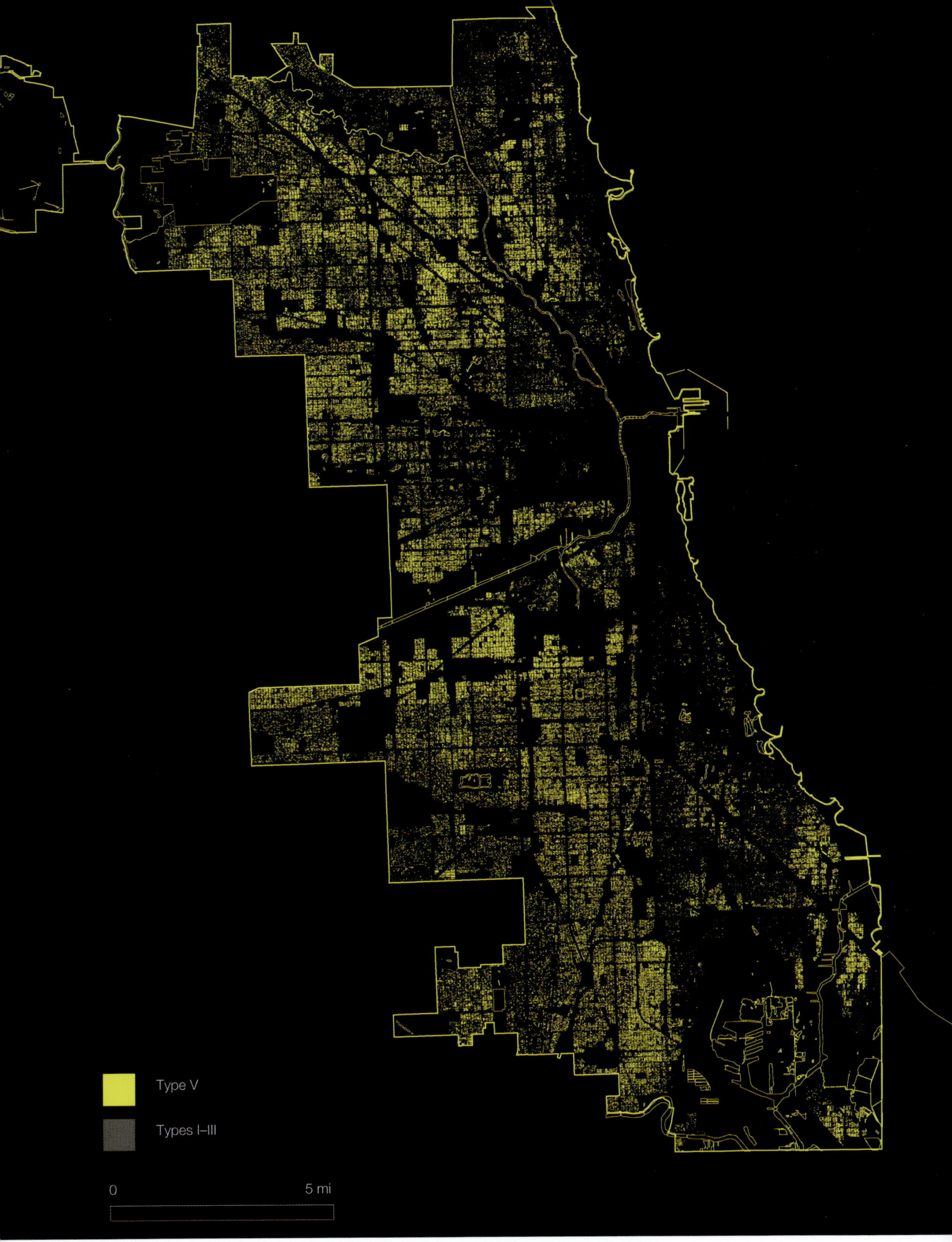

PLATE 1 *Chicago's contemporary residential Type V and Types I–III construction (2020).*

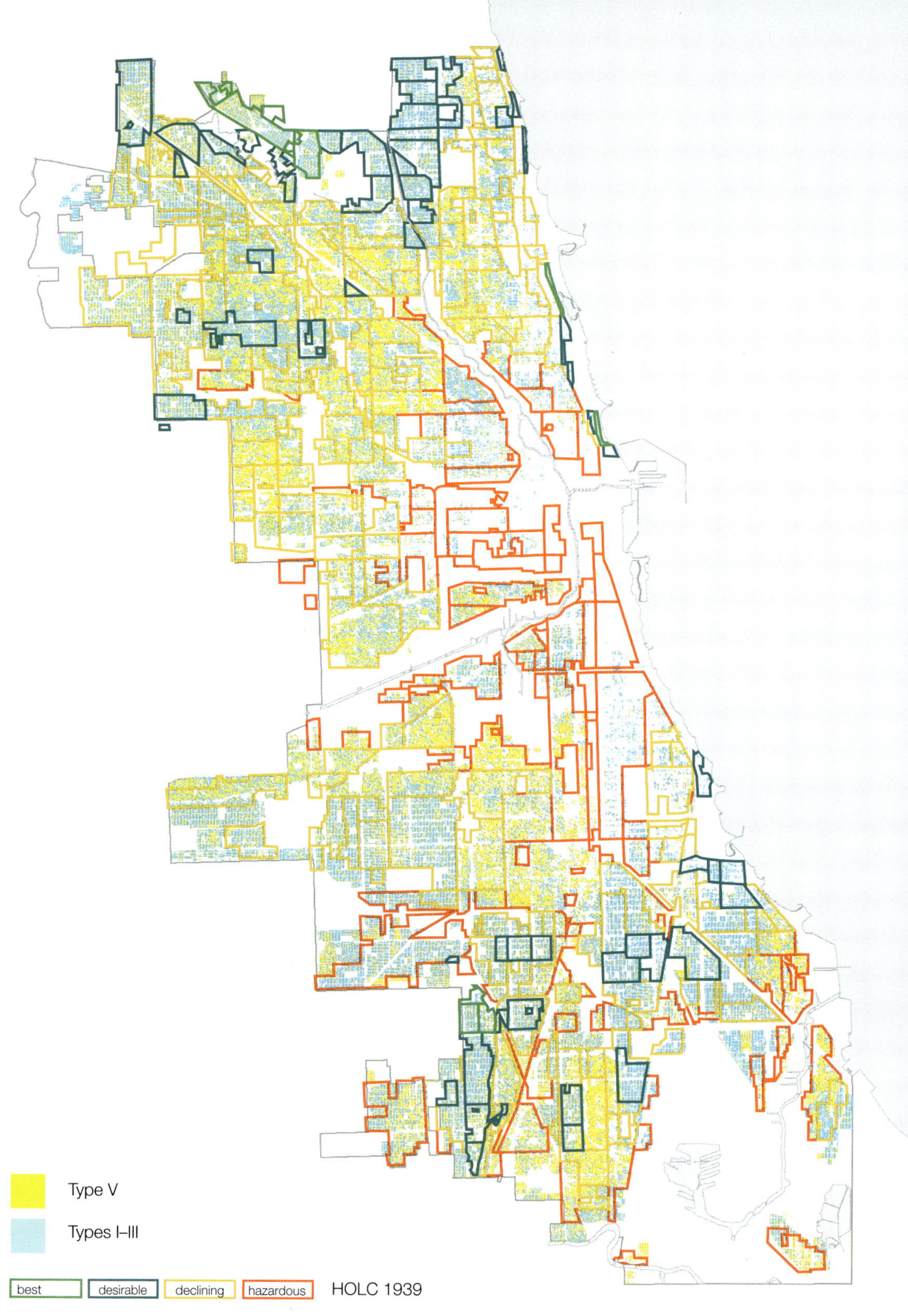

PLATE 2 *Chicago's contemporary residential construction materials (2020) and HOLC residential security map (1939).*

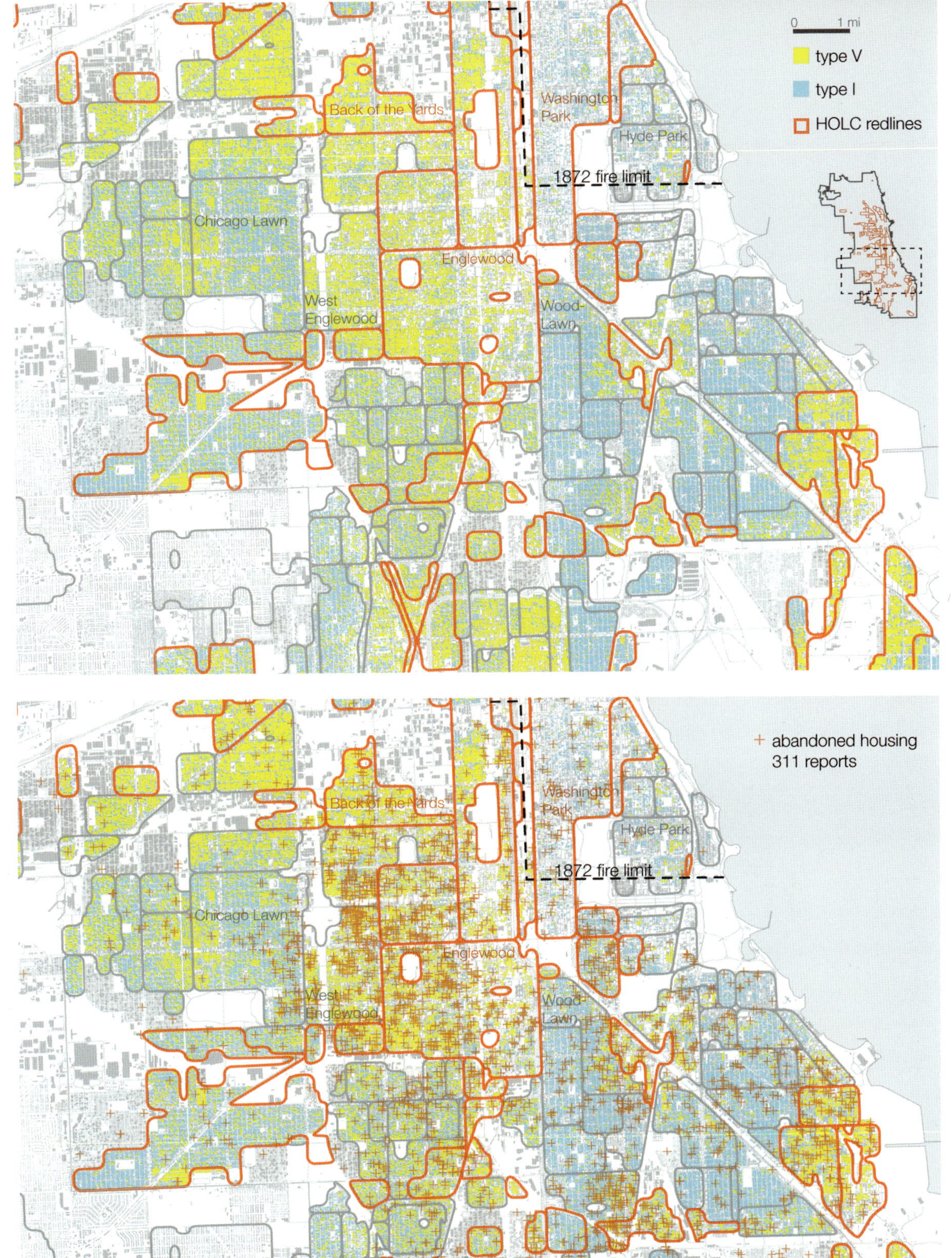

PLATE 3 a & b *(a) Chicago's contemporary residential construction types (2020) and HOLC "redlined" zones (1939); and (b) locations of abandoned building reports (2010–2019).*

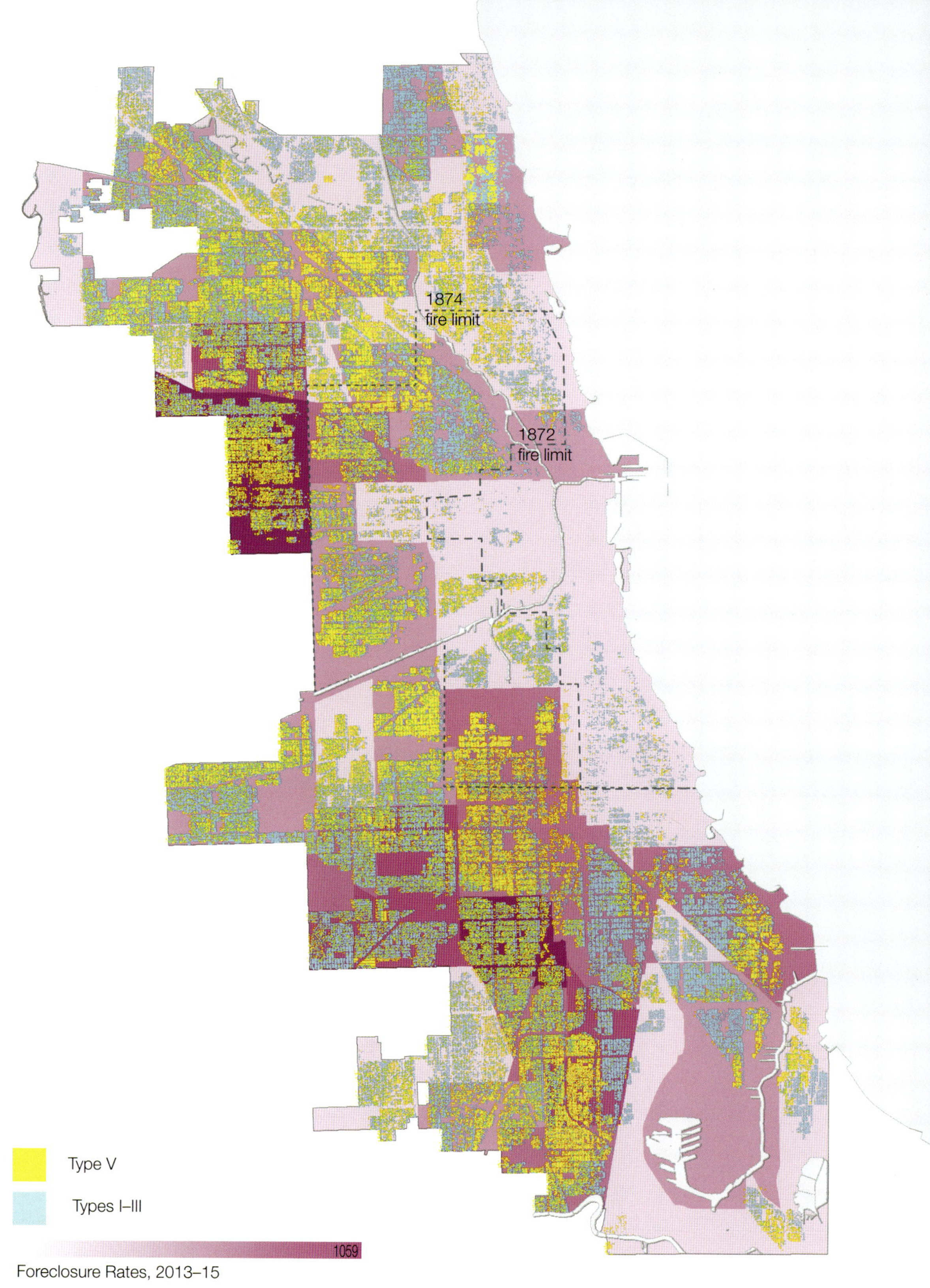

PLATE 4 *Chicago's contemporary residential construction types (2020) and Cook County Recorder foreclosure claims (2013–2015).*

PLATE 5 *New York City's contemporary residential Type V and Types I–III construction (2017).*

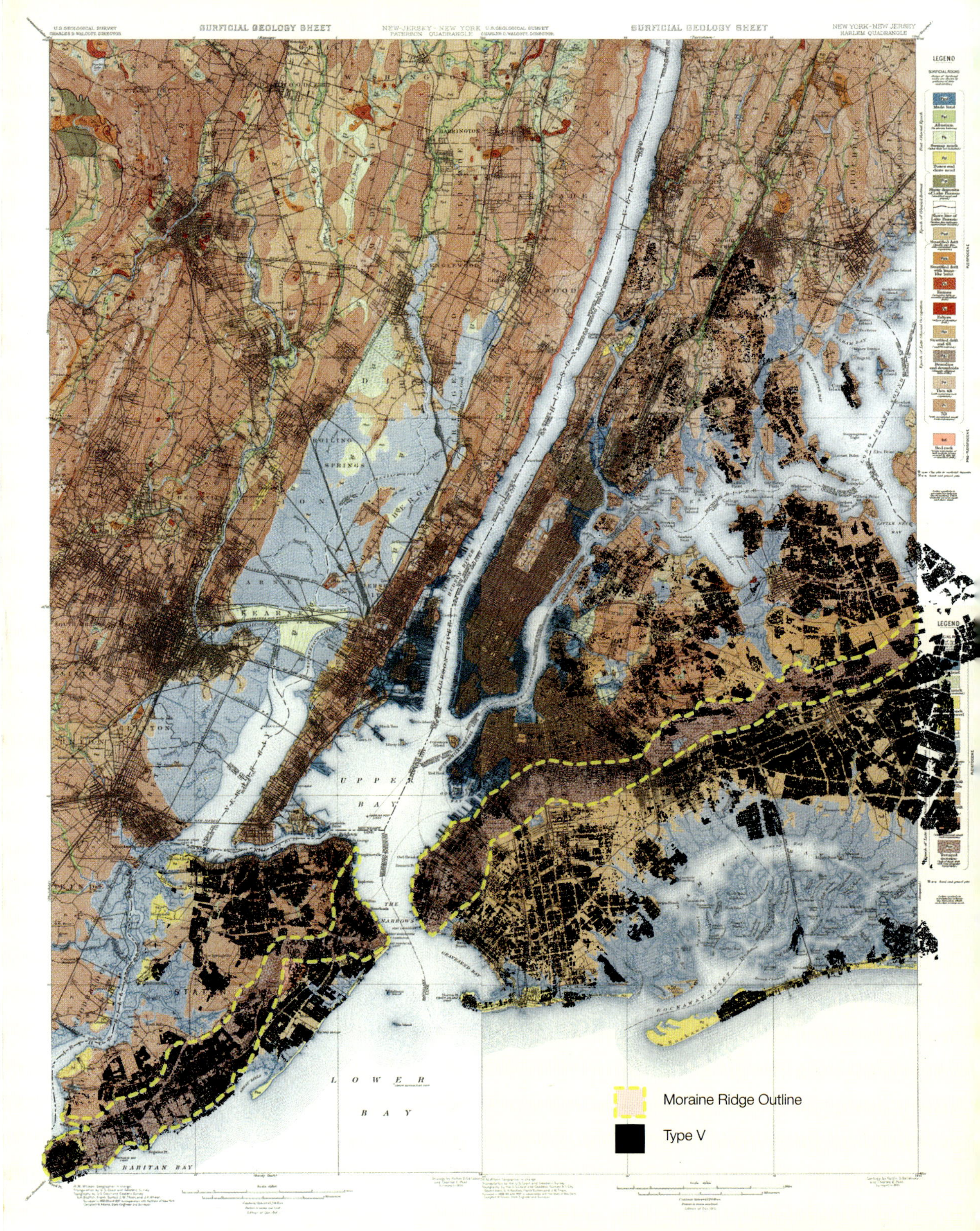

PLATE 6 *New York City's contemporary residential Type V construction (2017) superimposed on a US Geological Survey map (1897).*

PLATE 7 *New York City's contemporary residential construction types (2017) and coastal areas at risk of current and future flooding due to sea-level rise.*

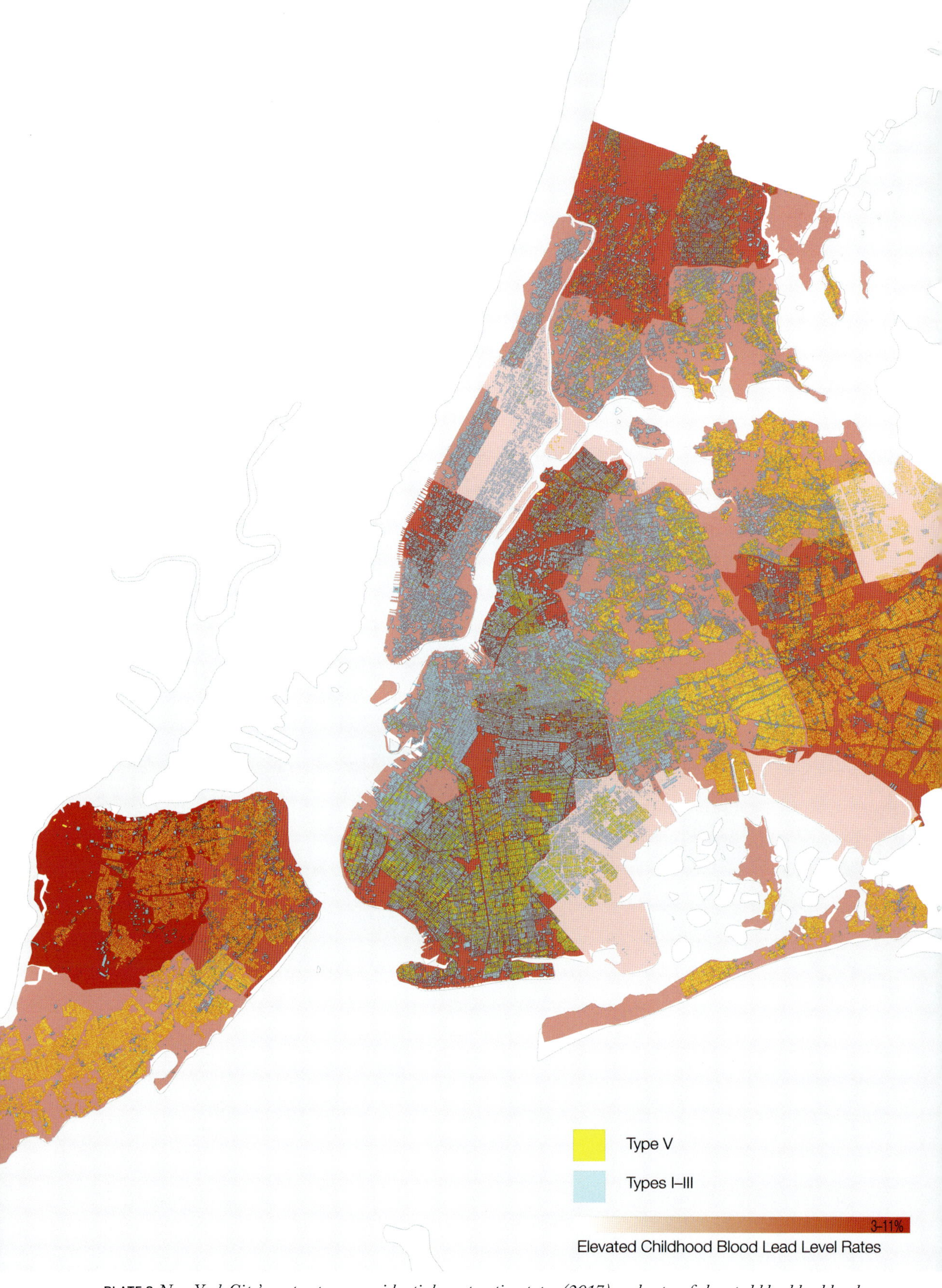

PLATE 8 *New York City's contemporary residential construction types (2017) and rates of elevated blood lead levels in children (2012).*

PLATE 9 *Philadelphia's contemporary residential Type V and Types I–III construction (2022).*

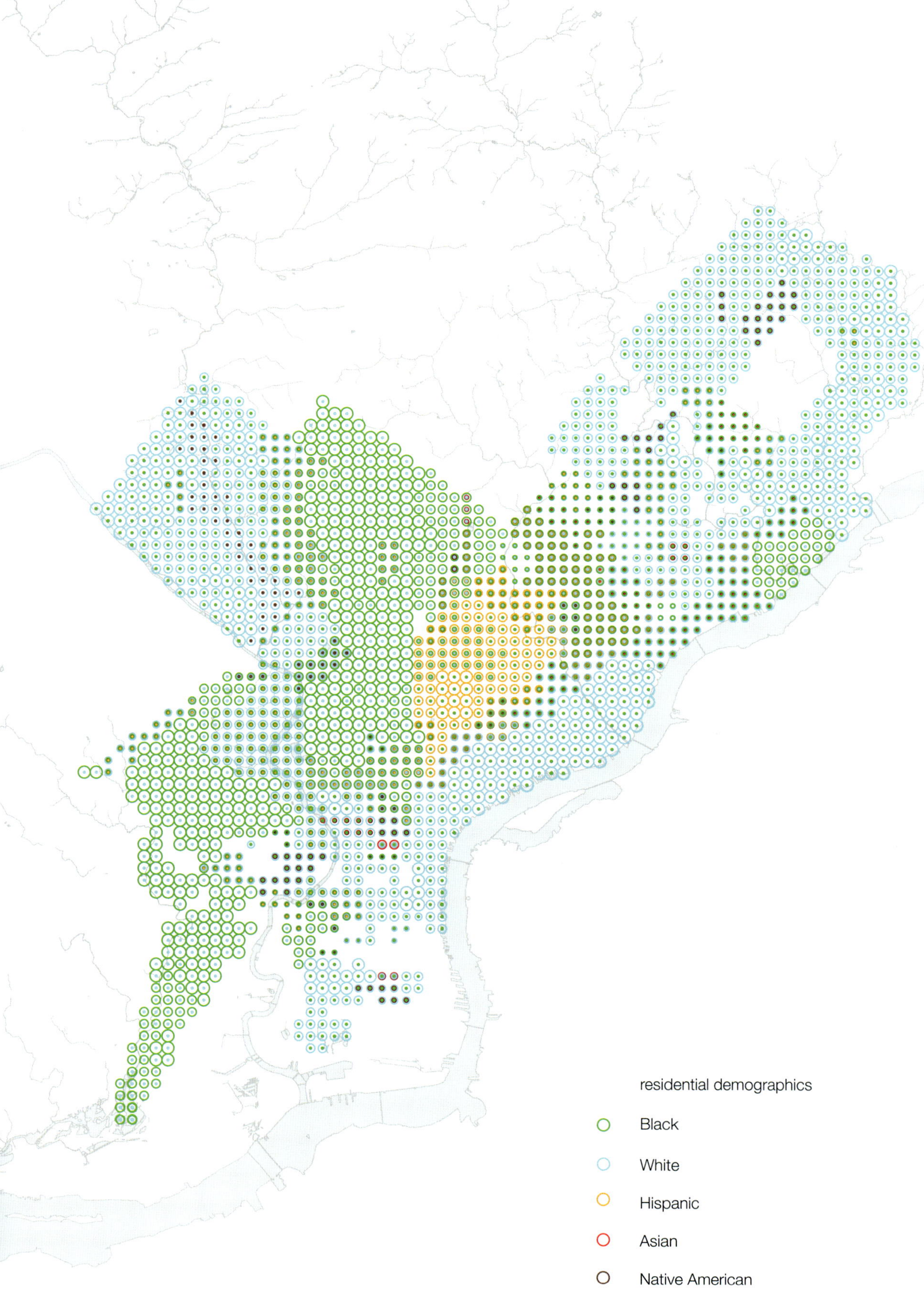

PLATE 10 *Philadelphia's contemporary residential demographics (2020).*

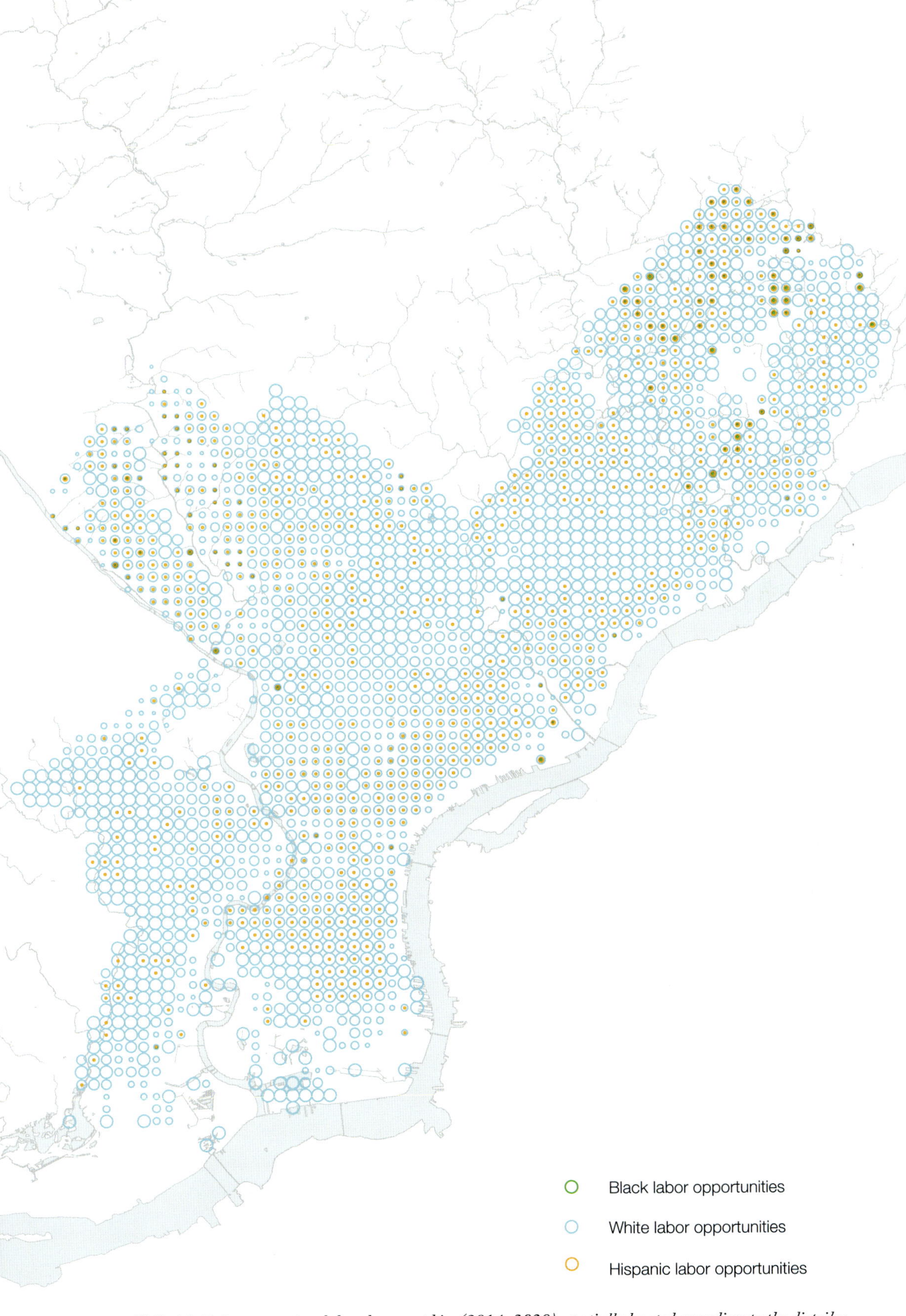

PLATE 11 *Philadelphia's construction labor demographics (2014–2020), spatially located according to the distribution of building materials.*

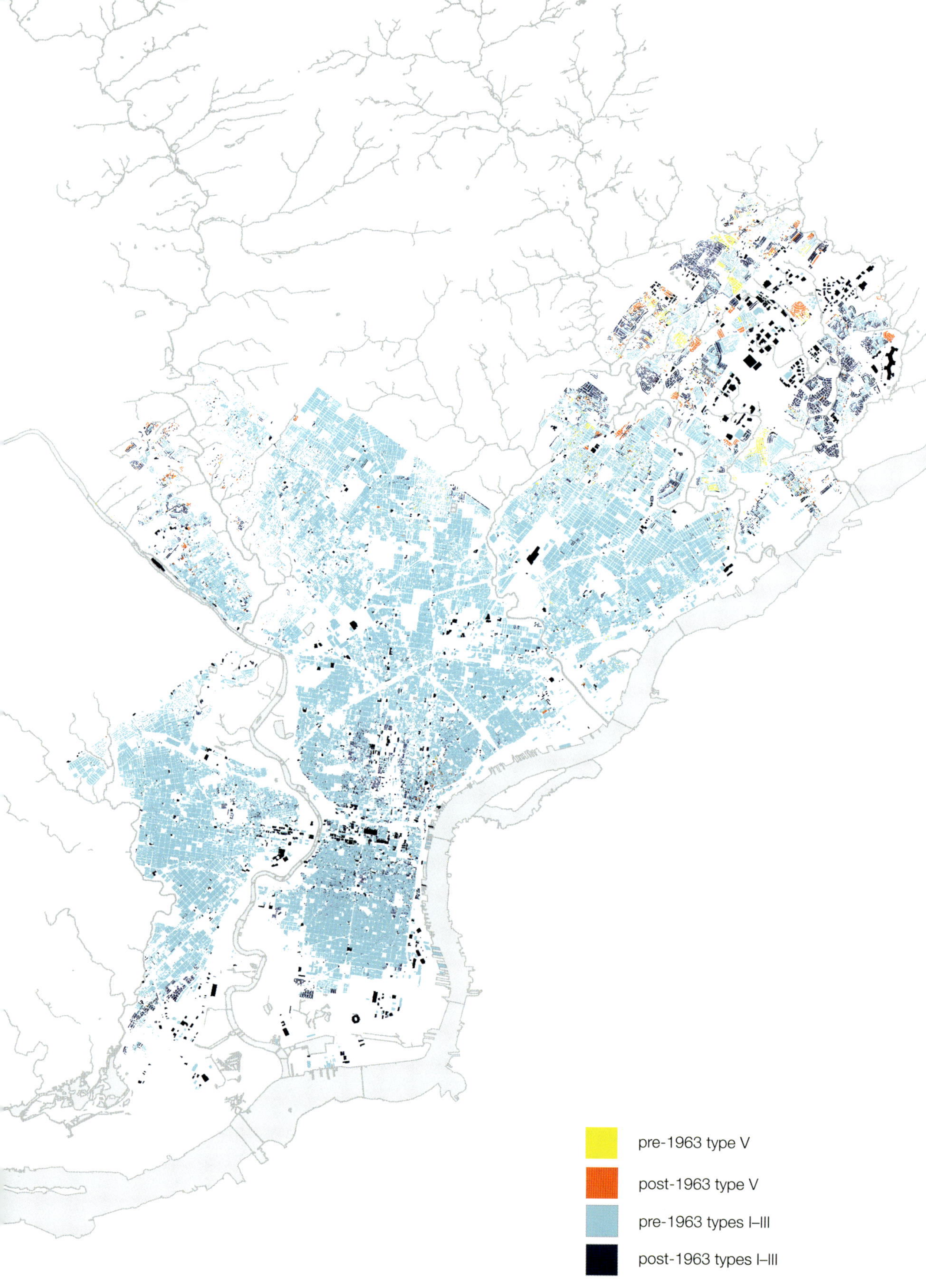

PLATE 12 *The Philadelphia Plan's labor reform was initiated in 1963. The majority of post-1963 construction was noncombustible brick masonry (shown as Types I–III).*

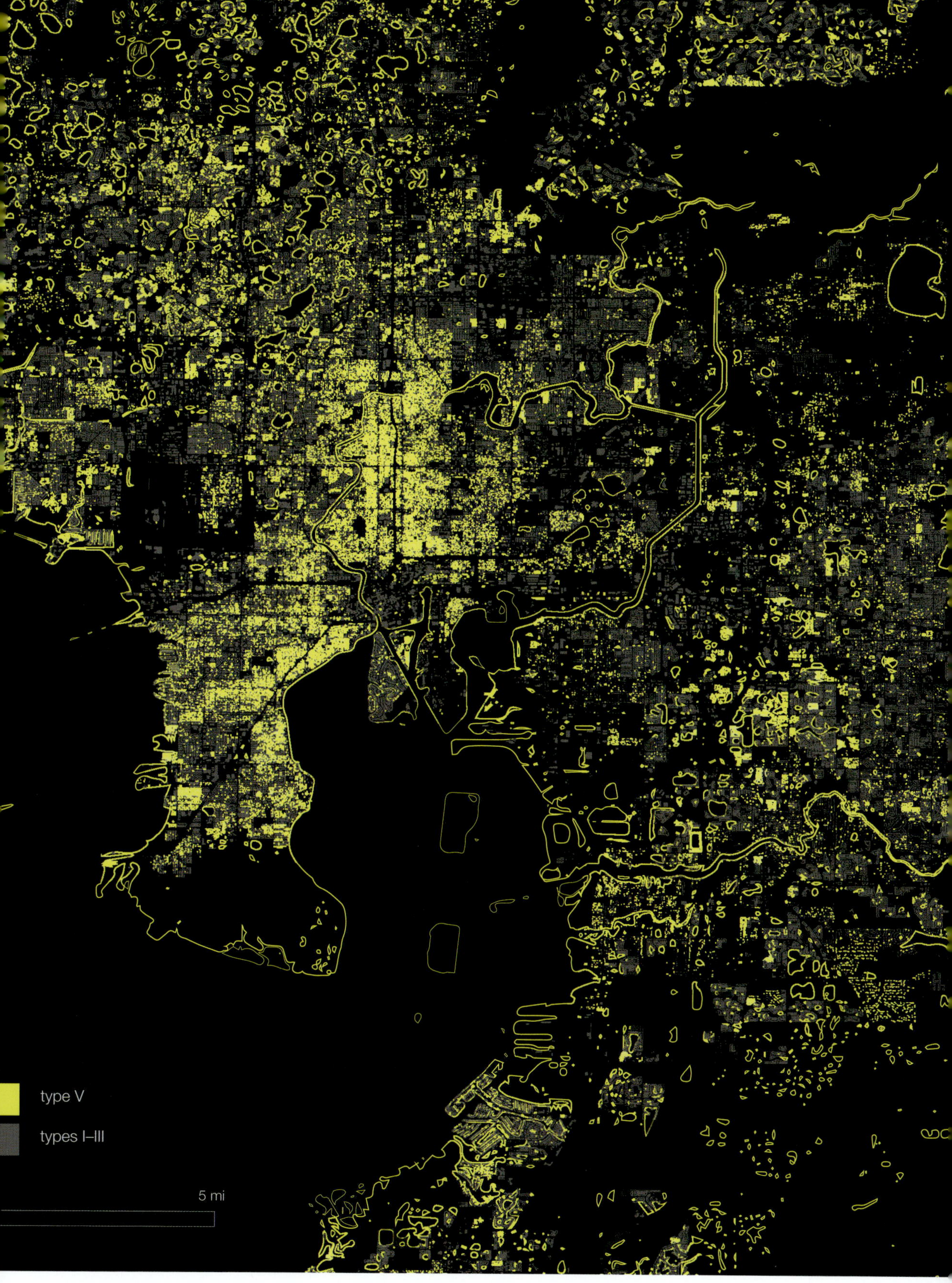

PLATE 13 *Tampa's contemporary residential Type V and Types I–III construction (2017).*

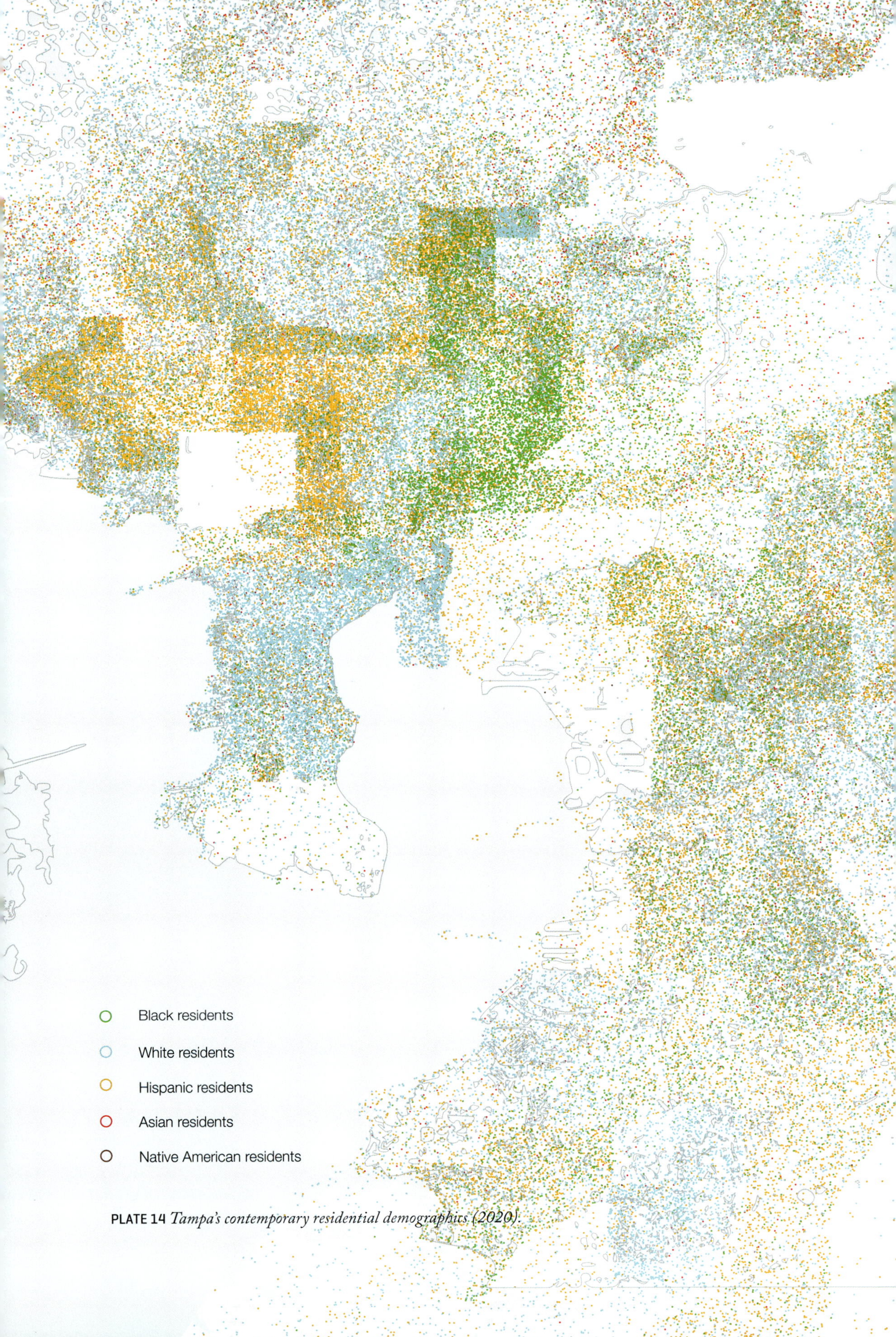

PLATE 14 *Tampa's contemporary residential demographics (2020).*

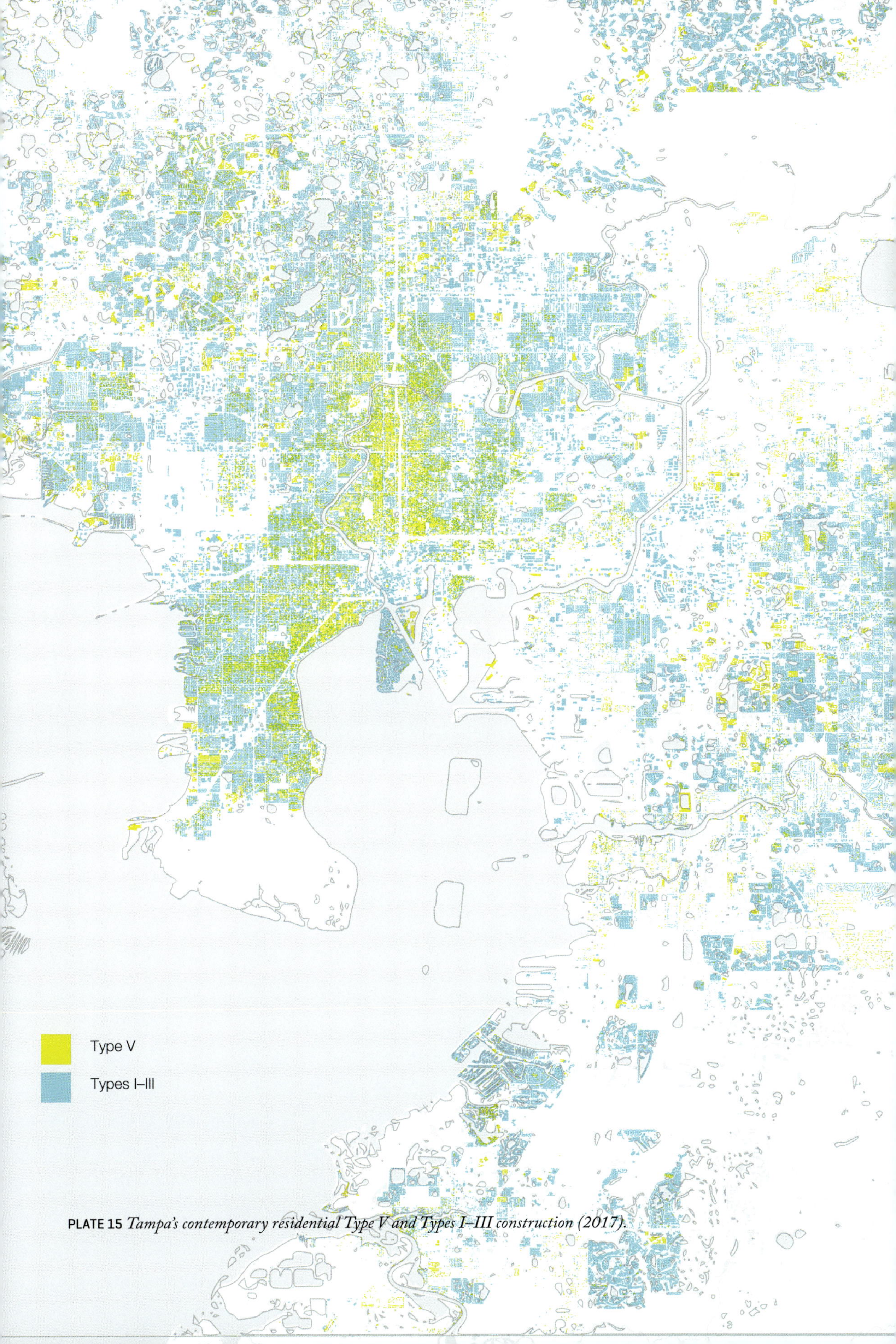

PLATE 15 *Tampa's contemporary residential Type V and Types I–III construction (2017).*

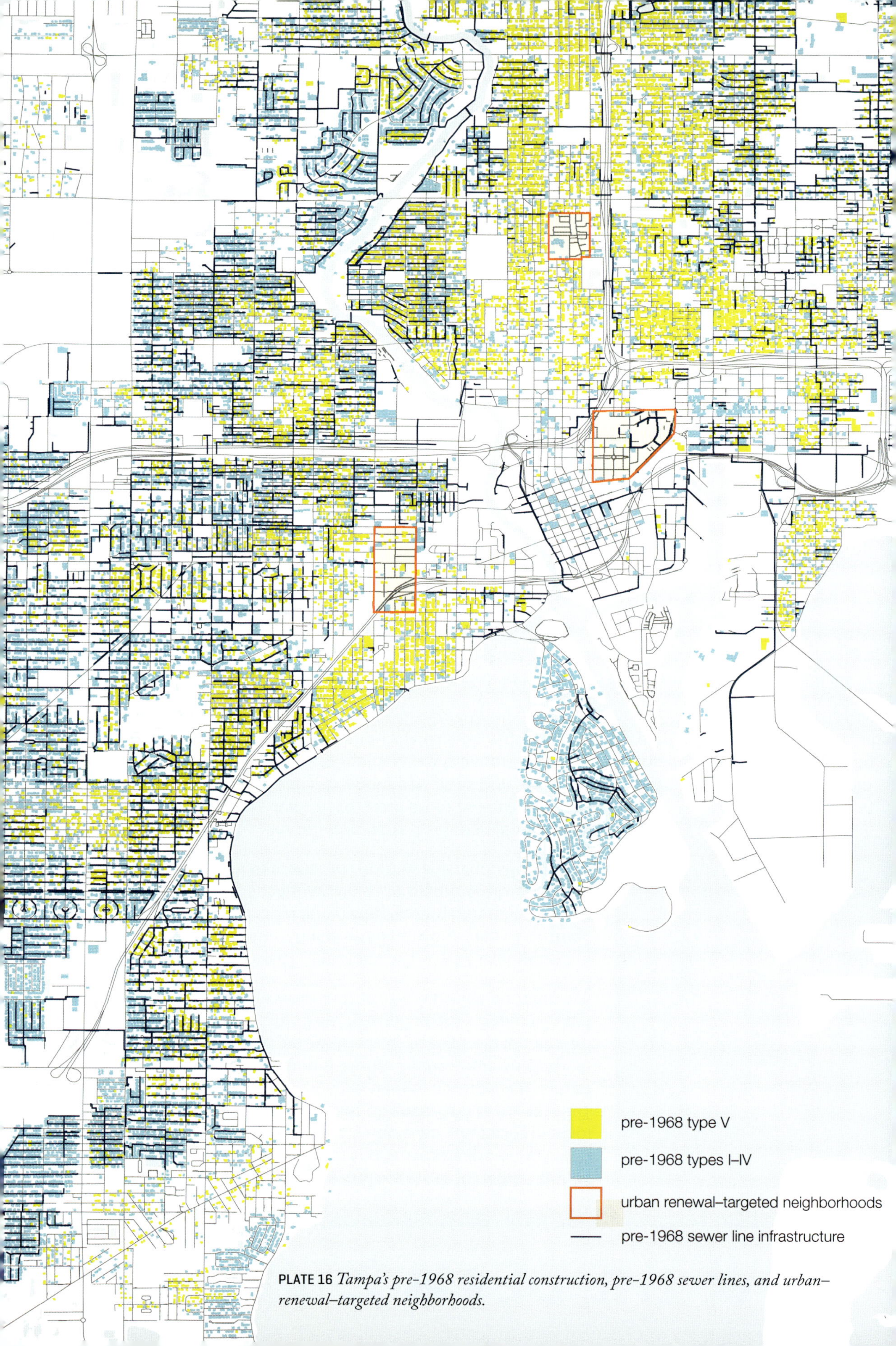

PLATE 16 *Tampa's pre-1968 residential construction, pre-1968 sewer lines, and urban-renewal–targeted neighborhoods.*

PLATE 17 *Seattle's contemporary residential Type V and Types I–III construction (2019).*

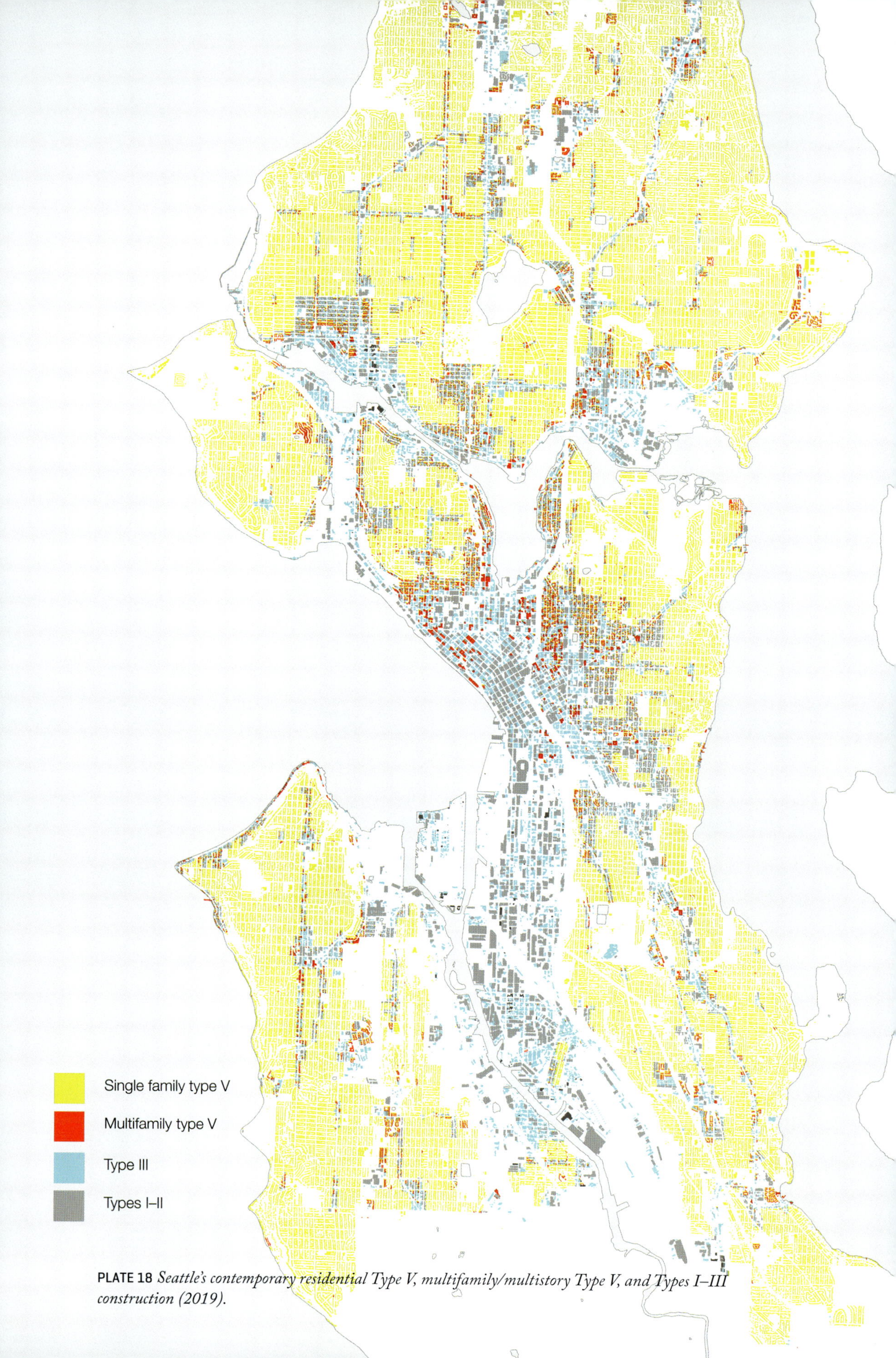

PLATE 18 *Seattle's contemporary residential Type V, multifamily/multistory Type V, and Types I–III construction (2019).*

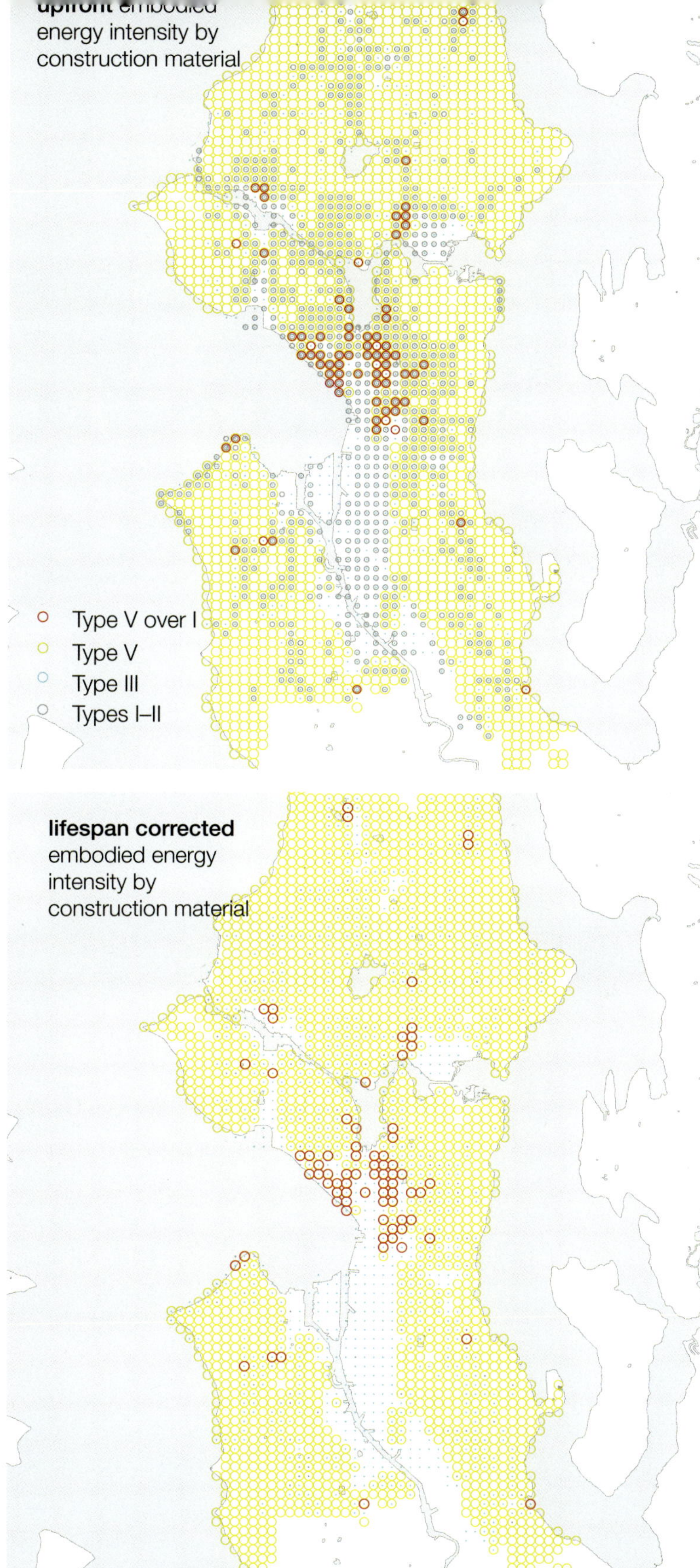

PLATE 19 *Relative embodied energy intensity in Seattle's residential building stock (2019), showing (a) upfront and (b) adjusted based on the average lifespan of each construction type.*

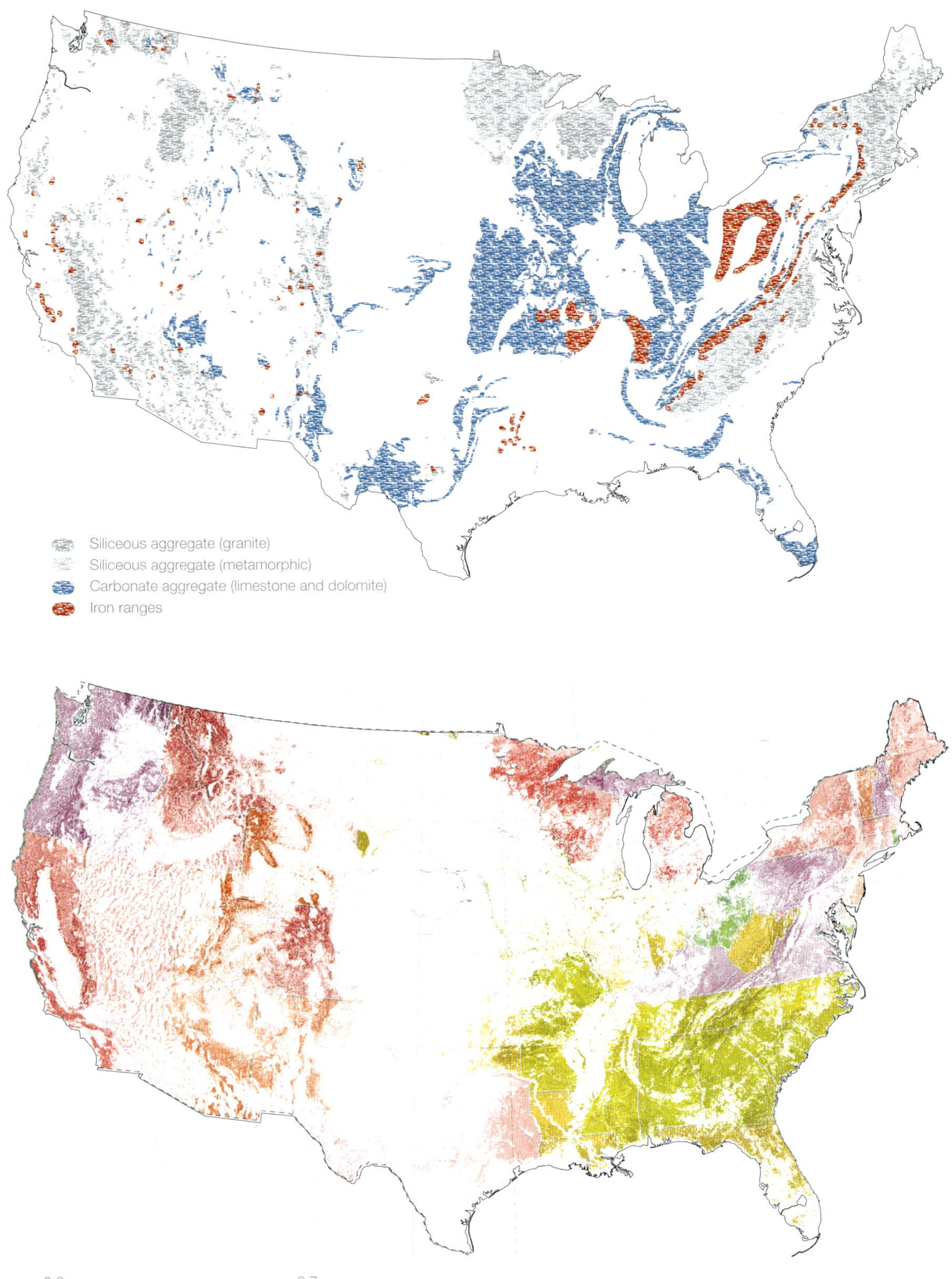

PLATE 20 *United States building material resource geographies for (a) concrete and (b) forest resources and their potential risks due to warming temperatures.*

INTRODUCTION

> They have no illusions as to the permanence of the establishment they are about to set up. It does not occur to them that they will spend their old age in the house, much less that the children will inherit it and live in it after they have gone.
>
> J. B. JACKSON, *THE WESTWARD-MOVING HOUSE*, 1953

> And there was, always, a geography to such things.
>
> D. W. MEINIG, *THE SHAPING OF AMERICA*, 1986

ALMOST EVERY AMERICAN CITY CAN be described as a "Type V city": a city with neighborhoods dominated by wood-frame construction. "Type V [five] construction" refers to exterior wall and structural systems defined by American building codes to mitigate combustibility risks. In the United States, Type V is synonymous with light, cheap, fast, and combustible wood-frame buildings, embodying the lowest upfront investment of labor and material in the building industry.

Building codes and their resulting material patterns offer a unique lens to view the social impact of American urban architecture. They are among the oldest forms of urban algorithms, designed to safeguard cities since their early stages of development. The construction types defined within these codes have shaped the aggregation of building materials for over a century, offering insights as urban formulas with outcomes extending beyond architectural technology. These rules, informed by public discourse, adapted to American cultural priorities, and confounded by societal paradoxes, reveal varied intentions across American cities. Their histories are so entangled with spatial, economic, environmental, and social pressures that their very logic nearly reversed into irrelevancy in recent years.

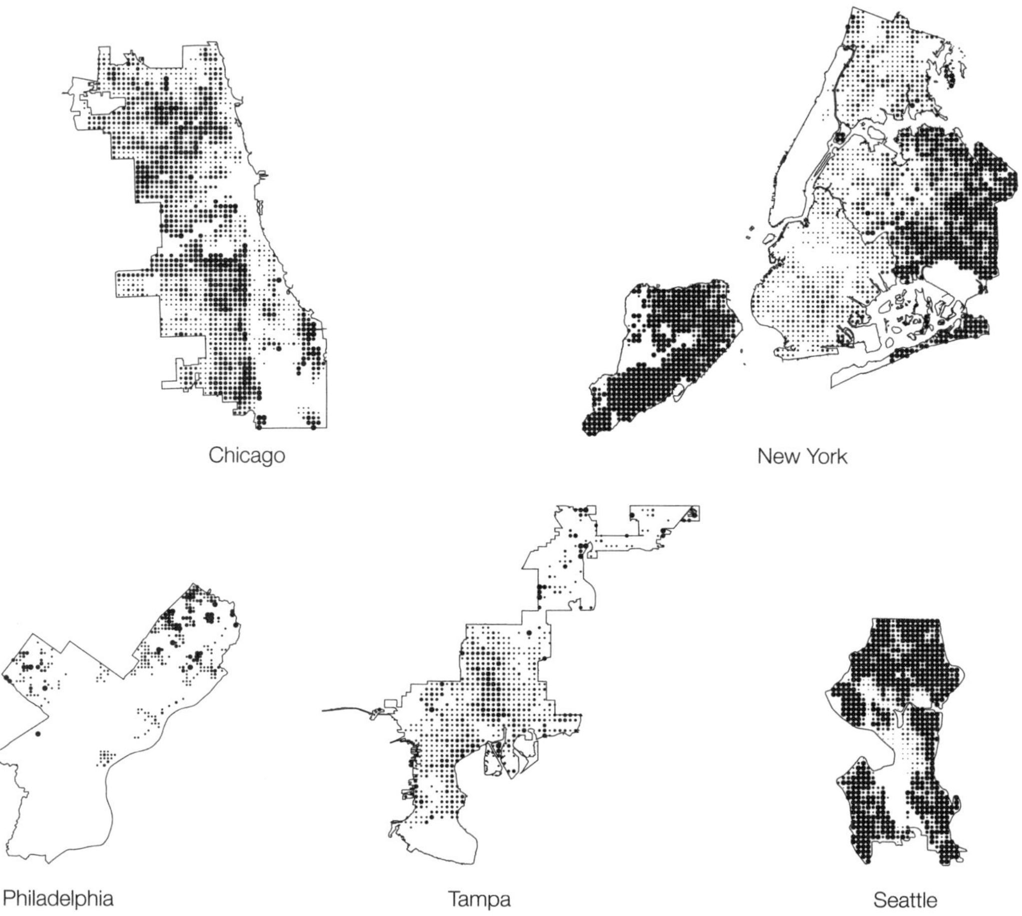

FIGURE 0.1 *Type V American cities; darker shades indicate higher concentrations of Type V construction.*

Governments increasingly turn to sophisticated data analysis to inform policy and infrastructure decisions, driven by the urgent need to design for resilience. However, the goals driving this data and the urban regulations it supports often rest on outdated assumptions. Rather than evaluating the extent to which cities are meeting urban safeguarding targets, they should be scrutinizing whether these targets are appropriate in the first place.

For example, American building codes, with their five construction types, primarily address the risk of urban fires—a concern rooted in early twentieth-century contexts. Today's urban vulnerabilities are far more diverse, encompassing economic decline, extreme weather events, public health issues, resource shortages, labor market shifts, and more. This century-long emphasis on mitigating one specific risk has shaped other vulnerabilities, while those in power prioritized or neglected additional concerns.

To design effective data-informed urban systems today, it is essential to consider both the successes and shortcomings of historical "expert-driven" rules. By examining building codes, we can uncover the logic and legibility of urban data structures across different cities and through the centuries. These codes and their consequences equip architects and city planners with the necessary tools to reassess American building objectives and their underlying assumptions. This process ultimately allows cities to articulate and debate more clearly the relationship between urban infrastructures and their core priorities.

In this context, it is fascinating to observe that construction types had a birth and death—a cultural emergence and eventual irrelevance—at particular places and times in American history. They crystallized in Chicago in the late nineteenth century amid a passionate public debate pitting ideals of self-reliance and social mobility against urban safety and sustainability. Chicago chose to isolate rather than eliminate the risk of urban conflagration, enabling the short-term economic utility of wood-frame construction to retain an urban foothold.

Chicago's codes managed material risk by delineating urban fire limits. However, Chicago subsequently complicated the codes' outcomes by classifying five construction types based on fire resistance, which still influenced the urban landscape, but with less predictability. These classifications range from Type I, featuring protected, noncombustible construction, to Type V, which offers minimal fire resistance.[1] Consequently, Chicago diverged from the typical urban material evolution seen in other developed cities, which transitioned from temporary, flammable structures to fireproof, more permanent buildings over centuries.

Chicago construction types sculpted its urban landscape, setting a precedent for other American cities. In doing so, Chicago showcased how building codes and material systems could morph according to cultural criteria, shaping interpretations of architectural objectives like safety, longevity, and environmental intelligence.

As American cities expanded, building codes reflected specific priorities and power dynamics. They secluded enduring business investments from unfettered yet impermanent real estate expansion, confined and eventually consumed vulnerable ecosystems, safeguarded labor interests for a select few, reinforced racial segregation, influenced social interaction through occupancy limits, and even masked disposable construction as ecological sustainability. These codes shaped material distribution and produced unintended effects on social and environmental systems such as economic investment patterns, human and ecological health, job access, spatial adaptive capacity, and material embodied energy.

As westward growth reached Seattle, Chicago's temporary material concession to maintain allowable wood construction in the city overtook the Northwest boomtown. Seattle embraced Type V construction, pushing regulatory limits and bolstering firefighting infrastructure rather than curbing the use of flammable materials. Seattle's early acceptance of the temporary economic benefits from Type V construction was so comprehensive that it cultivated a lasting culture of tolerance, eventually producing the codification of a more lenient and denser Type V infrastructure.

Nearly a century later, Seattle and its neighboring Northwest cities have expanded their concessions to fire risk and continued to embrace a more flexible approach to building codes. They leveraged this tolerance and robust firefighting infrastructures to pioneer a new form of multifamily wood-frame construction regulation. Their multifamily hybrid construction, known as five-over-one, allows up to five floors of Type V over one floor of Type I construction.[2]

After decades of permissibility in the Northwest, five-over-one was adopted nationally by model codes in 2015 and now dominates a generation of American building stock. Notably, it relies on modified balloon-frame construction—a variation of the framing method blamed for the intensity of the Great Chicago Fire (1871). While stronger firefighting infrastructure and fire-blocking details likely prevent the urban conflagration risk that drove building codes for over a century, the very objectives underpinning material regulation are now diluted into insignificance.

The paradox of contemporary building codes lies in their narrow focus on fire risk, even as they relax material restrictions to cut costs, thereby inviting alternative risks. Despite the erosion of consistent fireproof logic in the evolution of contemporary building codes, an estimated 75 percent of the codes still focus on some form of fire protection, while other social and environmental impacts are overlooked or disregarded.[3]

If Chicago opened a small window for cities to accommodate additional urban goals by compromising its fireproofing, Seattle expanded this opportunity into a vacuum of clear intentions by inverting the rationale of contemporary building codes. Still, the public, building professionals, and policymakers maintain confidence in the illusion that national building standards are neutral technological absolutes rather than the prioritization of select spatial and social values.

The American Institute of Architects (AIA) and the Rocky Mountain Institute recently conceded that the codes serve the interests of private industry more than climate imperatives.[4] Meanwhile, the US government invested billions in infrastructure funding, misguidedly prioritizing compliance with national model building codes under the guise of promoting resilient cities.[5]

In this rudderless regulatory context of the past decade, cities across the country embraced loosened rules and erected multistory wood-frame buildings with remarkable speed, claiming victory for affordability. Type V, wood-frame construction now accounts for 92 percent of all new single-family housing and 85 percent of all new multifamily residential buildings nationally.[6]

Cities continue to face significant threats to social and environmental resiliency, demanding recognition of the contradiction of current building strategies, an assessment of building code impacts over the last century, and a refocusing of city-building objectives to meet twenty-first-century challenges. As cities have eased stringent fire-resistance requirements in building codes due to advancements in firefighting measures, they must now consider a broader framework to guide urban material performance goals. Which competing objectives might now drive urban building-material performance: upfront costs, energy savings, durability, health, adaptive capacity, job opportunity, industry profit, varied occupancy? And who decides?

BUILDING CODES AS DISTRIBUTED SYSTEMS

To extrapolate insights from building codes as social and spatial rule sets, it is important to understand them not only as architectural technologies but as organizational systems with historically varied outcomes. How are they structured internally and influenced or assessed externally? And how have they interacted with other urban systems, in both intentional and unanticipated ways, to create socially inscribed landscapes?

The internal structure of building codes forms a complex matrix with precise yet often impenetrable objectives, leading to opaque relationships between codes and urban outcomes. American model codes, known as the International Building Codes (IBC), are maintained by the International Code Council (ICC), a nongovernmental organization (NGO) that includes both public and private representatives in the code development and voting process. However, the dense organization of these codes hampers public scrutiny, with construction types exemplifying this challenge. When Chicago shifted from geographically clear fire limits to the intricate rule matrix of today's construction types, it obscured the legibility of building-material standards and their urban impacts.

Consider the regulations governing a structural, exterior building wall. Within the IBC, fire resistance stands as the sole performance criterion dictating material *choice*. Chapters 5 and 6 of the IBC guide material selection based on fire resistance, tailored to the building's size and occupancy (e.g., business, assembly, residence). Chapter 7 further refines the fire-resistance requirement, considering the wall's proximity to the property line.

Once fire-resistance standards are met, additional regulations come into play, affecting openings, waterproofing, insulation, and structural integrity. Chapter 7 sets the *maximum* allowable openings, while chapter 12 mandates *minimum* openings for natural light and ventilation. Finally, chapter 18 details waterproofing requirements, and an entirely separate structural code ensures the wall's stability.[7] This regulatory approach focuses on individual parts, sometimes overlooking the whole—the building, cityscape, lifespan, and social and environmental contexts.

When regulations are organized by specific components, they are known as "prescriptive codes." By contrast, "performance codes" set holistic building performance standards, offering more dynamic and adaptable alternatives through calculations or simulation. Although the IBC allows for performance-based compliance, the simplicity, lower cost, and reduced liability of prescriptive codes often make them the default choice in the built environment.

Steven A. Moore and Barbara B. Wilson, authors of a comprehensive theoretical analysis of American building codes entitled *Questioning Architectural Judgement: The Problem of Codes in the United States* (2013), describe the primary logic of the IBC codes, which they describe as "prescriptive economic regulations":

> [Prescriptive codes] see the built environment as an assembly of technological objects and spaces in which the relationship between humans and their environment is ordered at a distance, by experts. . . . The principal problem with prescriptive codes is, however, that code-makers—perhaps owing to their training—tend to be unaware of the complexity of the systems they hope to regulate. Simply put, prescriptive codes tend to have unintended consequences.[8]

The current regulatory paradigm for building materials overlooks several critical factors. Building codes often operate within narrow frames, regulating a single piece of a single building in isolation rather than as part of a larger interactive urban system. Yet a building is not isolated from its dynamic environmental or social context. The requirements for exterior walls, for instance, do not consider the materials of neighboring buildings, local topography, or proximity to landscapes, industry, or resources. Nor do the codes respond to opportunities like job access, the social value of occupancies, or social vulnerabilities.

Just as the code objectives—health, safety, and welfare—are sociotechnical, the structures they measure perform through social and spatial intersections. For example, consider that urban heat islands disproportionately affect low-income residents, that "black children are three times more likely to suffer from lead poisoning than white children," and that communities of color in Chicago account for 87 percent of flood-damage claims.[9] Today's climate and social equity crises make painfully clear the need to couple social and spatial vulnerabilities, revealing a gaping void in regulatory analytical frameworks for buildings.

Current material codes also lack built-in adaptive capacity. Many risks reveal themselves slowly or even reverse over time. By contrast, material codes are static, assuming a neutral, short-term context reliant on the computability of upfront performance. Consider the striking contrast in time frames within the language of the codes versus the lifespan of urban buildings. Material construction types within IBC describe assemblies in terms of time: one-hour rated walls or three-hour rated assemblies refer to the time needed to evacuate a building in the case of a fire. There is no other mention of time or lifespan requirements in American model building codes. Yet the average residential building age is 88 years in Chicago, 90 years in New York, and 51 years in Seattle. Urban building lifespans consistently exceed the 40-year national average, underscoring the importance of lifespan considerations in city building.[10] Despite widespread concerns about building energy and resource consumption, today's material performance objectives focus on hours-long flame resistance rather than decades- or centuries-long durability and embodied energy targets.

THE EVOLUTION OF POWER AND PROTOCOLS

Building codes are legally enforceable minimum requirements for residential and commercial building design and construction that shape the fabric of our cities.[11] Although they dictate only a minimum set of requirements, building codes also organize and alter the functional characteristics of the built environment, increasingly aligning with national and international standards.

In their earliest stages, municipal governments defined building codes according to each city's individual needs and challenges. Nineteenth-century building codes were embedded within municipal ordinances as discrete building requirements such as structural rules of thumb and material flammability restrictions in designated areas. Over time, city codes began adopting regional and then national "model codes" to increase consistency and predictability across the industry.

Land-use scholar Eran Ben-Joseph highlights the expanding reach of standardized regulations. He notes, "What began in the early nineteenth century as a few local and national regulations throughout the United States and Europe is now a worldwide effort toward standardization."[12] Thus, model codes have become one of the most universal, yet often overlooked, transformative mechanisms in the built environment.

Complex negotiations between public and private entities drive building code development and influence their priorities. States hold the governmental authority to adopt and enforce building codes, while local jurisdictions must comply with state codes but can often add more stringent conditions. Today, all fifty states have chosen to adopt all or part of privately developed model codes while adding their own amendments. These American model building codes—crafted and maintained by an NGO comprising private industries, governmental representatives, and related professionals—are not binding or enforceable on their own.[13] However, they set a powerful baseline that is highly influential on a national scale. This interplay between private and public development and enforcement intentionally demands the negotiation of interests.

The contemporary American model code, the International Building Code, was first issued in 1997, resulting from the consolidation of several regional model codes.[14] The International Code Council, which develops the IBC, is a subsidiary of the American National Standards Institute (ANSI), an industry-led umbrella organization with origins dating back to World War I.[15] The ICC also maintains the International Residential Code (IRC) for "detached one-and-two family dwellings and townhouses not more than three stories above grade plane in height with a separate means of egress and their accessory structures not more than three stories above grade plane in height."[16] The IRC refers back to the IBC for material requirements when structures are densely situated (with less than five feet separation). Therefore, these essays will primarily reference the IBC while focusing on dense urban development.

The ICC describes its goals as expansively as its "international" title, asserting that its codes safeguard "public health, safety, and welfare."[17] However, these codes are primarily adopted domestically and are often criticized as privatized, "expert-driven," and lacking public accountability. The ICC updates its codes every three years, inviting public input during the development process but limiting final voting to government representatives.[18] Despite this seemingly balanced process, the ICC has faced criticism for actions that may tilt code development power in favor of private interests.

In 2019, *The New York Times* revealed "a secret agreement" that allowed the nation's homebuilders to more easily block changes to building codes aimed at addressing climate change.[19] The *Times* reported on an agreement between the ICC and the National Association of American Home Builders (NAAHB) to guarantee the NAAHB several seats on code development committees. Although government representatives vote on final decisions, this report highlighted the industry's outsized influence over what content reaches a vote.

Two years later, the ICC faced further criticism for removing model energy code updates from the public input and government voting processes, shifting them to a committee-controlled "standards process." This decision was opposed by many government representatives and organizations, including the American Institute of Architects.[20]

Climate advocate Mike Henrich of RMI (formerly the Rocky Mountain Institute) remarked: "The ICC chose to limit the input of local leaders in favor of industry groups resistant to change. The climate crisis won't wait for these opposing forces to come around, so the federal government and local leaders must work together to accelerate modern, healthy, zero-emissions buildings."[21] Critics fear that the ICC's close ties to the construction industry may perpetuate codes that prioritize economic interests over social or environmental well-being.

Sociologist Lawrence Busch has extensively explored the politics of standard-making. He notes that the fundamental challenge of expert involvement in this process affects both the creation and oversight of standards. Cost-benefit analysis and risk analysis are the primary methods used to assess the pros and cons of standards. However, Busch considers both methods to be fundamentally limited in scope and perspective. Like standard-creation, these evaluation processes are conducted by a limited set of experts and rely on significant assumptions of value.

> At best, [cost-benefit analysis and risk analysis] are somewhat heroic attempts to forecast the future, sometimes shedding light on real and important problems and opportunities. At worst, they are pseudoscience, means for obfuscating what is at stake and of concentrating decision-making in the hands of a technoscientific elite that falsely claims to have the answers. . . . Yet none of this is to argue that costs or risks should be ignored. . . . Therefore, the expert opinions of cost-benefit analysis and risk analysis must be inputs into a democratic decision-making process in which contingencies are revealed, and not prepackaged as outputs that obviate democracy.[22]

In the swiftly shifting landscape of today's regulatory environment, the need for a retrospective analysis of the last century's regulatory impact grows ever more crucial. The drive toward national or even global standardization often produces a deceptive sense of security. This overreliance on a single, authoritative standard stifles engagement with the codes among professionals and communities, curtailing nuanced negotiations unique to each city's distinct challenges and priorities. To truly understand the evolution of local built environments, greater clarity in the analytical framework is essential: What is measured? What outcomes do current regulations yield at the city level? Who reaps the benefits? These questions are vital in navigating the ongoing transformation of urban landscapes.

Building codes are internally organized through a distributed structure and externally controlled by a public and private network. In most jurisdictions, these codes interact with several parallel regulations that govern and impact buildings. Although building codes are often the only regulation to directly specify allowable materials, the applicable rules may be influenced by elective codes, zoning ordinances, and comprehensive plans. Understanding these relationships is crucial, not only to recognize overlapping influences but also because these parallel regulations demonstrate mechanisms to translate complex content, enhance public legibility, and promote intentional integration with other urban systems and objectives.

Elective codes are guidelines designed to improve the performance of a building according to additional, optional criteria often related to environmental sustainability. LEED (Leadership in Energy and Environmental Design) is one of the most well-known contemporary elective codes in the United States, managed by an NGO, the United States Green Building Council (USGBC). Some jurisdictions mandate that public buildings meet elective standards like LEED, while others use these codes as a template for adopting their own, more ambitious building performance standards. For instance, California developed its own CALGreen Codes, which became mandatory building standards in 2010.[23] Despite environmental advances in building codes and elective codes, most standards continue to protect the building or the indoor environment rather than the ecologies they inhabit.[24] However, they remain powerful mechanisms to define and broadly communicate alternative priorities in the built environment.

Cities and regulators often turn to elective codes to identify co-benefits and shape policies and incentives. Consider ESG (Environmental, Social, Governance) investment reporting, which ties cost-benefit and risk assessment to data analysis, raising new questions about how resilience is measured in the twenty-first century. ESG reporting often relies on elective codes when assessing building industry impacts and, in many markets, still struggles to guide "social" reporting mechanisms.[25] The European Union mandates that ESG reporting standards include social impact measures such as workforce and community impact. By contrast, US draft reporting mandates do not yet integrate social impact, though the US Securities Exchange Commission (SEC) promises future standards to measure "human capital" impacts.[26] The analysis of social impacts in Type V cities that follows highlights several methods to enhance current assessment mechanisms.

Zoning ordinances, like building codes, include mandatory building requirements. However, zoning primarily focuses on land use, controlling building bulk, land subdivision, building placement, and land and building use.[27] Zoning ordinances are more locally controlled than building codes, with states typically granting zoning authority to municipalities. While zoning ordinances rarely dictate building-material requirements directly, beyond occasional aesthetic restrictions, they play a significant role in setting uniform requirements for building use, size, and setback throughout a neighborhood, influencing the application of building code material combustibility requirements.

For instance, single-family zoning often limits building height to a range that qualifies for the building codes' lowest fire-protection restrictions—Type V construction. Additionally, zoning ordinances specify setback requirements, predetermining what, if any, building separation is required in a neighborhood. IBC requires more robust construction types for exterior walls located within five feet of the property line.

Zoning ordinances also permit building uses (called occupancy) in a neighborhood. Some occupancies will increase the fire-resistance requirements. By controlling building height, separation, and occupancy, zoning ordinances can either limit or enhance the applicability of certain building code material minimums.

Zoning ordinances differ from building codes in two important ways related to communication. Zoning ordinances employ both text and graphics, describing land-use requirements and regulations while drawing maps to illustrate their geographic impact. By contrast, building codes rely primarily on written text, rarely visualizing the spatial implications of their rules.

Significant changes to zoning ordinance are often preceded by comprehensive plans, which publicly articulate goals for future land uses, density, and public amenities.[28] Comprehensive plans typically include maps and sometimes diagrams to convey the implications of zoning proposals. Building codes lack comparable goal-setting or communication processes that might foster public scrutiny. One could envision expanding comprehensive planning processes to incorporate building codes, allowing localities to interpret, debate, and challenge the suitability of state and model code requirements.

Urban and social impacts of zoning receive much more public and scholarly attention than building regulations, perhaps due to the relative opacity of building codes.[29] Extending building code scholarship to urban contexts allows the following essays to further explore building regulation as mechanisms of social and spatial infrastructures.

BUILDING SYSTEMS AND SOCIAL CONSEQUENCES

The necessity of modest beginnings, opportunism afforded by abundant wood resources, and self-reliant settlers drove America's historical dependence on wood-frame construction. Growing cities reconstructed American forests as "Type V cities" throughout the twentieth century. Rapid growth spurts, financial incentives, and skilled labor influences propelled Type V cities to become a national material and spatial form of organization.

As twentieth-century American cities expanded, geographic fire limits, construction types, municipal zoning, and product-scale standardization divided cities into building-material territories. Entire neighborhoods were distinguished by the prevalence of one dominant building material. Figure 0.1 presents a material "fingerprint" of several American cities, mapping the locations and density of Type V construction. Despite shared historical influences, unique regulatory decisions and urban dynamics produced distinctive material patterns and landscapes of risk across cities.

The history of construction types is bookended in Chicago and Seattle, where they were most definitively developed and then disregarded. In between, regulations confronted different contexts and cultures, producing varied social consequences. These histories challenge the logic of applying a universal approach to unique environments and the notion that building codes automatically create a safe, healthy, resilient city, instead raising the question, "For whom?"

Building codes serve as important tools of urban analysis, both as a subject and a springboard to consider more generative, adaptive spatial infrastructures. Each of the following essays follows the negotiation between a city and its building codes, dissecting interactions between building materials and other urban systems that ultimately shaped communities, habitats, and cultures.

Five American cities—Chicago, New York, Philadelphia, Tampa, and Seattle—serve as case studies for the essays in this book, tracing the material development of American urbanism and building regulation. Chosen for their distinct regions, cultures, climates, and eras of growth, each city presents unique opportunities to examine material rules and their social consequences. The themes within each essay include durability and disinvestment in Chicago; saturation, health, and environmental systems in New York; labor and affordability in Philadelphia; occupancy opportunity and urban vitality in Tampa; and adaptive capacity and longevity in Seattle. Each essay also explores the connections between building materials, building codes, and the power structures that shaped their evolution. These stories not only highlight the actors and interests behind building code development but also reveal a rich collection of related social challenges and spatial consequences over time.

In Chicago, the story of the Type V city begins with workers marching through the streets to defend their newly invented balloon-frame wood construction that so quickly democratized home ownership before engulfing the city in flames. Following the Great Fire, the city's workers, industrial moguls, and real estate investors debated whether to ban wood-frame construction but ultimately compromised, dividing the city into two distinct zones, both socially and materially. Soon after, Chicago's construction types effectively privatized the logic and legibility of building-material standards and urban analysis. This essay describes shifts in public awareness, starting with building material as the subject of protest marches and ending with an invisible, self-perpetuating system, rarely measured or mentioned.

While the architectural impacts of Chicago's Great Fire are well documented within the fire limits, historical accounts often overlook the architecture that evolved outside of conflagration constraints. These neighborhoods remain dominated by wood-frame buildings, demonstrating the lasting economic impact of the city's material and regulatory compromise. Chicago's spatial and material patterns suggest urban disinvestment as an unintended consequence when building codes and consumer markets fail to recognize the impact of material durability.

In New York, relentless development pressure created an early and persistent test bed for density, habitation, and health. Land speculators and regulators repeatedly failed to incorporate environmental logic into the city's material rules, perpetuating a pattern of unregulated Type V construction in wetlands, lowlands, and sunken urban spaces. Real estate pressures drove the heedless expansion of Type V construction in New York's outwash plains, defying centuries of conventional construction wisdom and decades of local health and environmental warnings. New York's building codes were later refined to conspire with newly invented zoning codes. These two code systems isolated and neglected vulnerable ecosystems, buffered risk with flood insurance, and feigned resilience through chemical protections with untested health consequences.

The New York narrative also describes the dramatic evolution of wood construction over the twentieth century, increasing its absorption and expanding its vulnerability. In New York, macro- and microstructural challenges converged as increasingly absorptive, vulnerable urban wood buildings clustered in low-lying urban floodplains. The story of New York's material evolution traces shifting wood construction practices, the absorption challenges they introduce, and the "flood-resistant" codes that now perpetuate material risk.

Philadelphia was historically the most exclusive of the cities, restricting both what could be built and who could build it. Local labor unions exerted considerable control over building codes and municipal policies, producing an early noncombustible construction mandate to protect both jobs and buildings in a city that evolved as a union town built primarily of brick. By the early 1960s, centuries of job exclusion for Black workers reached a boiling point. Local leaders famously claimed that the city was not hiring any Black skilled workers for construction projects.

Philadelphia's protests expanded nationwide and resulted in affirmative action programs aimed at construction labor. However, the resulting Philadelphia Plan failed to consider local building regulations that might restrict or promote specific types of skilled labor. Although intended to expand job access, the plan omitted the bricklayers union, the trade required throughout the city by building codes. Labor unions' political influence led to over a century of noncombustible material protection in Philadelphia. However, when unions and federal regulators failed to share access to the labor opportunities protected by building codes, support for these restrictions declined, as did the affordability of robust construction for local populations.

This story shows that affordability is not just about reducing upfront costs but also enabling local job access. In this context, building codes are not only instruments of risk mitigation but also tools to create or restrict social opportunity. Labor demographic data offers a chance to share and spatialize relationships between job access and material outcomes, thereby broadening the definition of affordability.

Tampa's vibrant Central Avenue district afforded a range of material occupancy possibilities—from dance halls to bakeries to in-home laundry businesses. Tampa exemplifies the connection between racial segregation and building material in the American South because postbellum settlements were constructed beyond many southern urban fire limits. Central Avenue grew into an unusual urban mix of wood-frame and noncombustible construction characterized by dense housing, boarder lodging, home and business ownership, live-work entrepreneurship, and community mutual support.

Variations in occupancy and building material grew out of resistance and resilience under the limits of Jim Crow segregation. Yet Central Avenue's sociospatial value was disregarded during urban renewal. Instead, Tampa's exclusively white government translated racial bias into double standards in material risk assessment and uneven urban infrastructural investment. Tampa's story highlights the importance of building code occupancy restrictions, in that code restrictions designed to regulate fire and evacuation parameters also served as mediators of spatial social interactions and urban vitality.

The story of construction types ends in Seattle as America transitioned to almost ubiquitous reliance on Type V construction. The abundant wood resources of the American Northwest combined with seismic risks and cycles of urgent growth to elevate the role of Type V construction in boomtown building. From mill town to technology hub, Seattle's speed-minded building community prioritized material convenience to meet capital demand, often sacrificing common safety standards and longevity in the process. Seattle's unique material leniency among these case-study cities offers an in-depth examination of wood and building lifespans, revealing that short-term building drawbacks outweigh most lifetime carbon and energy benefits of light-wood-frame construction.

Seattle's tradition of risk-tolerant fire codes and multifamily short-term housing gave rise to its invention of America's new hybrid multistory standard: five-over-one construction. While these buildings offer upfront cost savings, they also multiply expansion and contraction challenges and limit spatial adaptive capacity. Over time, the upfront affordability benefits of five-over-one may be eclipsed by diminished functional capacity and durability.

ADAPTIVE CAPACITY, ENVIRONMENTAL GEOGRAPHY, AND GENERATIVE POTENTIAL

American cities used building codes as tools for risk isolation or obfuscation rather than as instruments for uniform protection. Consequently, their urban histories serve as a means to expand and illuminate alternative building-material priorities. Three umbrella categories encapsulate the broader frames of analysis suggested by these narratives of social material performance—adaptive capacity, environmental geography, and generative potential.

Spatial adaptive capacity, rooted in American vernacular architecture, can promote flexibility and longevity. However, the potential to build for adaptation or indeterminacy is often hindered by building regulations and material choices. Additionally, resource geographies and local environmental systems exert a profound influence on material and urban health, durability, and resource economy. Finally, material infrastructures can transcend their role as defensive isolation mechanisms and evolve into generative labor and occupancy opportunities, fostering affordability and neighborhood vitality.

The Type V city reveals broader tangible impacts of building materials beyond those overtly described within codes, challenging prevailing narratives of urban resilience, sustainability, affordability, and equity in the American built environment. By shifting the scope of material analysis from short-term performance to interactions across communities, environments, economies, and centuries, an expansive definition of urban welfare comes to light. Narratives of the Type V city highlight building-material codes as the prioritization of values with social consequences, ultimately empowering cities and designers to reimagine the goals and interactions shaping our urban landscape.

TYPE V CHICAGO

Durability and Disinvestment

> To forbid all wooden structures inside the whole space that . . . is named on the map Chicago, means to stop the further growth of the city . . . nothing less than suicide.
>
> ANTON CASPAR HESING, *STAATS-ZEITUNG*, JANUARY 16, 1872

> I cannot doubt for one moment that, in no long time, if we can build as we should the fire-proof house, be it mansion or cottage, will be the cheapest as well as the best. . . . Let us never sacrifice a lasting security for a very transient advantage.
>
> REV. ROBERT COLLYER TO MR. A. C. HESING, *CHICAGO TRIBUNE*, JANUARY 19, 1872

"A THOUSAND LUNATICS" AND THE ORIGINS OF THE TYPE V CITY

On the evening of January 15, 1872, a historic debate unfolded in the streets of Chicago. A group gathered between Market and Illinois Streets to protest a citywide ban on wood-frame construction, a measure of protection under consideration in the aftermath of the Great Chicago Fire (October 8–10, 1871). The protest eventually swelled to over a thousand residents marching toward city hall. They carried signs reading "Leave a Home for the Laborer" and "No Tenements."[1] The day after the protest, a local paper described the demonstration, stating that "a thousand lunatics storm[ed] City Hall and [drove] out the aldermen."[2]

This event marked a pivotal point in the heated argument between the "fireproofers" and the protesters that unfolded through public speeches

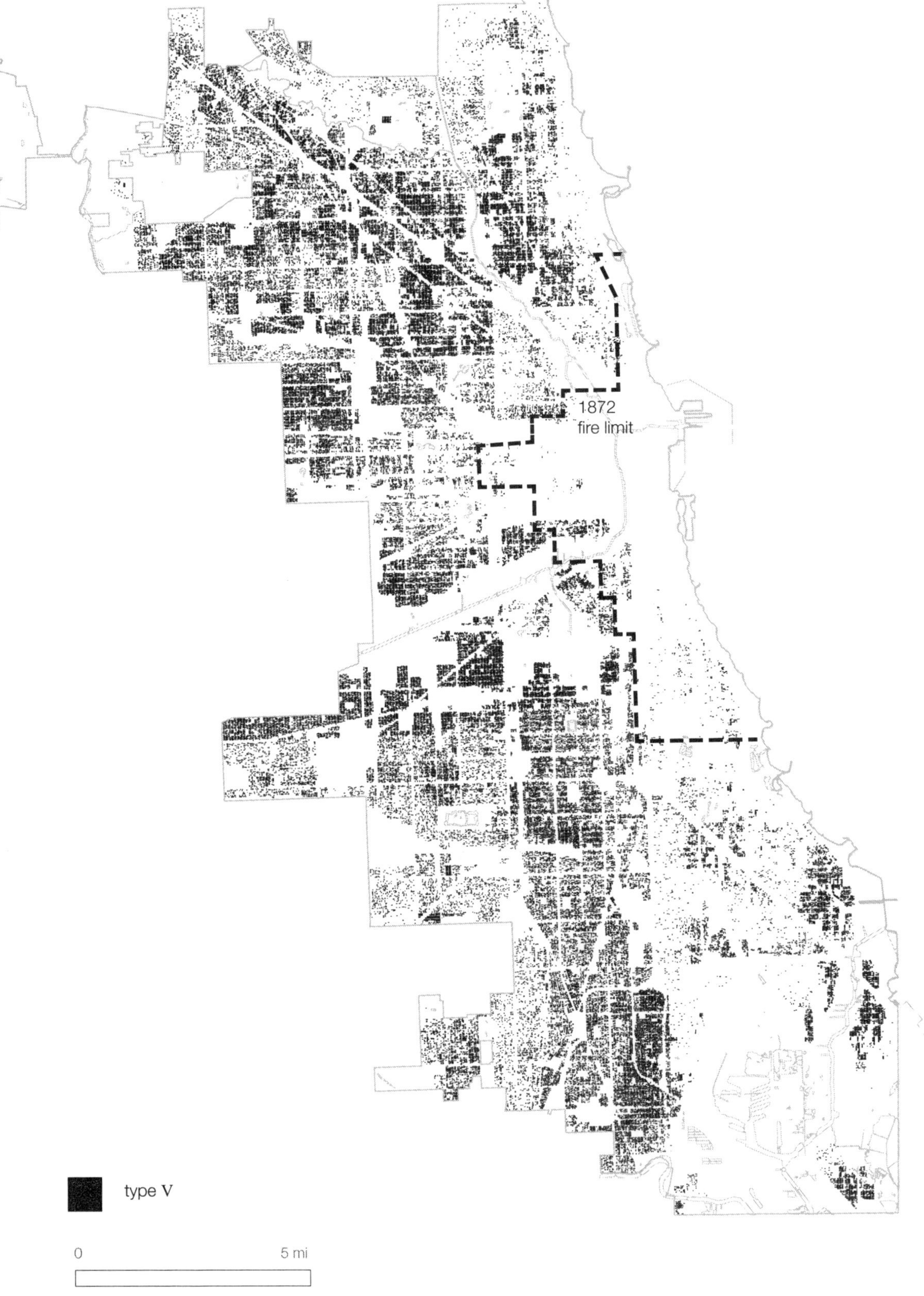

FIGURE 1.1 *Chicago's contemporary residential Type V construction (2020) and fire limits (1872).*

and open letters in newspapers in the days and weeks after the fire. This conflict condensed competing ideals of public safety and upward mobility into a battle for the identity of American building vernacular.

In 1872, after the Great Fire, Chicago was at an architectural turning point. Disaster had wiped out its center city, and while residents united in their commitment to rebuild, they remained divided by social structure and by tolerance of material risk. In particular, they struggled to determine the future of wood-frame construction.

Prominent public voices disagreed on the geographic material boundaries for a restored city. Business leaders, real estate speculators, and heads of industry wanted to push fireproof construction limits to the edge of the city limits, protecting Chicago for future generations. However, workers, already grappling with affordable home ownership, demanded that the limits only encompass the business center. Wood construction would allow its inhabitants to maintain their fragile grasp on economic mobility.

Chicago's debate was driven by intertwined material and social priorities, marking an origin story of American building codes and American material culture. The crowd of "1000 lunatics" and the opposing fireproofers were impassioned by the short- and long-term stakes embedded in this city-building decision. Ultimately, the fireproofers failed to ban wood-frame construction throughout the city. Urban wood construction did not become a footnote in the nation's early building improvisations; instead, it remains a persistent element of the American urban material fabric, reinforced and enabled by building codes.

The revised 1872 city codes, drafted after the debates and protests, approached material protection by segregating risk rather than eliminating it. Codes safeguarded business interests in one area while appeasing the workers' risk tolerance in another. This compromise resulted in the establishment of two tiers of urban material standards: combustible and noncombustible, light and heavy, short- and long-term, vulnerable and durable. A geographic "fire limit" zig-zagged around the central business district, separating two material environments and delineating the physical and regulatory isolation of risk geographies.

The evolution of architecture within Chicago's 1872 fire limits is extensively documented and analyzed. It was the test bed of architectural innovation, accommodating a business boom with new structural materials meeting the most stringent fire standards. From within the fire limits, the second city launched a technological volley with New York, learning as it built and competing for the tallest, most innovative new construction. Building and experimentation advanced so rapidly within Chicago's fire limits that scholars often refer to this architectural era as the Chicago school. However, the architecture outside of this boundary did not benefit from stringent regulation, investment, or related material invention.

Instead, the neighborhoods of unregulated material thoroughly escaped performance scrutiny and revision.

By 1894, Chicago's building codes had undergone another significant change. City ordinances began supplementing the geographic fire limits that had garnered so much attention and debate with a component-based system, the beginning of "construction types."[3] This shift, while not as overtly controversial as the 1872 fire-limit debate, was a significant milestone in the evolution of Chicago's building codes. It marked a transition from geographic restrictions to more nuanced, component-based regulation. This change did not provoke the same public response as the 1872 protest; it did not lead to marches or letters to editors by prominent political figures. Yet this code change ultimately marked a significant transfer of power with a long-lasting impact on the future of the city.

As Chicago's building codes moved toward standardization based on building components, they sacrificed spatial legibility. The component-based regulation did not easily reveal its potentials or consequences, hindering broad scrutiny. Instead, private entities such as the insurance and mortgage industries maintained the only aggregated data maps to spatially analyze material risk and building code consequences throughout the twentieth century. This form of rule-making masked insight and muted debate, replacing public awareness with private industry interests.[4]

Chicago's buildings of wood sticks and studs are now classified as Type V construction. Type V is the component-based label most American building codes now use to describe a combustible exterior wall and structural system, most often light-wood-frame construction. Chicago's Type V neighborhoods remain a distributed network today, visibly skirting around the 1872 fire limits (fig. 1.1).

The following pages examine how Chicago's early construction-material compromise affected its residents' social and economic well-being by analyzing the city's material usage patterns and the underlying values and systems that shaped them. The two-tiered material character of Chicago neighborhoods aligns with today's patterns of disinvestment, suggesting that urban economic risk patterns may be amplified by building material, a danger felt most intensely by Chicago's most vulnerable communities.

Additionally, Chicago's building codes fail to make their impacts clearly visible or to provide consistent economic protection, calling into question their claimed purpose to protect public welfare. This analysis ultimately points to a material durability blind spot in the current consumer market and in urban policies, perpetuated by the illegibility of increasingly complex component-based codes.

American cities were poised for a building-material debate by the time Chicago burned. A century earlier, visitors to the United States observed an emerging national material character, perceiving a connection between the prevalence and impermanence of wood and the restless opportunism of American society as it expanded west. The sociophysical relationship between enterprising Americans and their resourceful use of wood buildings was a striking deviation from the European preference for permanence using brick and stone masonry.[5]

As settlement spread across the American landscape from the seventeenth through the nineteenth centuries, dense forests still blanketed the entire eastern half of the United States. Faced with this abundance, early settlers generally saw woodlands as something to be tamed and cleared away rather than preserved or even extracted for valuable uses.[6] In this context, wood construction was a necessity. As the United States grew, some argued for an increased sense of permanence in American craft and construction.

Thomas Jefferson famously stated in his *Notes on Virginia* in 1785 that Americans must pursue enduring improvements to the country. He suggested brick and stone as lasting investments in nation-building and future stability.

> A country whose buildings are of wood can never increase in its improvements to any considerable degree. Their duration is highly estimated at 50 years. Every half century then our country becomes a tabula rasa, whereon we have to set out anew, as in the first moment of seating it. Whereas when buildings are of durable materials, every new edifice is an actual and permanent acquisition to the state, adding to its value as well as to its ornament.[7]

A contributor to *The American Museum* in the eighteenth century expressed a similar sentiment, stating:

> The evil in our architecture lies principally in this—that we build of wood. From this custom much immediate, as well as remote inconvenience, is to be expected: and certainly, however suddenly felt may be the comfort arising from celerity and dispatch, the numerous considerations of perishableness and want of safety, and call for repairs . . . will very much weigh with an enlightened people. . . . Bachelors only ought to build of wood—men who have but a life estate in this world, and who care little for those who come after them. Those who have either children or a wife to leave

> behind them will build of brick, if they wish to leave monuments of kindness, rather than a rent-charge.[8]

Despite perspectives favoring durability, the higher priorities of speed and material access as well as reliance on unskilled labor propelled wood construction to dominate the emerging American landscape. Advancements in wood transportation, processing, and building techniques enhanced the affordability and convenience of an already plentiful material supply, with Chicago at the center of this transformation.

By the end of the nineteenth century, rail lines had established material flows from New England to the Midwest, with cities rising to prominence when they acted as points of exchange. Chicago, in particular, became a massive transfer point for material converging from all directions. It was not just a hub for the distribution of wood but also a processing junction, transforming raw material to lumber with predictable dimensions at its wholesale docks and riverside mills. Lumber was then shipped east as freight cargo or distributed west for farm fencing and railroad ties.[9]

Historian William Cronon vividly describes the wooden cityscape that emerged in Chicago, stating: “In no other city on the planet was there a neighborhood to compare with the vast, strange landscape of stacked wood that dominated the South Branch of the Chicago River. In no other city did so large a lumber fleet gather to deliver so immense an output from so many different sawmills. And in no other city did so many customers from so extensive an area gather to buy so much wood.”[10]

FIGURE 1.2 *C. E. Noble,* Map of the Great Central Route and Its Connections, *“the most central, attractive, direct, and reliable thoroughfare between the eastern and western states” (1856). (Courtesy of the Library of Congress, Geography and Map Division)*

FIGURE 1.3 *"The Lumber District of Chicago." (*Harper's Weekly, *October 20, 1883)*

Readily available dimensional lumber provoked the invention of a new building technique in residential construction. Builders initially called this method of building a "balloon frame" because it was extremely light and "might blow away at the first strong wind."[11] St. Mary's Church in Chicago was among the first of these buildings on record in 1833. This accessible form of construction radically transformed homebuilding in the United States. Balloon framing was fueled by the newfound availability of dimensional lumber and the advent of mechanically produced nails. Additionally, cast-iron stoves replaced the need for hearths and chimneys, and pattern books propagated the opportunity to build one's own home without skilled labor or costly materials.

One of these pattern books, written in 1859 by D. H. Jacques, described wood construction as a short-term utility. Jacques stated that not only was wood available and affordable, it was also suitable for "the unstable and migratory character of our people." Jacques justified wood construction, asking, "Why should [the builder] seek a more enduring material? He will need the building but a few years; and his sons, perhaps have all 'gone West' or shall sell the paternal mansion so soon as it shall come into their possession and build for themselves."[12]

Jacques also explained that necessity drove the country's tolerant sentiments.

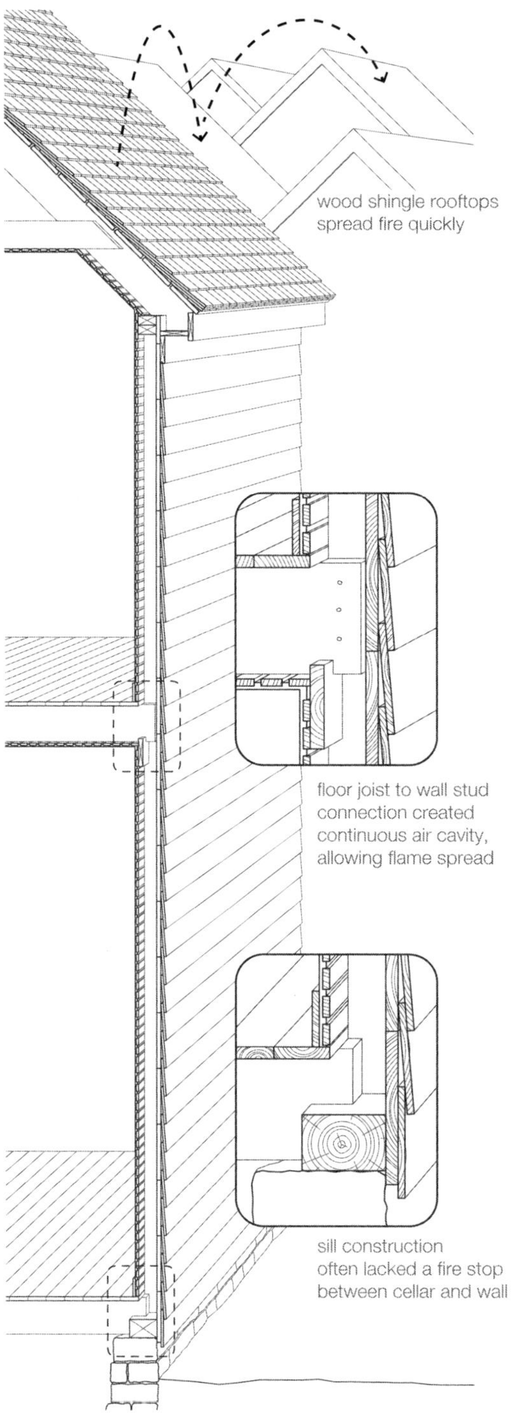

FIGURE 1.4 *Balloon-frame construction wall section.*

> While wood is abundant and comparatively cheap, it will necessarily continue to be employed by those who must build cheaply or not at all. Rent-paying is distasteful to our people, who choose rather to live in houses of low cost owned by themselves. . . . We are proud of the flimsy, unsubstantial structures, so sneered at by foreigners, which dot the whole face of the country. They are the homes of the people, who will by-and-by build and own better ones.[13]

Americans used wood construction to serve incremental needs as they developed pride in ownership. Looking back at this era from a contemporary perspective, historian Carole Shammas went so far as to claim victory for light-wood-frame architecture in America, stating that it "conquered all classes and remains the principal method for constructing homes today."[14] Contrary to Jacques's prediction, the tie between wood construction and American upward mobility ensured its enduring presence in construction practices long after early westward expansion had ended. However, the triumph of wood construction also faced its share of resistance. In large cities, conflagration hindered the spread of urban wood buildings and codified the limits of material choice.

CONFLAGRATION, CODES, AND ECONOMIC SEGREGATION

During the development of early American cities, large fires erupted frequently. However, few urban tragedies matched the scale of destruction caused by the Great Chicago Fire. After rapid expansion in the mid-nineteenth century, Chicago burned in October 1871. The fire covered an area four miles long and one mile wide in Chicago's city center.[15] It began near the South Branch lumber yards, where stacks of wood acted like a fuse, driving the flames toward the wood-framed Conley's Patch, located south of the business center.

Neither the masonry business district nor the river could effectively stop the intense blaze. The fire jumped the river and razed an expansive area of wooden workers' housing called the North Division until it was dampened by rain two days later. The conflagration ultimately destroyed 17,500 buildings and 2,600 acres. Eighty thousand people—one in three Chicago residents—were left homeless by the tragedy, with an estimated loss of three hundred lives.[16]

This catastrophe revealed the vulnerability of balloon-frame construction. Despite its speed and cost efficiency, the balloon frame concealed a flaw within its wall cavities that made it alarmingly combustible. Unlike earlier and later wood construction methods, the floor of a structure built with a balloon frame did not entirely block or interrupt vertical wall cavities (fig. 1.4). Consequently, each structure featured numerous continuous vertical shafts that effectively functioned as small chimneys, facilitating the rapid spread of flames.

Chicago's fire is often credited with revolutionizing construction in the United States, but few realize that despite its widespread destruction, the city did not abandon wood construction in its aftermath. The fire occurred one month before a mayoral election and sparked the formation of new political parties that championed construction methods as their central platform. The "Fireproof Party" emerged victorious, backed by local business owners keen on safeguarding speculative new office buildings in the city's center. They pledged to extend stringent noncombustible building requirements to the city limits. However, by the time the new mayor assumed office, thousands of wood-frame buildings had already sprung up in the city center. Moreover, the city required consensus among its aldermen to pass new legislation, and those neighborhood representatives backed competing proposals for the future of Chicago's buildings.

Although most Chicago residents agreed that eliminating vulnerable wooden buildings would improve the city's safety, they disagreed on the feasibility and affordability of rebuilding only with fireproof materials. The upfront cost of masonry construction was a significant barrier that was magnified in some areas by Chicago's raised streets, which required substantial basement foundations just to meet grade level.

Anton C. Hesing, a prominent representative of German immigrants in the North Division and longtime publisher of the newspaper *Staats-Zeitung*, spoke at length during a meeting of property owners near Lincoln Park in January 1872. Hesing appealed to the group to delay the implementation of a citywide fire limit, stating:

> The condition of the poor man in Chicago was far better than that of his neighbor in New York and Cincinnati, where he was compelled to live in the sixth story of some high building. By passing such a stringent fire ordinance, the poor man would no longer own his house, but would be reduced to the same condition as that poor class, and vice, and ignorance, and immorality would follow fast. . . . Let those men be, as they were before the fire. And they would in a short time be ready to build just such substantial brick buildings as Mr. Proudfoot was about to erect.[17]

Immigrant workers owned land in most of the burned area north of the river, and they could not afford to rebuild if the city outlawed wood construction. For the laborers, stricter building codes posed obstacles to maintaining the immediate value of their land, regardless of their potential to reduce future risk.

Representatives of the working class were not the only ones who argued for material leniency. Chicago's first mayor, William Butler Ogden, argued that the city should concede to allowable wood construction after the fire, despite having lost considerable personal and business property himself.

> We made our money generally in Chicago while living in cheap wood houses and stores. As soon as we were able we moved them back, and rebuilt of brick, stone, and iron. I apprehend it is wise, if not inevitable, in the burnt district of residences, chiefly on the North Side, that this be allowed to be done again. . . . If the people are left, in districts heretofore occupied chiefly by residences, shops, and small stores, to rebuild of wood or brick, as their means will admit, they will thrive; and, as their ability increases, they will . . . build anew upon the old sites, of brick and stone.[18]

Ogden was concerned about the depopulation of the North Side should a complete ban be enacted. Like most Americans at that time, Ogden saw wood construction as a temporary solution that would be eliminated as citizens prospered or commercial development evolved. Some scholars have suggested that he and other North Side landowning investors opposed the wood ban because their own speculative land interests would be well served by short-term construction. According to historian Christine Rosen, "[Ogden] and his fellow landowners had no intention of constructing durable brick tenements that were difficult to demolish or move, since their personal long-range plans for the land were to profit from future commercial development."[19]

Chicago residents proposed creative solutions such as pooling money toward the financing of higher-quality construction. A letter to the editor of the *Chicago Tribune* in 1872 suggested that citizens should unite to create $400,000 to $800,000 in total starting capital, enabling workers to join the association for a weekly fee and benefit from low-entry home ownership of a "quite substantial home" that would be paid off over time.[20] However, the proposal failed to gain traction. No financial mechanism was produced to enable affordable construction upgrades, perhaps owing to the opposition of some of the primary landholders, like Ogden, whose interests would benefit from less permanent construction.

Many charity organizations emerged after the fire, but none focused on enabling fireproof material upgrades. Instead, relief housing provided by the Citizens' Relief and Aid Society was just as poorly built as the inadequate speculator housing decried by the fireproofers.

The fireproofers' proposal to entirely ban wood construction within the city limits failed to gain support of the aldermen. Instead, the city adopted a new ordinance in 1872 that slightly expanded the previous fire limits geographically and offered districts the choice to "opt in" to increase fireproofing standards.

Only two years later, in 1874, the city revised the ordinance again and fully expanded the fire limits to be coincident with the city limits.[21] A. C. Hesing once again addressed the fire limits in the *Tribune*, noting rapid changes: lower brick masonry construction costs now made the implementation of expanded fire limits feasible.[22] However, Hesing failed to mention that the idea of expanded fire limits would naturally be more acceptable to a population that had already rebuilt.

Two years was enough to crystallize Chicago's 1872 fire limit into a contrasting urban building stock that persists today. As Chicago's central business district expanded beyond the river in the mid-twentieth century, fireproof construction still struggled to gain a foothold in neighborhoods filled with wood-frame housing built immediately after the fire. Chicago's line of compromise between opposing American values is still visible in the city's material fabric a century and a half later (see fig. 1.1).

Christine Rosen described Chicago's failure to pass an immediate wood construction ban in *The Limits of Power: Great Fires and the Process of City Growth in America* (2003). Rosen points out that allowing a tradition of low-quality worker housing in the city perpetuated "a legacy of slum housing," impacting the city and its social welfare for the remainder of the twentieth century. Rosen also describes the mistaken impression that low-quality buildings would be temporary, stating:

> What observers . . . never seem to have fully realized was that there would always be people who were too poor to obtain something better. This was a reality that not only made the construction of [poorly built] structures inevitable in the absence of any laws prohibiting their construction, but also made the voluntary abandonment of the buildings virtually impossible once they had been built.[23]

Rosen highlights another important element of the rebuilding pattern, noting that the fire limits ultimately expanded over some worker housing areas but not all. The wood-frame area known as Conley's Patch, just south of the former commercial business district, was quickly enveloped within the fireproof limits and expanded business district. Rosen notes: "The commercial redevelopment of the burnt-out slums on the southwest boundaries of the old business center forced the impoverished former residents to leave the area by replacing their demolished houses and businesses with first-class business buildings that rented at prices no worker could afford."[24]

The center city's poorest residents were displaced from Conley's Patch with little hesitation. By contrast, the North Division's land-owning laborers, armed with mechanisms for political representation and organized public advocacy, benefitted from the codes' compromise along with the business investors expanding the city center. The 1872 city codes, therefore, served the city's labor *and* investor interests by segregating risk, preserving the option of low-durability structures in the previously burned North Division, and enabling an enlarged business center to quickly consume Conley's Patch.

Considerable lore surrounds the Chicago fire within the field of architecture. It is often considered a significant stimulus for fireproof construction codes that turned the fervor of financial speculation toward architectural innovation. This is only part of the story.

In reality, the codes drafted after this overwhelming disaster left most of the burned acres to be rebuilt unchanged. The city even retained its lumberyards yards on the south branch of the river. The preservation of Chicago's Type V construction resulted from a collective choice to reap the economic benefits of differentiated durability zones throughout the city.

PRODUCT-ORIENTED RULES AND INDUSTRY INFLUENCE

When Chicago preserved its identity as a Type V city, it also solidified a mode of American city building that protected economic interests but fell short of public safety or resilience for all. As Chicago's building codes developed, the city's residents slowly surrendered their input and assessment of urban building materials to product manufacturers and the insurance industry.

Two trends initiated this transfer of power, and they happened so slowly that residents seemed hardly to notice. First, the codes shifted toward the regulation of buildings as isolated objects rather than elements of geographically organized material codes. The new rules responded to the conditions of a single building rather than those of a neighborhood, limiting collective interest. Second, the standardization of building rules coincided with industrial material standardization, and industries appropriated code development interests and input.

Material standardization developed in Chicago building ordinances relatively early. In the codes published immediately after the fire, building requirements still relied on rule-of-thumb material guidelines such as height to wall-thickness ratios.[25] "All buildings which shall, or may hereafter, be erected or constructed within said fire-limits, shall have outside

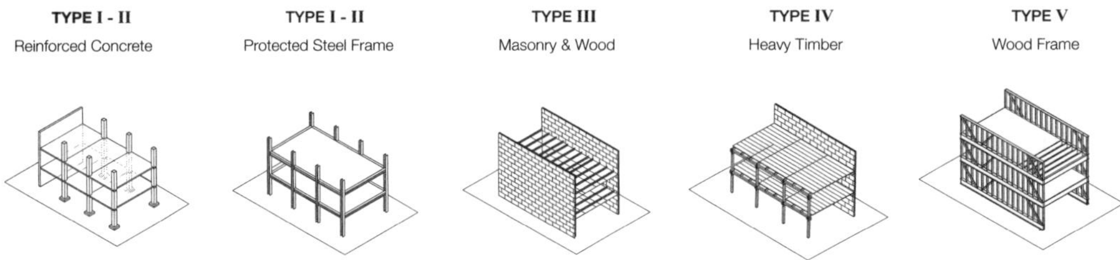

FIGURE 1.5 *Common materials within each building code construction type classification.*

walls of not less than one foot in thickness; and if any building shall be more than two stories in height . . . the outside walls of the basement and first story shall not be less than sixteen inches in thickness."[26]

Just a decade later, Chicago's 1881 codes still referred to masonry rule-of-thumb thickness, but they also started to introduce industrial standardization of materials. The 1881 codes stated that "composition roofs shall be made of not less than three-ply No. 2 felting" and "glass in all sky-lights, if not 'prismatic lights,' shall be protected by screens made of No. 10 (or heavier) wire, with meshes not exceeding 1A inches."[27] These 1881 codes also carry traces of the city's heightened fire sensitivity, describing, for example, a six-month imprisonment for a false fire alarm or "false outcry."

Chicago's quick adoption of material standardization was likely due to its substantial rail and manufacturing industries. The railroad's *Car Builders Dictionary*, published in 1879, was one of the first and most substantial records of early industrial standardization.[28] Therefore, 1881 was still early to see language referring to specific standard thicknesses and dimensions in building codes. Most industries achieved only limited success in implementing product standardization until the turn of the century.[29] Chicago's quick adoption of material standardization was an early indicator of product-based regulatory development and industrial influence.

Fire codes also drove the development of new industries, and those industries subsequently looked to regulatory policies to sustain them. Until 1873, the only terra-cotta factory in the United States was the Chicago Terra Cotta Company, established in 1866.[30] New fire codes called for protection surrounding steel-frame structures, which prompted a massive expansion of the terra-cotta industry. At its pinnacle, as many as seven plants resided within three hundred miles of Chicago. In 1932, as the terra-cotta business began to decline, the National Terra Cotta Society unsuccessfully lobbied the US government to require terra-cotta in all federal buildings.[31]

Much later, Chicago initiated a midcentury review to advance its building codes, which once again demonstrated the pressures of the building products industry on regulatory development. Henry T. Heald, president of the Illinois Institute of Technology, led the Citizens Building Code committee. During the committee's work, intense lobbying by material industries garnered local news media attention. Heald was "astonished and ashamed" when a subcommittee of the code council introduced last-minute amendments to the code. These changes appeared to cater to the Chicago Plastering Institute's request to increase the required thickness of plaster walls, slipping them into the fire safety requirements at the eleventh hour.[32]

By 1894, in keeping with the evident influence of industrial standardization, Chicago's building codes integrated new component-based fire-resistance requirements. They defined a set of classes according to building height and purpose and a corresponding set of fire resistance categories. "Fireproof," "skeleton," "ordinary," and "slow-burning" construction were defined in 1894 and became the precursors to today's construction types.[33]

The most stringent "fireproof construction" required all load-bearing elements and all stairs and elevator enclosures to be made of "incombustible material" and protected by brick, terra-cotta, or thick plaster on metal lath. "Slow-burning" and "mill-construction" allowed combustible interior structural elements with the types of protective materials mentioned above. Mill construction also required specific cross-section sizes for heavy timber, similar to today's Type IV, heavy-timber construction. Ordinary construction was defined as masonry walls surrounding unprotected wood-frame infill, like contemporary Type III.[34]

Building code construction types are designed to control material performance to protect both individual occupants and limit cumulative urban risk. During the earlier eras of geographic fire limits, the spatial impact of building codes was obvious. As cities developed beyond the fire limits, they increasingly relied only on construction types to regulate material, and the results were harder to envision. The rules now operate as a distributed matrix within the codes, and their impact is spread incrementally, through individual buildings across the city.

The shift toward construction types tied an individual building's characteristics more closely to its material combustibility requirements but eventually reduced the role of external risk and concealed collective urban impacts.[35] Despite targeting a fundamentally urban risk, conflagration, construction types only assess the performance of a single building or component.

The construction type classification within codes relies on meticulous tests of each material's behavior when exposed to extremely high heat using a custom "vertical tube furnace" (fig. 1.6).[36] However, despite their precision in one category of performance, the codes completely neglect several significant performance factors, failing to account for the environmental risks of the surrounding context or to evaluate the urban-scale consequences of material rules.

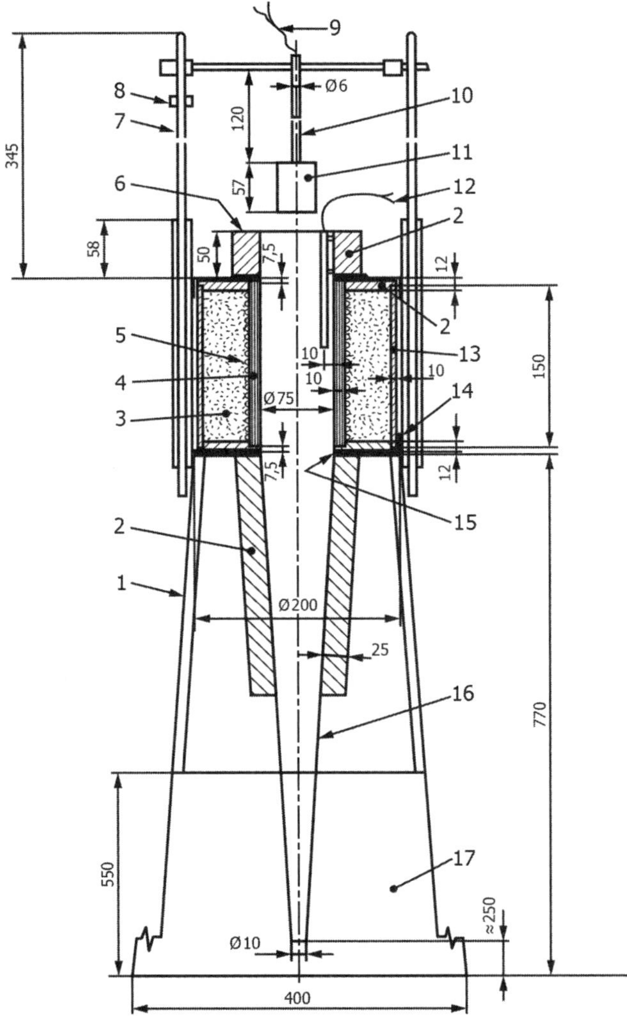

FIGURE 1.6 *Standard test method for assessing combustibility of materials using a tube furnace with a cone-shaped airflow stabilizer, at 750°C. (Courtesy of ASTM International, E2652-22)*

The construction and manufacturing industries were not the only for-profit entities influencing building code development. The fire insurance industry also played a substantial role, including the development of its own geographic risk analyses. However, like the codes themselves, the fire insurance industry did not necessarily aim to uniformly limit fire risk. Their focus on ensuring profitability could lead to varied incentives to protect individual buildings.

In her thorough history of fireproof construction, historian Sarah Wermiel explains that fire insurance encouraged risk by socializing the potential cost, thereby creating a safety net for risk-taking. Wermiel says that

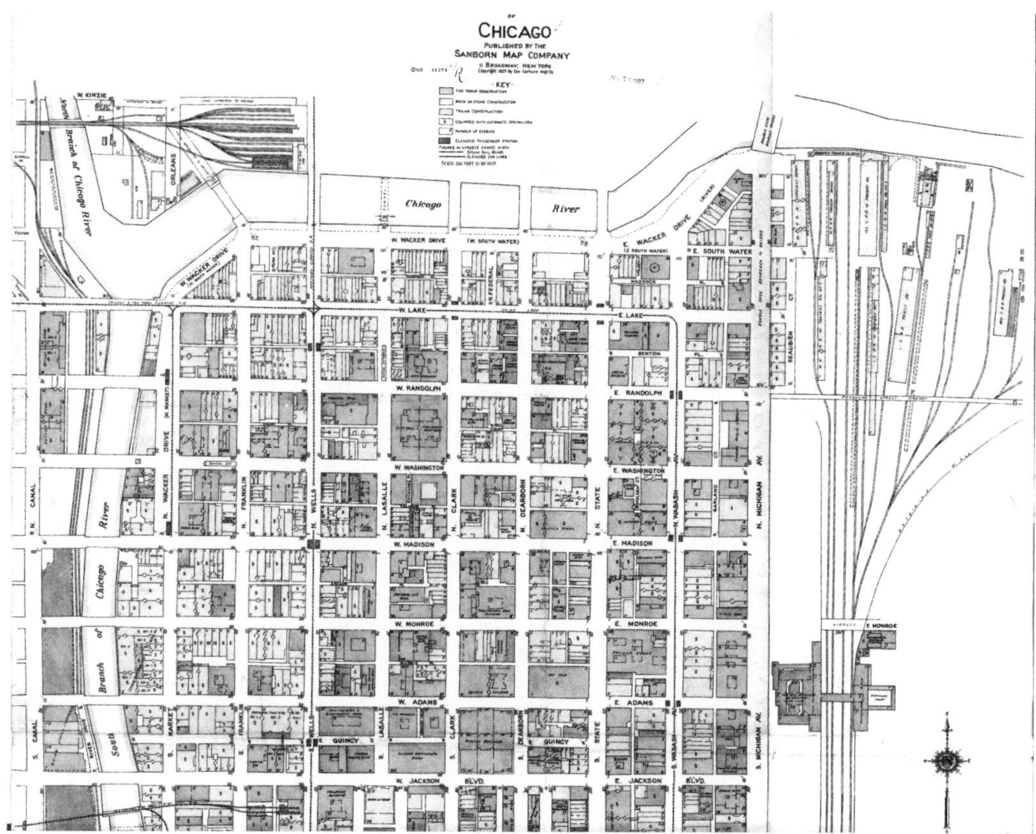

FIGURE 1.7 *Sanborn fire insurance map from Chicago, Cook County, Illinois (1927). This map shows three material designations: masonry, fireproof construction, and frame construction. (Courtesy of Library of Congress, Geography and Map Division, Sanborn Maps Collection)*

"people could shift the cost of protection from themselves to others by purchasing fire insurance."[37] This phenomenon will be discussed further in the next section as a "safe development paradox" related to flood insurance.

Wermiel further explains that the insurance companies were not risk-averse for individual buildings: "To a stock fire insurance underwriter, it made no difference how many individual properties burned so long as he earned enough in premiums to cover losses and expenses, and pay dividends to stockholders. In fact, the risky properties, for which he charged high premiums, could be profitable for agents and companies: they brought the former higher commissions and the latter more income to invest."[38]

While the fire insurance industry may not have protected collective risk evenly, they did maintain one of the only forms of urban building-material analysis in the absence of geographically clear building codes. The Sanborn Map Company began recording and mapping building-material patterns in 1867 (see fig. 1.7).[39] Sanborn maps documented building locations, heights, and exterior wall materials across American cities; Sanborn then sold their maps to insurance companies to give them precise material, geographic, and spatial information to assess risk exposure.

The Sanborn maps initially operated alongside municipal fire limits. Early on, both public municipal codes and private industry analyzed and controlled urban material from a geographic and spatial perspective. However, by 1894, as Chicago shifted from fire limits toward construction types, it effectively shifted the geographic and spatial understanding of urban building-material distribution to private industry. For several decades in the early twentieth century, as much of Chicago's building stock was established, only the fire insurance industry, mortgage lenders, and federal agencies maintained a legible overview of urban material patterns across the city.

The Sanborn Map Company's work eventually transitioned away from mapping urban material when insurance companies turned to alternative risk calculation methods. In 1997, the Library of Congress acquired and made publicly available approximately one million historical Sanborn maps.[40]

MORTGAGE LENDING AND DISREGARD FOR DURABILITY

At the turn of the century, Chicago's building codes arguably shifted from protecting the public to serving industry interests. Industry influence over building-material regulation produced a corresponding transition from clear material geographies to component-based obscurity in building codes.

The subsequent phase of building control and priority-setting was led by the mortgage-lending industry. Like the insurance industry, mortgage lenders maintained their own forms of urban material analyses, and they demonstrated an increasing disregard for the economic impact of material durability, reinforcing a lack of public awareness with problematic consequences.

In the 1920s and '30s, Chicago economists played an important role in shaping decades of mortgage-lending investment by pioneering new forms of spatial and socioeconomic analyses. The now-infamous economist Homer Hoyt was at the forefront of this research with his influential studies of Chicago's land values and real estate projections. Hoyt's PhD dissertation, titled *One Hundred Years of Land Values in Chicago* (1933), was the first work to analyze market land value according to geographic and social patterns.

However, Hoyt's work over the next decades also underpinned discriminatory property valuation methods. These methods focused on race and ethnicity as measures of economic risk, leading to significant disparities in property valuations and access to credit that perpetuated racial and economic inequities.

Hoyt's methods and the lending practices they engendered are of particular interest to this study of Type V cities for two reasons. First, Hoyt's temporal study of land valuation provides valuable insights into the economic repercussions of the 1872 fire limits. Second, his early writings and subsequent publications on federal lending reveal a shift in the perception of material durability as a measure of investment value, a concept that was previously fundamental to real estate appraisal.

In the book printed from his dissertation, Hoyt described the significant impact of the fire limits established after the Great Fire on the city's land valuation and development patterns. He argued that rebuilding outside of the fire limits was so exuberant that it temporarily lowered the value of the land inside the fire limits. In addition,

> the fire had also another very important effect in that it accelerated the building of a belt of workingmen's cottages in a semicircle around the outskirts of the city. An ordinance, enacted after the fire, had prohibited the erection of wooden buildings near the center of the city. As the workers could not afford to live in no other kind and also found that new [rail] carshops . . . were all being located on the edge of the built-up area, they began to seek homesites outside of the fire limits. . . . This encircling belt of frame houses grew rapidly during 1872. . . . In addition to this belt, seven miles long and one mile broad, that adjoined the solid growth of the city, there were streamers of a straggling growth of frame cottages radiating from Englewood along the railroads, northward toward fifty-fifth Street, southwestward toward South Englewood and Washington Heights and southeastward toward Grand Crossing and South Chicago.[41]

Later, Hoyt concluded that "the best use of some urban land at that time was for cheap frame dwellings. The extension of the fire limits since that time to cover almost the entire city has now been looked on as an advantage, preventing, as it does, the erection of cheap frame houses that would lower property values."[42]

At the time, economic valuation was closely linked to material durability. *One Hundred Years of Land Values in Chicago* references real estate valuation theories by influential scholars like H. A. Babcock, who advocated for assessing real estate value based on exterior wall material, among other factors. Historian Carole Shammas also describes the basis for this approach in early American appraisal guidelines: "To determine a dwelling's valuation, the government instructed these [appraisers] to consider

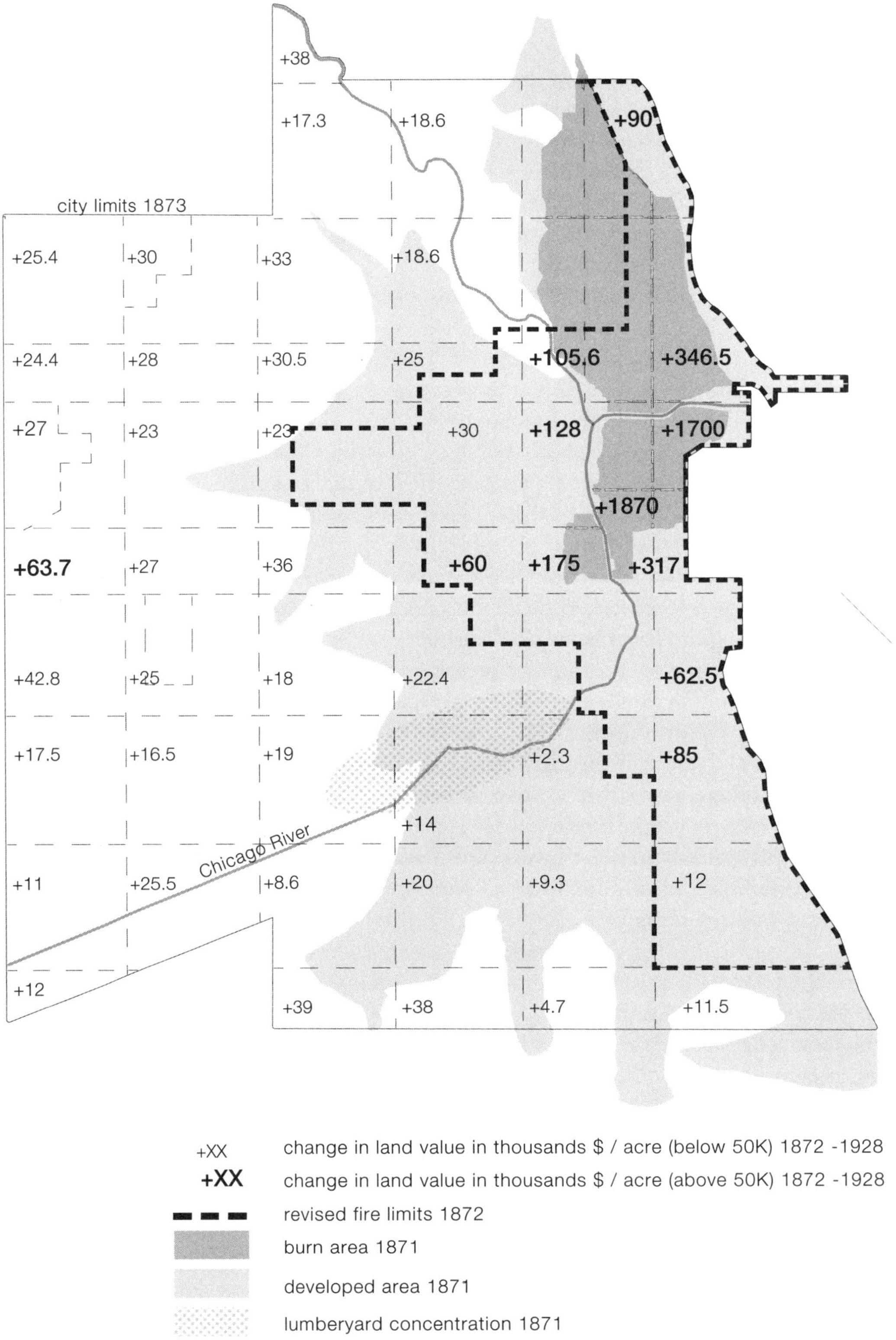

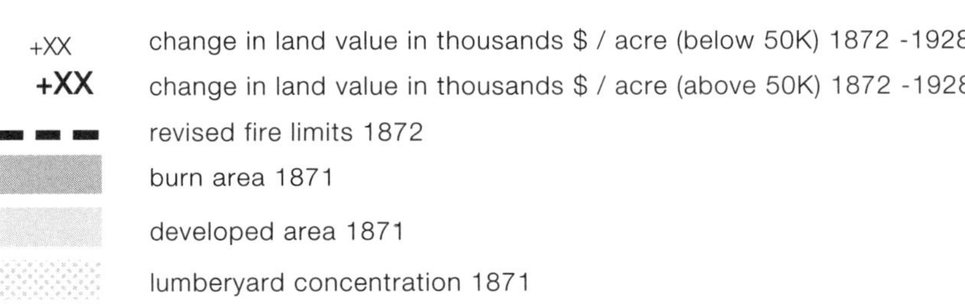

FIGURE 1.8 *Fire limits (1872, 1874); burn, lumberyard, and developed areas (1871); and land value appreciation rates (1872–1928).*

not only the structure's state of repair and square footage but also the type of construction (brick, stone, or wood), number of stories, and number of glazed windows and panes."[43]

Underscoring the typical view of material value at the time, Hoyt often used qualifiers that indicated low value when mentioning wood-frame buildings: "cheap frame," "frame hovels," or "frame cottages."

Hoyt's research formed the basis of further analyses related to material economics. Figure 1.8 shows the 1872 fire limits compared to changes in land value over the sixty years following the fire.[44] Hoyt's observations, which linked frame structures to lower property values, are particularly relevant here. Properties within the 1872 fireproof area saw the fastest-growing values, while properties initially allowing flammable construction experienced slower value increases.

The establishment of the 1872 fire limits was not just a matter of safety but also a reflection of neighborhood wealth. Neighborhoods outside of the business district had an opportunity to voluntarily join the bounds of the fire limits. By 1874, the fire limits were expanded to the city limits, but the material character of the inner-ring neighborhoods was already established and continued to influence the rate of property value appreciation for decades to come. Thus, material regulation boundaries responded to relative neighborhood wealth and locked it in place.

In 1934, the US government named Hoyt chief economist at the Federal Housing Administration (FHA). Within the FHA, Hoyt reinforced the view that a neighborhood's building material would impact its economic risk. However, Hoyt also added demographic characteristics to the urban and housing properties he studied as indicators of market value and investment risk. As part of his work for the FHA, Hoyt measured and mapped rental occupancy, nonwhite occupancy, building material, and building age, among other characteristics.[45] He coined the term "overlay mapping," a method of analyzing spatial and economic trends by substituting demographic and housing attributes as proxies for economic risk.[46]

In his FHA publication *The Structure and Growth of Residential Neighborhoods in American Cities* (1939), Hoyt describes his use of map overlay as follows:

> In order to bring out at a glance the areas in which a concentration of the desired housing facilities exists, a technique has been devised for superimposing a series of patterns on each other. . . . This procedure is easily flexible—the area finally delineated will depend on the factors and the limits chosen by the investigator. In other cities, a different choice of factors might be advisable—other than white occupancy, for example, a characteristic which may be

used with justification only in southern cities as a measure of the poorest housing conditions. In northern cities, the worst slums are occupied by whites, and some cities have a relatively small Negro population.[47]

Hoyt stated that spatial separation of housing types was beneficial because "the value of any single home is affected by the condition, type, and value of surrounding homes." He also claimed that segregation of race and nationality was beneficial because "racial mixtures tend to have a depressing effect upon land values—and therefore upon rents."[48] However, unlike most theories that he justified with maps and numeric analysis, Hoyt provided only anecdotal evidence to back his claims on racial segregation. Hoyt's failure to justify discriminatory arguments suggests that prevailing societal attitudes at the time did not demand justification.[49]

A great deal of the logic of American neighborhoods—in particular, the creation of distinct pockets of material, racial, and ethnic homogeneity that persist in Chicago today—was reinforced by New Deal–era investment practices. Within the Home Owners Loan Corporation (HOLC) "redlining maps," diminishing attention to material-durability economics is evident. The HOLC maps are significant because they demonstrate another mechanism of material risk analysis that was available to and valued by the mortgage and insurance industries but was unavailable to the public, and they show that cultural priorities, such as racial and ethnic biases, overshadowed material durability concerns.

The HOLC was a New Deal–era relief effort predating the FHA. It was designed to save failing mortgages from foreclosure. From 1933 to 1936, the HOLC refinanced over one million mortgages, "saving eighty percent of the homes for the original owners."[50] When homeowners were having problems making the payments on their mortgage loans, the HOLC refinanced the loans for the borrowers, often at longer terms and therefore lower monthly cost. This program was good for both lenders and borrowers and helped to stabilize the markets. However, the HOLC and the banks did not grant loans for all homes, to all people, or in all neighborhoods.

In 239 cities, the HOLC produced the now-infamous Residential Security Maps, which designated neighborhood-level mortgage risks to lenders. Kenneth Jackson dubbed this practice "redlining" in his book *Crabgrass Frontier* (1985). These maps documented mortgage-lending risk by overlaying a red shade to neighborhoods considered high risk or "hazardous" and a yellow tone to "declining" neighborhoods. The term "redlining" implies that federally backed lenders denied capital investment to these neighborhoods.

Although HOLC predated the FHA, the redlining maps were based on Hoyt's earlier theories developed while he was a student in Chicago.[51]

Figure 1.9 compares Hoyt's later Chicago map, published with the FHA in *The Structure and Growth of Residential Neighborhoods in American Cities*, to the almost identical HOLC redlining map showing neighborhood classifications.[52] Kenneth Jackson also notes that additional influential appraisal guides at the time emphasized similar, racially biased methods and the importance of building-material durability, including Frederick Babcock's *The Valuation of Real Estate* (1932) and Stanley L. McMichael's *Appraising Manual* (1931).[53]

Like the Sanborn maps, the neighborhood-level assessments conducted by the HOLC and FHA were primarily designed as tools to support private industry. An interagency report from 1939 described lender access to FHA neighborhood surveys.

> The Division has copies of the summary reports from all of these [property inventory] surveys and, in addition, block tabulations from many of them. The collection of material includes thousands of maps covering hundreds of local areas, including several hundred maps prepared in the Division. Many of the maps are available not only in Washington but in the field offices where they are available to representatives of local lending institutions who may wish to consult them.[54]

The FHA publicly outlined its policy logic in its publication "The Structure and Growth of Residential Neighborhoods," but its data was only shared with lenders.[55] HOLC maps, which considered neighborhood-level material assessment as a factor when calculating economic risk, were not made public until many decades later. This catering to lenders by the government and mortgage industry restricted public access to material geographic trends and limited public awareness of the long-term impacts of building-material patterns.

By viewing economic risk as a matter of interest only to investors and not as valuable information for city residents, city-builders allowed financial institutions to perpetuate material segregation and disinvestment for some residents, under the guise of protecting collective economic stability.

Furthermore, HOLC maps demonstrate that financial risk assessment related to material characteristics, such as maintenance quality, long-term durability, or even combustibility, was easily overshadowed by cultural demographic biases. In several instances, HOLC's Chicago surveys recorded high-quality building materials dominating zones still labeled "hazardous" due to racial demographics.[56] Although material characteristics featured prominently in the HOLC survey notes, they appear to be less influential than racial and ethnic biases in determining neighborhood ratings.

FIGURE 1.9 a & b *(a) The HOLC residential security maps for Chicago (1939); and (b) Homer Hoyt's Chicago assessment published in* The Structure and Growth of Residential Neighborhoods in American Cities *(1939).*

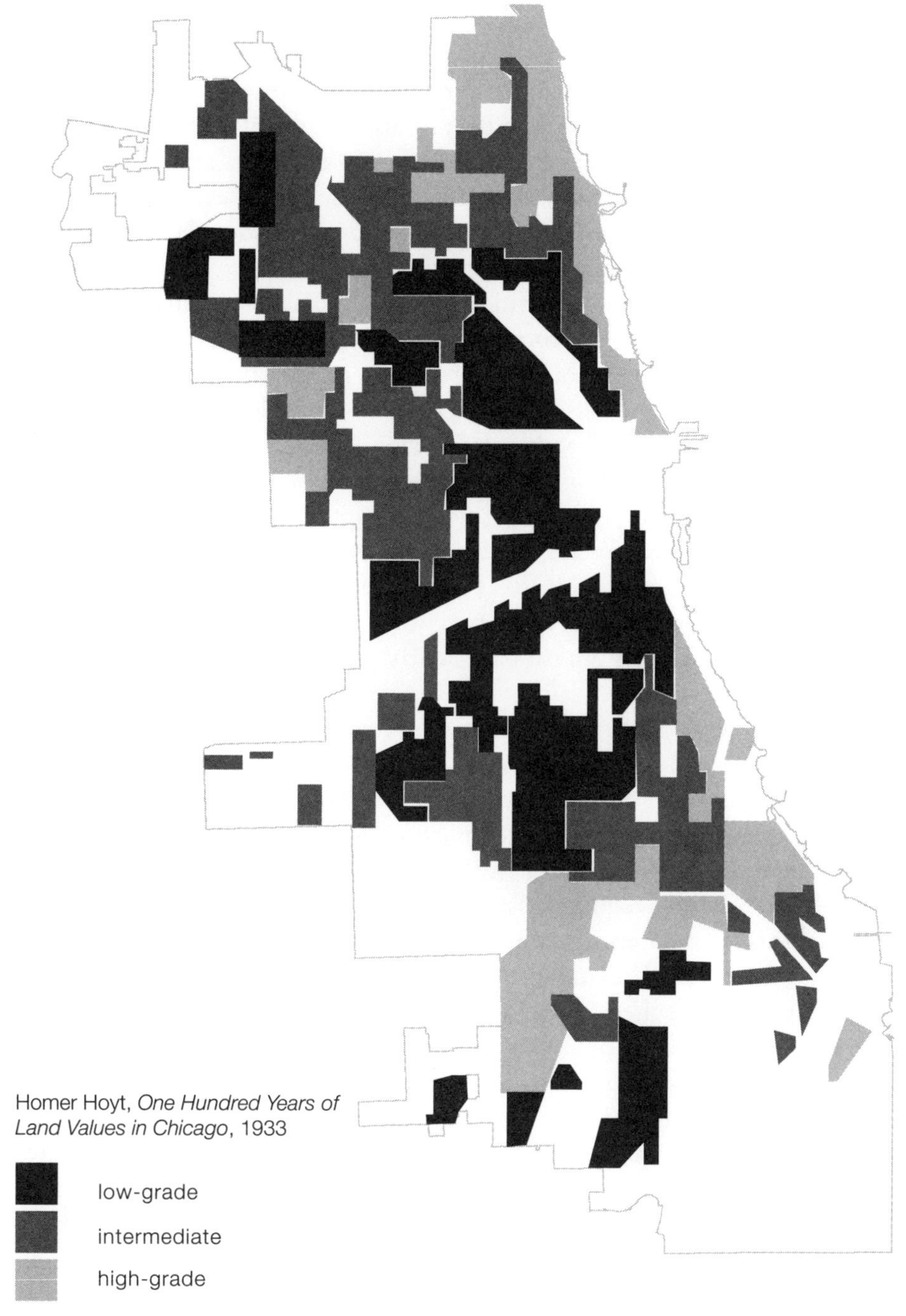

Homer Hoyt, *One Hundred Years of Land Values in Chicago*, 1933

At the same time, the US Census of Housing ceased collecting and publishing building-material trends across cities, further demonstrating an emerging disregard for material risk or social impact. Until 1940, the Census recorded these trends, but by 1950, it had shifted focus to spatial characteristics and services (such as bedroom counts, plumbing features) rather than structural or exterior wall materials.[57]

Contemporary material maps still appear to follow the old HOLC boundaries. Plate 2 demonstrates that mid-twentieth-century boundaries drawn around economic priorities produced persistent material patterns in the city. One can see a correlation between the HOLC rating system and today's material distribution, particularly in the ring of neighborhoods outside of the central business district that Hoyt described in his 1933 book.[58] Most neighborhoods rated yellow (declining) still contain the city's densest collections of remaining wood-frame structures, while those rated blue (desirable) and green (best) also retain more substantial Types I–III residential construction today. Hoyt's theories and investment patterns documented by the HOLC further entrenched existing material and social segregation. This segregation, coupled with a disregard for durability as a collective risk, has proven particularly problematic for socially vulnerable populations.

Before delving into the analysis of contemporary material durability impacts, it is important to highlight another lasting influence of New Deal–era mortgage lending on urban material trends. The FHA, acting as an insurer rather than a direct lender, influenced the uniformity of construction within blocks and neighborhoods. Houses guaranteed by FHA-backed loans required inspection to ensure that they met FHA standards. This led builders to replicate the same FHA-approved model house plans.[59] The massive demand for rapid home construction coupled with FHA policies resulted in clusters of repeated construction types across entire neighborhoods.

To ensure investment quality, the FHA published a set of standards outlined in "Circular 2, Property Standards: Requirements for Mortgage Insurance Under Title II of the National Housing Act." These criteria later became known in the industry as the HUD Minimum Property Standards (MPS). Similar to the standards developed for post–Chicago fire insurers, the federal MPS focused on combustibility as the primary consideration in determining material choice based on density and occupancy.[60] Although the FHA intended the MPS to serve as a backup in the absence of local codes, by 1958 they had surpassed many local codes and became de facto building codes for the highly repetitive neighborhoods that defined post–World War II urban and suburban construction.[61]

Additionally, loans almost exclusively funded white applicants due to a range of racist lending practices.[62] This racially biased lending combined

FIGURE 1.10 a & b *"Color(ed) Theory." In her exhibition at the Museum of Contemporary Art (2017), artist Amanda Williams shows (a) images of painted wood-frame homes slated for demolition; and (b) gold-painted bricks. (Photographs by Tom Harris)*

with repetitive construction further solidified Hoyt's economic ideas, leading to the creation of racially, ethnically, and materially homogeneous neighborhoods.

Since the publication of the HOLC maps in *Crabgrass Frontier*, scholars have debated their accessibility and purpose. Some argue that they were not widely distributed enough to dictate lending; rather, they recorded typical lending practices by banks at the time.[63] Whether they operated as surveys or guides, the maps lay bare a pervasive set of racist practices and historical injustices that shaped American cities.[64]

The HOLC maps reveal how socially constructed priorities overtook technical considerations in judging risk and value in real property investment. They were part of a mortgage-lending structure that further isolated and homogenized urban material, concentrated analytical capacity in the hands of industry, and limited public awareness of the economic risk associated with urban building-material patterns.

CHICAGO'S MATERIAL BLIND SPOT

"Color(ed) Theory," a widely acclaimed 2015 project by artist and architect Amanda Williams, featured boldly painted abandoned wood-frame homes in Chicago's South Side. Williams selected color shades and structures to represent the local neighborhood culture, painting and photographing houses prior to city-sponsored demolition. When Williams showed her work at the Museum of Contemporary Art in 2017, striking images of colorful wood-frame structures occupied the gallery adjacent to a stack of gold-painted bricks (fig. 1.10).

Williams described the artwork as a comment on the value of salvaged brick as a material export from struggling South Side neighborhoods. "All of a sudden you start to think of what [that] translates into in terms of commerce, or economy, or value that's not being mined in the neighborhood."[65]

A century and a half after the Great Fire and its ensuing great material compromise, Chicago's wood-frame neighborhoods remain vulnerable. The city's economic challenges disproportionately impact its most vulnerable communities. The Englewood neighborhood on the South Side stands as a stark example, as one of the hardest-hit areas during the economic and foreclosure crisis that began in 2008. Facing waves of home abandonment, the city marked clusters of wood-frame homes in Englewood with red Xs to signal to firefighters that the buildings were abandoned and need not be saved. In 2012, the city spent $14 million to demolish 736 vacant buildings, and former mayor Rahm Emanuel closed fifty schools in many South Side neighborhoods with declining populations.[66]

Economists describe urban disinvestment as a contagious phenomenon, where the risk can spread from one house to the next, similar to the spread of disease or the devastating conflagrations that led to new building regulations. Economist Brian Melzer highlights the economic dangers associated with maintenance costs in vulnerable neighborhoods. His research reveals that owners burdened with negative debt (owing more than the property is worth) "cut back substantially on home improvements . . . and maintenance relative to owners with positive equity."[67] This reduction in upkeep expenditures can increase visible signs of neighborhood deterioration and create a spiral of underinvestment.[68] In short, the decay or abandonment of one property can increase the risk for neighboring properties and contribute to an overall decline in value. Some types of building construction require more frequent maintenance, exacerbating economic strain and its visible consequences.

Plate 3 shows abandoned properties reported to the City of Chicago between 2010 and 2019. This image shows the pattern of abandonment spreading like contagion through the patchwork of neighborhoods, each with its own building-material character. The red outlines in plate 3 indicate redlined neighborhoods in Chicago, or those neighborhoods rated hazardous and excluded from New Deal–era investment. The gray outlines in the image are neighborhoods that were sufficiently developed at the time to receive a more positive rating from the HOLC.

As discussed above, redlining in the early twentieth century produced decades of underinvestment and is seen today as a predictor of many physical and social vulnerabilities. Yet abandonment patterns more closely follow wood construction in these neighborhoods than redlining, and the problem intensifies when the two combine.

These maps raise pivotal questions: Does material vulnerability heighten the risk of disinvestment, especially when coupled with another social risk? Is Type V construction uniquely susceptible to neighborhood disinvestment? Plates 3 and 4 compare abandonment and foreclosure rates with material patterns. Material properties show a statistically significant correlation to these forms of disinvestment. In fact, foreclosure and abandonment patterns in Chicago more strongly correlate with the density of wood-frame construction than any other social vulnerability factor as defined by the Centers for Disease Control and Prevention. These social vulnerabilities include poverty rate, minority rate, unemployment rate, lack of vehicle access, low educational attainment averages, and crowded housing, among other factors.[69]

Poverty rates are the second-most significant predictor of foreclosure and abandonment, behind the concentration of Type V building. Overall, the density of wood-frame housing within a neighborhood predicts 7 to

9 percent of abandonment and foreclosure rates, constituting a significant yet overlooked risk factor in a complex urban environment. Given that neighborhood-level economic decline and disinvestment are persistent urban issues, potentially impacted by building-material performance, these findings underscore the crucial need to expand the analysis of building-material performance at the urban scale.

The potential connection between Type V construction and economic stability at the neighborhood level has practical implications for policymakers, architects, and urban economists. Contemporary city data analytics departments would be the first to warn that correlation is not causation in urban analysis.[70] Instead, correlations can help identify the right questions and guide more detailed analysis. Economic stability can also be evaluated in more detail at a smaller scale using measures of building component durability.

Durability refers to a building component's capacity to withstand change, decay, or wear. Many factors can influence a building assembly's durability, including climatic conditions and construction quality. However, the average service life of the building's outermost layers generally predicts the frequency of maintenance requirements.

Home inspection literature and product warranties provide insights into building-material durability and maintenance cycles. Maintenance cycles are important in terms of ongoing expenses for individual owners. As noted by the economist's earlier description, they might also impact the rate of contagious urban disinvestment, a crucial consideration for urban well-being.

Figure 1.11 compares upfront construction costs with the service life of materials commonly used in construction Types I–III (noncombustible) versus Type V (combustible) construction assemblies.[71] Type V wood structures require a lower initial investment, but some components may demand more frequent maintenance. On average, Type V systems will incur maintenance costs more often, necessitating double or triple the maintenance frequency of some Type I–III systems. Moreover, Type V load-bearing elements are highly vulnerable to moisture and decay if the outermost weather barriers fail.[72]

Figure 1.11 also shows these maintenance timelines in relation to residential ownership timelines, including tax and financial structures that may influence ownership patterns. The American Community Survey (ACS) conducted by the US Census Bureau and published in 2021 reports that the current average ownership tenure of American homes is thirteen years, a generally high number compared to the historical average of six to seven years.[73] If Americans are only occupying a home for close to a decade, a typical buyer may be disinterested in long-term durability and maintenance cycles.[74]

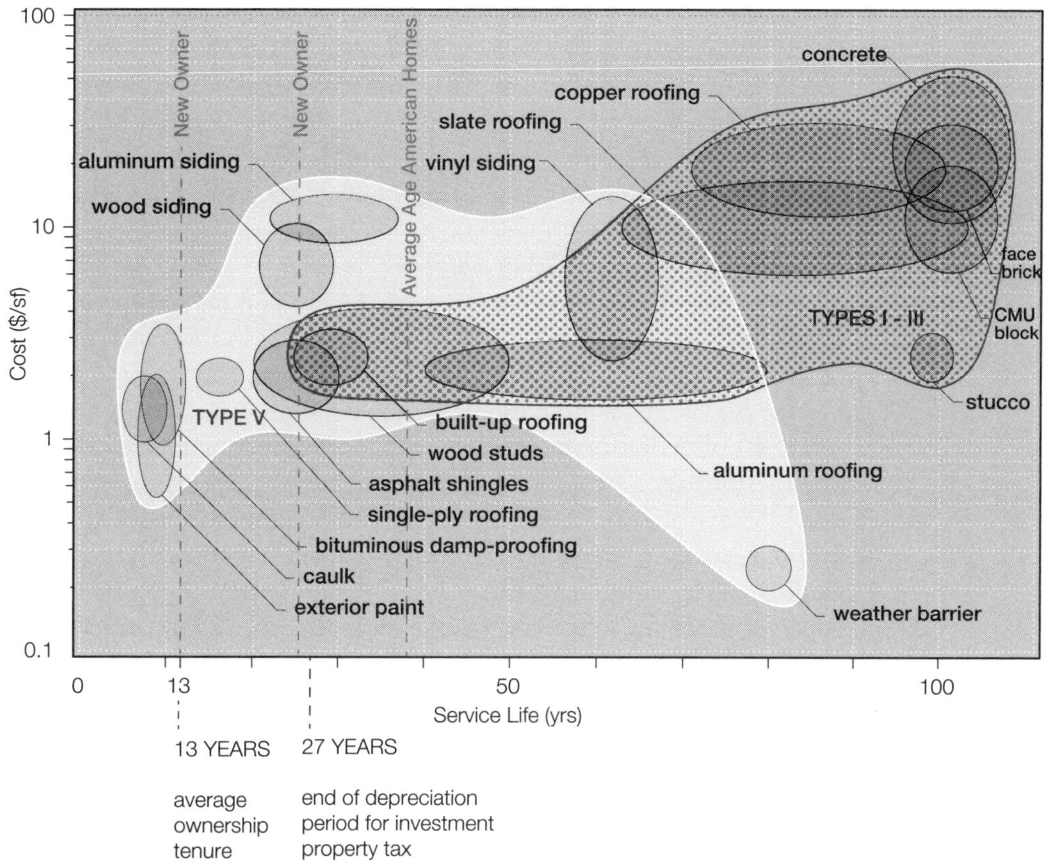

FIGURE 1.11 *Upfront cost and service life of construction type building components.*

Although Type V, wood-frame construction may require more frequent maintenance to prevent visible deterioration, not all wood construction will lead to disinvestment or decline. Instead, a concentration of wood-framed structures in a neighborhood may act as an amplifier for other forms of economic risk.

Maintenance cycles are also likely to increase over time as the structures age, and the average Chicago wood-frame home was built in 1925.[75] A century later, varying levels of upfront investment in material across neighborhoods create physical risk disparities that intensify the economic exposure for some communities and raise questions about public awareness and municipal assessment of these risks.

Most contemporary city assessors, including Chicago's assessor, manage their own geographic property data—including building-material data—for the purposes of property valuation and tax assessment. Building and land assessment is an appraisal, an estimate of property value, by the government for tax purposes. To distribute the tax burden, a city's base property taxes rely on a multiple of the property's assessed value, including land and building (sometimes called improvement) value.

Building-material information is collected because historical tax guidelines instructed assessors to consider exterior wall material in their home valuations. However, building material seems to have no bearing on home assessment values in Chicago today. An analysis of Chicago's contemporary residential property data shows no statistically significant relationship between material and assessed value.[76]

The disconnect between economic assessment and building and planning in cities is a significant issue that can be addressed with a more holistic approach to building-material health, safety, and welfare. Building technology scholarship presents a compelling case for the importance of exterior wall material on a range of contemporary social and environmental performance issues. Exterior walls and roofing largely predict a building's lifespan and operational energy.[77] Similarly, exterior walls and load-bearing elements are the primary determinants of a building's embodied energy and embodied carbon.[78] Despite these well-established parameters regarding the impacts of building material, neither Chicago nor the ICC publishes spatialized analysis of collective material vulnerability or the health, safety, and welfare consequences of building codes.

Real estate markets also disregard building material when it comes to property valuation. Property values reflect occupiable square footage and bedroom counts but rarely adjust on the basis of the material construction of the home. The durability gap between Type V and other forms of construction occupies a blind spot in the real estate market that also extends into studies on urban disinvestment and environmental justice.[79]

Historically, economists and appraisers distinguished between building materials according to value and risk, and early city builders believed that wood framing was a form of temporary construction. Today, the city and the public have more access than ever to building-material data, and yet cities and real estate markets seem to ignore exterior wall material when evaluating and valuing property. A century after building-material debates dominated Chicago politics, Chicago has golden bricks in its galleries, abandoned wood frames spreading through vulnerable communities, and an overlooked link between building material and economic vulnerability.

Throughout its history, Chicago's material and investment boundaries reinforced each other, first creating then perpetuating the Type V city's material and social segregation. Chicago workers thrived within balloon-frame structures and then defended the Type V city while accepting its separation from the protected business center.

Over the course of the twentieth century, Chicago's building codes underwent significant changes. They shifted from geographically designated fire limits within city ordinances to material rules contingent on individual lot and building characteristics. This change was accompanied by increasing influence from related industries, particularly the fire insurance industry. While the fire insurance industry privately maintained urban assessment of building-material patterns throughout the early twentieth century in Chicago and across the United States, the codes no longer made material geographies clear to the public.

The debate surrounding urban building-material goals and trade-offs waned with the lack of public awareness and engagement on this critical issue. Investors and economists later codified urban risk assessment and valuation to minimize building stock durability and emphasize growth opportunities and racial segregation.

This analysis of Chicago suggests urban disinvestment as one unintended consequence of building-material regulation, specifically due to the lack of attention to durability. It offers an additional perspective for analyzing and prioritizing material construction.

City builders once consciously allowed the construction of "temporary" wood buildings in certain areas, anticipating their short lifespan. However, a century later, widespread impacts like abandonment and foreclosure are particularly evident in neighborhoods with dense wood construction. What was once a deliberate choice to accept durability risk as a temporary urban necessity has now become a neglected but lasting threat for many city residents.

Contemporary construction increasingly trends toward layered, stick-frame, Type V construction, signaling a growing preference for short-term cost savings over long-term durability. Increasingly complex building codes and less legible impacts of urban materials have created a significant oversight in both the real estate market and municipal policy priorities.

Urban material vulnerability not only exacerbates social and economic risks within neighborhoods but also highlights deeper issues. If building codes remain opaque to the public while cities continue to prioritize only the immediate concerns of combustibility risks and upfront construction costs for housing at-risk populations, they may inadvertently perpetuate a cycle of uneven disinvestment and instability.

TYPE V NEW YORK

Saturation and Health

> We breathe an air tainted with every putrid and nauseous exhalation. We live in multitudes, crowded together atop undrained swamps and made grounds. Our quarantine establishments are very imperfect. Thus surrounded by dangers—we sleep in the midst of them or only adopt the same hackneyed and unavailing measures of precaution. We sweep the surface of our streets, then fold our arms, trust fortune, and shut our eyes.
>
> A HOUSEHOLDER, *NEW YORK GAZETTE*, 1805

THE SATURATED CITY

In 1805, New York City struggled to balance health, hydrology, and housing as its population swelled. An early Manhattan resident, claiming the identity only of "A Householder," published a series of letters to the *New York Gazette* questioning the health consequences of New York's tendency to fill wetlands, build over them, and disrupt drainage patterns. The householder indicated a connection between the former marshlands and locations of frequent disease outbreaks.

The writer insisted that a shared desire for urban prosperity and common sense would alter construction practices. After all, "the Island of New York, as formed and situated by nature, was calculated to be a healthy place." Yet "the manner in which it has been laid out, built upon, and altered, has in many particulars tended to make it *unhealthy*." The householder asked of their neighbors, "Are no further means to be taken for the preservation of the city? Are there any measures by which all or most men agree would be beneficial? What are these measures? And are they within our power to accomplish?"[1]

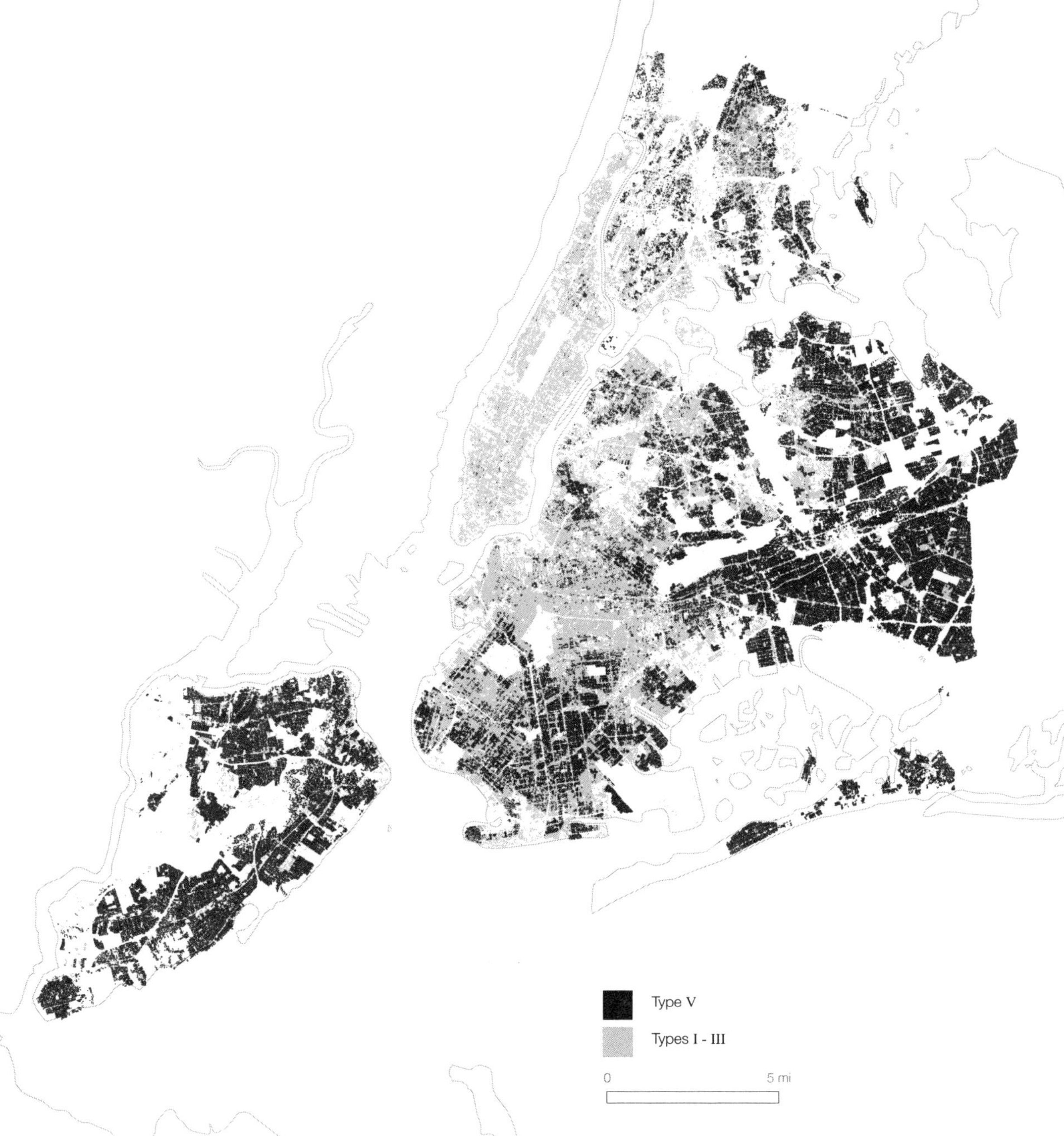

FIGURE 2.1 *New York City's contemporary residential Type V and Types I–III construction (2017).*

Waves of disease, including yellow fever, cholera, polio, tuberculosis, and influenza, are considered defining drivers in shaping New York's built environment, determining centuries of building regulation that sought to balance density and health.[2] And, as noted by the householder, New York's coastal ecology operated as another catalyst, ordering the city's early resource economies, growth, and health challenges.[3]

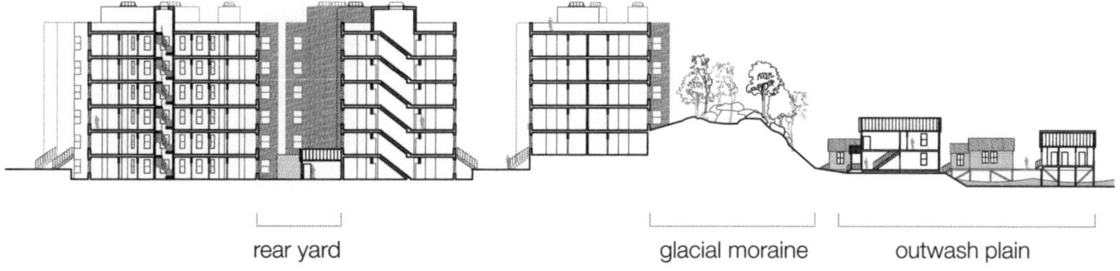

FIGURE 2.2 *A diagrammatic construction section across New York City's geological landscapes.*

Given the coevolution of New York's built environment and its formidable health and environmental obstacles, the city's building codes might be expected to adapt in sophisticated ways to address environmental ecologies and human health. Instead, New York City's development and regulatory history is a dizzying cycle of reactions to disease and water challenges with building codes that often exacerbated both.

Galvanized by development pressures and unconstrained by conventional wisdom and lessons learned, New York codes guide its most lightweight, water-sensitive material toward its most disaster- and flood-prone environments. The codes mitigate material indiscretion through biocide and heavy metal treatments that create waste toxicity challenges, particularly near groundwater. This essay examines the forces and follies that shaped the eco-logics and health consequences of New York's building-material codes.

"DISCIPLINE AND DRAIN"

> Of all the world's cities, New York has the most destroyed itself in order to grow.
>
> RICHARD SENNETT, *FLESH AND STONE: THE BODY AND THE CITY IN WESTERN CIVILIZATION*, 1996

Environmental humanities scholar Rod Giblett describes New York City's approach to its wetland ecosystem as "discipline and drain." This hubristic strategy is evident in a range of hydrological inclinations, including the construction of its building policy infrastructures.

Throughout most of the eighteenth century, Manhattan's drinking water came from a seventy-acre-wide, sixty-foot-deep reservoir known as Fresh Water Pond, later called the Collect Pond. During this time, the pond marked the northern boundary of the city's fire limits, providing the framework for a sustainable city by delineating areas for masonry construction and delivering water resources. The *Laws of New-York: From the Year 1691* directed that "every Dwelling-House or Building whatsoever, whether publick or private, that should be erected . . . within the said City, to the Southward of Fresh-Water, should be made of Stone or Brick and roofed with Tile or Slate."[4]

By 1803, city ordinances referred to the water body as the Collect Pond. When describing the fire limit, the ordinance drew a line connecting it to "the swamp of Anthony Lispenard" (present-day Canal Sreet).[5] Historical descriptions of the area by Edwin Burrows and Mike Wallace illustrate the function of waterways and marshes as natural barriers to development.

> A stretch of marshes and swamps between modern Chambers and Canal . . . nearly cut the island in two, blocking the northward flow of population. One outlet, a sluggish stream, ran along modern Canal Street before losing itself in the swampy wooded salt marshes known as Lispenard's Meadows, where for decades gentlemen had taken guns and dogs to shoot woodcock and snipe. To the southeast, a second outlet ran through a smaller tidal marsh, known as "the Swamp," and along the course of Roosevelt Street, a foul muddy alley, to the East River.[6]

The earliest codes treated Manhattan's water systems as convenient boundaries, but they also were entities outside of the codes' restrictions and precautions. From the beginning, building codes in the city excluded hydrology from their purview, protections, and logical considerations. They left the construction within and around the water bodies to proceed unregulated. Slaughterhouses and tanneries moved to the outskirts of the Collect Pond, producing runoff that was detrimental to water quality.

By 1795, a local medical man, Dr. Valentine Seaman, noticed that "musquetoes were never before known, by the oldest inhabitants, to have been so numerous as at this season, especially in the southeastern part of the City."[7] Pollution and population growth had increased the risk of mosquito-borne disease spread. Health experts had not yet linked yellow fever transmission to mosquitos, but they quickly tied the location of outbreaks to the wet and polluted areas of the city.

By 1800, a contributor to the *Daily Advertiser* called the pond "a shocking hole . . . foul with excrement, frog spawn, and reptiles . . ., a very sink and common sewer. It's like a fair every day with [residents] washing their clothes, blankets, and things. . . . Sudds and filth are emptied into this pond, besides dead dogs [and] cats."[8]

A health crisis was emerging in the growing city, forcing it to establish a Common Council to regulate health, sanitation, and quarantine. The council voted quickly to drain and fill lower Manhattan's swampy ground, including the Collect Pond. By 1807, a drain cut through present-day Canal Street to carry much of the moisture away, and the Collect Pond was filled. However, underground spring water remained, producing "a boggy tract that oozed and sank unevenly. . . . The principal street had to be laid with planks to be passable, and the cellars of the buildings that soon covered it were constantly full of water."[9]

Five- to six-story brick masonry tenement buildings soon occupied the newly created blocks over the former pond, creating a neighborhood known as Five Points. The buildings were constructed in a manner typical of the area, including deep cellars, sunken privies, and lower rear yards that were often inhabited by smaller wood structures such as utility buildings, outhouses, and sometimes additional tenant quarters (fig. 2.2).

Rear yards were a full or half story below street level. At the site of natural springs and low topography, flooding frequently filled cellars and kitchens, overflowed privies, and settled in the rear yards. A medical report in 1824 noted this concerning condition, pointing out "the old and decayed state of many of the houses. . . . [They] must certainly be considered of a nature to aggravate the disease, when brought about by other causes—namely, the state of the ground in the rear of the houses . . . [which is] considerably below the ordinary level; and, therefore liable to accumulate matter."[10]

Five Points became a notorious option of last resort for those seeking housing, yet it remained crowded with an ever-growing immigrant population. The neighborhood also remained the epicenter of disease outbreaks for the next century, including typhoid, polio, tuberculosis, cholera, and yellow fever.

Medical professionals disagreed on whether the sources of the diseases were local or imported, and whether they were caused by environmental conditions or moral failings. Those who blamed local environmental causes pointed to the "new ground, which renders a considerable part of the city [at] a low level." They claimed the filled wetland and related challenges required a different building strategy, calling them "changes which place us in a situation different from any previous period."[11]

Early city dwellers recognized the geographic concurrence of poor drainage, poor housing, and health hazards but still found it challenging to isolate precise causes of disease outbreaks or agree on infrastructural solutions. In addition, the city's water challenges were not limited to poor drainage but also included a lack of access to water and ineffective sewage systems. Issues such as conflagration added to the risks. These combined crises spurred the New York City Board of Health into action, regulating both water infrastructure and housing development.[12] However, regulators addressed the two challenges—healthy housing and water management—separately, treating them as technologically distinct problems despite their many integrated dynamics.

The city incrementally extended its fire limits, marching the line restricting wood construction further north five times between 1812 and 1834. By 1834, fire limits bisected lower Manhattan roughly along 14th Street and terminated once again just south of a former marsh on the East River near today's Tomkins Square.[13] Meanwhile, Manhattanites transformed marshes into navigable piers and swamps into streets as they moved development north. The original landscape of hills, rocks, and wetlands was leveled and seemingly erased.

In 1845, the city inspector of New York, Dr. John H. Griscom, published a landmark report that would initiate tenement reform in the city: *The Sanitary Condition of the Laboring Population of New York.* Griscom focused primarily on sanitation, ventilation, and overcrowding as health concerns. He again pointed out the relationship between ventilation, dampness, and cellars or rear yards occupying low ground: "There are two features of a cellar residence which more especially render them objectionable; 1st, the dampness, and 2nd, the more incomplete ventilation. . . . The moisture, whose escape is thus prevented, is in itself a very prolific source of disease."[14]

Griscom had spent significant time working in New York City's medical dispensaries for the poor. Rather than just citing facts and figures, his report called for building and health regulations that grew from his firsthand experience. An unreceptive board of aldermen fired Griscom in response.[15]

Twenty-two years later, the Tenement House Act of 1867 was passed, which addressed several concerns outlined by Dr. Griscom. It required that all privies and cesspools be watertight, that roofs not leak, and that building drainage connect to a sewer where possible. It also limited the occupation of cellars based on height and ventilation and required that the cellar must be drained.[16]

By 1901, the revised Tenement House Act further addressed damp-proofing, maintenance, and ventilation restrictions for basements and cellars.

> Such damp-proofing and waterproofing shall run through the walls and up the same as high as the ground level and shall be continued throughout the floor, And the said cellar or lowest floor shall be properly constructed so as to prevent dampness or water from entering. . . . All shafts, courts, areas and yards shall be properly concreted, graded and drained, and shall be properly connected with the street sewer so that all water may pass freely into it.[17]

These regulations required waterproofing measures to protect individual buildings, relying on the municipal sewers to compensate for the city's failure to protect natural drainage infrastructures during development. The early tenement laws also required further ventilation of interior rooms, eventually producing seemingly misguided improvisations such as interior wall "tuberculosis windows."[18]

New York's building regulations tended toward stop-gap treatment of symptoms rather than causes. They confronted impractical topography with street drains and disease with interior windows. Meanwhile, the *source* of sanitary problems—sunken buildings in unprotected marshland blocks—remained unresolved.

The city was by now cognizant of the importance of planning around natural waterways. Late nineteenth-century New York City engineer Col. Egbert Viele was an influential advocate of natural drainage infrastructures. Viele famously surveyed the island of Manhattan in 1865, developing a map of the city streets superimposed over predevelopment topography and water systems (fig. 2.3).[19]

Viele updated and expanded his maps over ensuing decades, publishing a larger water atlas in 1875 and writing about the errors and lessons from New York City's lack of attentiveness to watercourses up to that point.

> Any attempt to carry out a plan not based upon the topography must necessarily end in failure. When I speak of drainage, I do not include sewerage. Drainage and sewerage are entirely distinct, and can seldom be combined, and then only to a limited extent. . . . All that is necessary to do is to make the plan of the town conform, if only in a general way, to the topography of the surface. The streets and avenues, instead of being impediments to drainage, may serve to facilitate it. . . . The city of New York affords the most striking example of the errors committed in this respect. . . . Miles and miles of running streams, fed by innumerable perennial springs, permeate the original topography in every direction. Over these the streets have been graded, the intervening blocks filled up, and acres of buildings erected, and beneath lies the undrained saturated soil giving off its damp chilling malarious air. . . . Startling as all this is, every city and town in the United States is following recklessly in the footsteps of New York, and all in the end will pay the same penalties.[20]

Viele's analysis remains relevant today and demonstrates a remarkable early synthetic analysis of hydrological and urban systems. However, city ordinances evolved in the opposite direction, growing more analytically discrete, assessing the behavior of each piece rather than the relationship between environments, health, and infrastructure.

New York City began issuing stand-alone building codes in 1899, expanding the technical specificity of building requirements far beyond

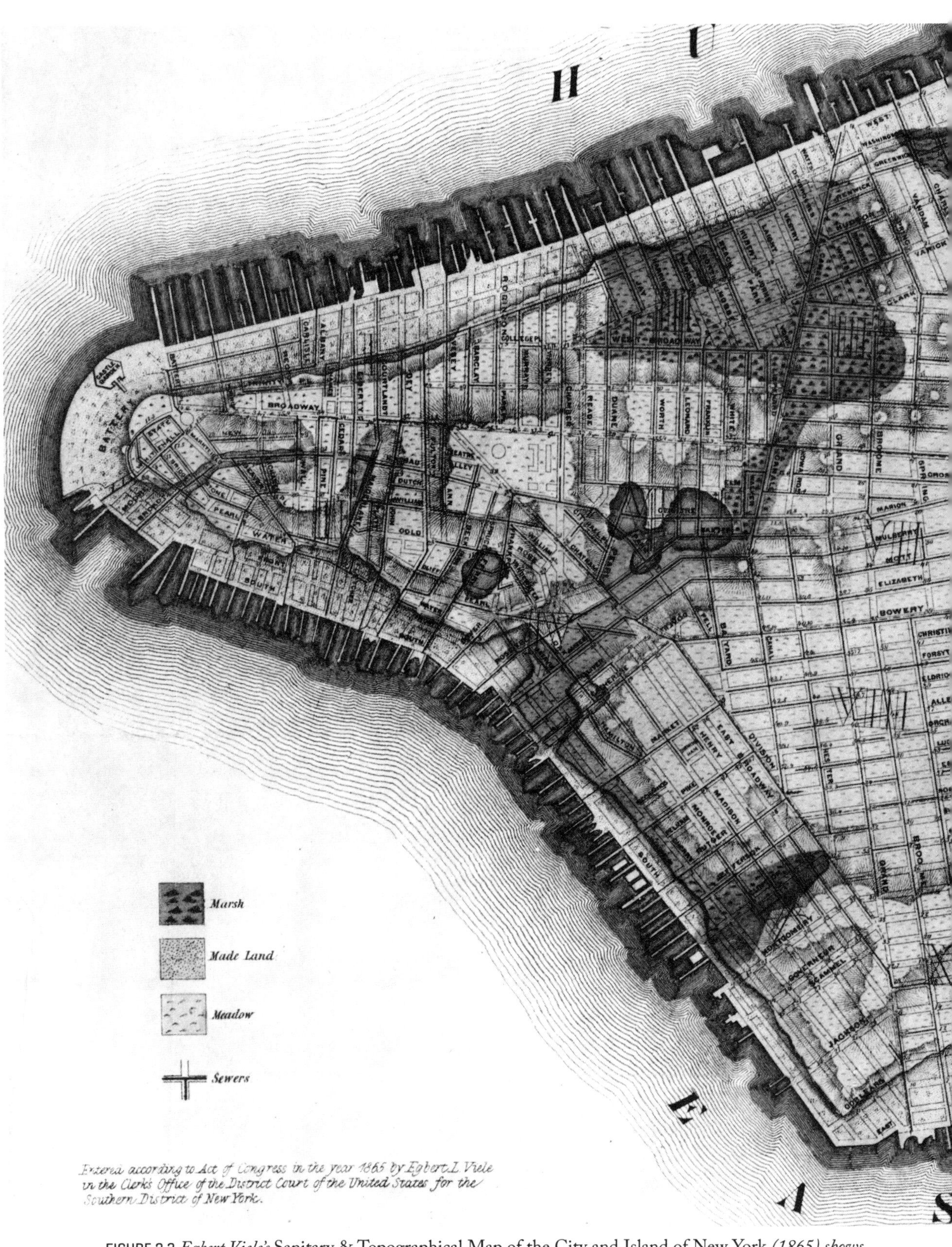

FIGURE 2.3 *Egbert Viele's* Sanitary & Topographical Map of the City and Island of New York *(1865) shows predevelopment waterways, including the Collect Pond and Lispenard's Salt Marsh. (Courtesy of the Library of Congress, Geography and Map Division)*

the single chapter of older city ordinances. These codes began to integrate specific foundation requirements relative to soil-bearing capacity and even prescribed wood species more impervious to wet environments.

> Stud partitions which may be placed in the cellar or lowest story of any building, shall have good solid stone or brick foundation walls under the same, which shall be built up to the top of the floor beams or sleepers, and the sills of said partitions shall be of locust; or other suitable hard wood; but if the walls are built five inches higher of brick than the top of the floor beams or sleepers, any wooden sill may be used on which the studs shall be set.[21]

While these early codes integrated the properties of different wood species, this consideration was later omitted. They also addressed soil types, indicating a shift toward construction that responds to geological conditions. However, the codes still failed to improve protections for waterways or consider sensitivity to existing topography.

Following Chicago's example, New York eventually replaced its urban fire limits with building classifications—restrictions based on individual building properties rather than an urban area. This shift away from a geographic approach and toward classification and standardization was typical of the reductionist analysis of the industrial age. Ironically, New York City adopted Chicago's geography-blind building code logic just as it expanded development into its largest floodplain—the outer boroughs of Brooklyn and Queens.

TYPE V LOWLANDS

Roughly eighteen thousand years ago, the two-mile-deep Laurentide ice sheet that covered North America began to melt and retreat.[22] As it moved, the glacier left behind rocky debris that formed a ridge known as a terminal moraine. This ridgeline cuts through New York's outer boroughs and stretches for thousands of miles across the northern United States.

In New York, the glacial moraine is recognizable as a strip of parkland that still bisects the city. Because its rocky terrain was difficult to build on or farm, this area was mainly used for parks and cemeteries.[23] Adjacent neighborhoods in Staten Island, Brooklyn, and Queens are named for their elevated locations, such as Crown Heights, Bay Terrace, Park Hill, Bay Ridge, Prospect Heights, Ridgewood, Forest Hills, and Hillcrest. South of the glacial ridge, ancient streams deposited sand and sediment to form a broad, flat outwash plain with fields, marshes, and wetlands. Neighborhood monikers like Flatlands and Flatbush describe these low landform areas today.

In 1679, a visitor described the wet, coastal outwash ecosystem.

> There is toward the sea [the bay], a large piece of low flat land which is overflown at every tide, like the schorr [marsh] with us, mirry at the bottom, and which produces a species of hard salt grass or reed grass. Such a place they call valey and mow it for hay, which cattle would rather eat than fresh hay or grass. . . . Their adjoining corn lands are dry and barren for the most part. Behind the village, inland, are their meadows, but they also were now arid. All the land from the bay to the Vlacke Bos [flat bush] is low and level without the least elevation. There is also a tract that is somewhat large, of a kind of heath, on which sheep could graze, though we saw none upon it. This marsh, like all the others, is well provided with good creeks which are navigable and very serviceable for fisheries.[24]

By the late nineteenth century, south Brooklyn and Queens still maintained a much lower population density compared to Manhattan's crowded conditions. One historian describes the outer boroughs in the late 1800s as "one immense garden,"[25] while others noted still-expansive marshlands in and surrounding Jamaica Bay.[26]

Gertrude Vanderbilt Whitney, the famed Brooklyn resident and founder of the Whitney Museum, remarked in 1881 that the last traces of village life in the lowlands were protected by the glacial moraine. She described it as "the ridge of hills that long kept back the . . . tide of human life in the adjoining city."[27]

A geological survey from 1902 provides context for Ms. Vanderbilt Whitney's observations: "The moraine has controlled in large measure the development of the island. The surface of the moraine is so uneven that it was not well adapted to cultivation, and was very generally left in forest, while the less rolling lands on either hand were brought under cultivation."[28]

As transportation improved access to the outer boroughs in the early twentieth century, the appeal of open land quickly led to development in the outwash plain. The Brooklyn and Jamaica Railroad Company, a short-lived predecessor to the Long Island Railroad, established an early route just south of the moraine, connecting the city to its farmland and marshy waterfront. Developers began purchasing farmsteads and creating subdivisions of single-family homes near the ridgeline. Closer to the coast, the Rockaway and Canarsie neighborhoods began as small vacation homes with densely packed lots and narrow streets.

Between 1914 and 1916, New York City passed several new regulations that together shaped the future of building in the outwash plains. Up to this point, the fire limits and development had incrementally expanded with the growing city. Unlike Chicago, the buildings in Manhattan quickly transitioned to fireproof construction within each expanding boundary. In 1914 and again in 1916, the city published new building codes. These codes set the boundary for fireproof construction at the edge of the glacial ridgeline and enabled looser restrictions for building in the low outwash plains and marshes.[29]

In 1916, New York City famously passed the first United States zoning ordinance to apply both land-use and building-size restrictions to the entire city. New York's 1916 zoning resolutions are extensively referenced for their profound influence on American urban form and land-use patterns. However, an often overlooked yet equally significant driver of urban form is the city's *building* codes, also revised in 1916. These codes operated in tandem with the zoning ordinance, providing a greater degree of control over the scale of development in some areas of the outer boroughs.

The 1916 zoning ordinance left several fringe areas of the city, particularly the areas that were wetlands prior to development, designated for "undetermined" use (fig. 2.4).[30] The 1916 building codes then filled in these gaps by creating a new geographic designation just beyond their ridgeline fire limits called the "suburban limits." Within the "suburban limits" the codes created an exception to combustibility requirements, allowing wood frame construction only for residential purposes at a limited scale. This building code loophole ensured the dominance of small-scale development patterns and wood-frame construction in sensitive peripheral areas of the city with lasting impacts.

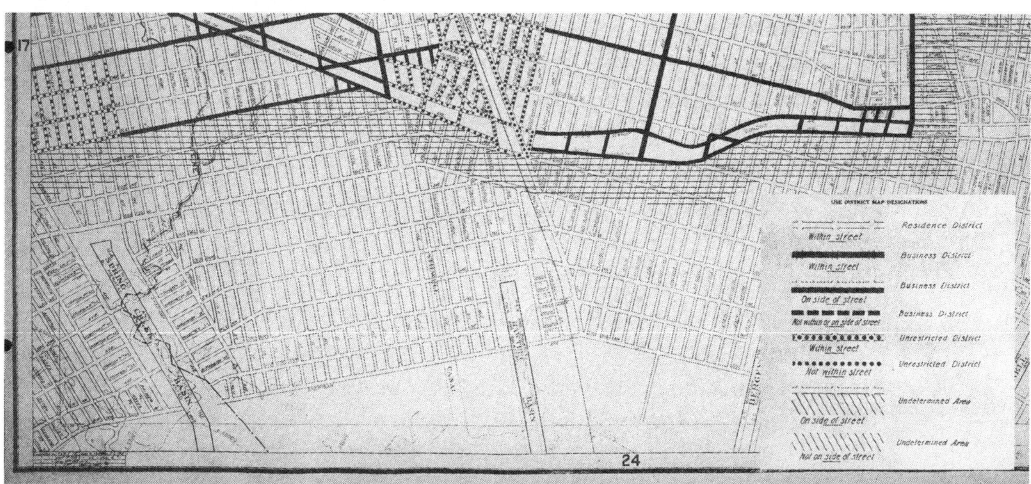

FIGURE 2.4 *Use district map within New York City's zoning ordinance (1916) shows the neighborhoods of Lindenwood south of Stanley Avenue and Howard Beach as "undetermined" districts. (Courtesy of the New York Public Library)*

> No frame or wood structure shall be built hereafter within the following areas of limits hereinafter referred to as "Suburban Limits," . . . provided, however, that nothing herein contained shall prevent the erection, maintenance or occupancy of any frame building to be used exclusively for residence purposes with not more than 15 sleeping rooms and covering not more than 85 per cent of the width of the lot.[31]

At the time, the city's tenement areas—still accounting for one-quarter of city construction—maintained an unhealthy reputation that many homeowners and developers hoped to avoid in newer neighborhoods.[32] Using exceptions to fireproof construction mandates, new building codes incentivized the expansion of single-family, lower-density construction. The city maintained the same exceptions throughout the twentieth and twenty-first centuries, still allowing wood-frame construction within low-scale residential districts today.[33] New York's outwash plains were locked in as de facto Type V zones by the combined early adoption of single-family residential zoning and building code material exceptions. Once again, sensitive water ecosystems were omitted from protection.

The 1914 codes were the first in New York City to adopt "construction classes," initially seen in Chicago's 1894 codes.[34] These rules were based on building properties rather than urban areas, determining allowable materials based on occupancy and building area limitations rather than a fire limit map. This approach was a precursor to today's construction types.

Additionally, 1914 code leaned toward standardized requirements based on products with few acknowledgments of hydrological considerations. References to water-resistant wood species were eliminated and replaced by requirements for foundation drainage.[35] The building codes also created a new geographic zone approximately matching the area of the outwash plain. Instead of recognizing it as a flood limit, they designated this "suburban limit" to be built with porous, absorptive materials.

Despite its advancements, building regulation during this early development phase lacked the urban and environmental logic recommended by Viele. The city was simultaneously grappling with conflagration, water resources, and drainage, but regulations failed to address the interplay between these issues, particularly those related to material absorption until long after most of New York was built. Instead, the city repeatedly treated wetlands as "undetermined zones." These were specifically labeled in the 1916 zoning ordinance or simply overlooked and excluded from the early fire limits, leaving critical gaps in the city's regulatory logic.

Fire limits were established by 1765, along with corresponding mandates for material and construction protection. Remarkably, it took another two centuries for the city to draw its first regulated flood zones, which were not created until 1983.[36] While the early codes responded to fire with specific building strategies, they did not set water limits to link the city's environmental geographies with absorption-specific siting and material guidelines, street drainage logic, or environmental protections.

New York's building regulations reacted to localized drainage problems rather than proactively positioning buildings and materials to address known ecological and human health considerations. Consequently, Type V construction repeatedly became the city's default strategy for building in flood zones.

HARDENED EDGES AND FLOODING

Since the outer boroughs could not grow up, they grew out and pushed the limits imposed by marshes and estuaries at their edges (plate 6). Just as Manhattan underwent significant landform transformation centuries earlier, the Jamaica Bay watershed in southeast Brooklyn and Queens experienced extensive topographic and watercourse alterations as the city developed. The area originally had nearly a dozen freshwater creeks and four freshwater aquifers.[37]

As recreational and residential interests in the area grew, they overshadowed the early ecosystem economies that depended on fisheries and oyster habitat. In their book *Coastal Metropolis*, environmental historians Carl Zimring and Steven H. Corey describe the conflict between the ecosystem-based economy and the growing recreational and residential interests: "The region represented a classic tension between a production landscape where local interests were involved in resource extraction and a consumption landscape where outside interests focused on consuming the amenities of the place during short visits. In almost all of these histories, large-scale business interests win out over local interests, and that was the case in Jamaica Bay."[38]

In the early part of the twentieth century, Jamaica Bay became the new dumping ground for refuse from the nearby growing population, including sewage and dead animals.[39] In 1921, *The New York Times* announced: "Jamaica Bay, which sends 300,000 bushels of oysters to the New York City market each year, will no longer be a source of supply. The waters have become so polluted as to constitute a menace to health, and the Health Department announced yesterday an order that will put a ban on the oyster beds."[40]

The *Times* also reported health challenges similar to those in Manhattan's early polluted marshes. Articles highlighted the prevalence of typhoid in neighborhoods surrounding the bay, even suggesting a link between the bay, its pollution, and "Typhoid Mary," the infamous asymptomatic cook responsible for sixty cases and twenty deaths in the city.[41]

The area struggled with repeated flooding. As early as 1888, the city government stated that "[flood relief] claims are constantly coming up" in Brooklyn's coastal districts.[42] By the 1920s and '30s, residents of lower Brooklyn and Queens grappled with frequent floods. Headlines from this period read, "Flood in Brooklyn Cuts Water Supply" (1928), "Flood Damage Here from 36-Hour Rain . . . Sidewalks Cave In" (1929), "Storm Sweeps City . . . Many Cellars Flooded" (1932).[43]

Government "improvement schemes" eventually called for the "elimination of all marshes and meadows," the bulkheading of the bay and its peripheral lowlands, the pumping of aquifers, and the channeling of streams. Robert Moses, the infamous New York City urban planner, expanded boulevards and bridges along the Brooklyn shore to Jamaica Bay, dredging and filling to make way for housing, parkways, and airfields. First, Floyd Bennett Field was created by filling Barren Island in 1931. Later, the city filled creeks and marshes to make way for the Marine Parkway Bridge and the Belt Parkway. Finally, in the 1940s, it covered estuaries to construct Idlewild Airport, the future JFK International Airport.[44]

The hardening of New York's outer borough coastline recalls the discipline-and-drain errors of early Manhattan development. Reminiscent of the rear yards in Manhattan's flood-prone tenements, which were filled with wood-frame sheds and privies, the vulnerable outwash plains were occupied by wooden, Type V single-family houses. Risks to these structures worsened over time as the bay's hardened ecology deteriorated.

Wetlands act as crucial absorption barriers against storm surges. The hardening and degradation of the Jamaica Bay ecosystem altered the material risk calculus for these coastal neighborhoods. The rate of marshland loss in the New York City lowlands increased from an average of ten acres a year at the turn of the twentieth century to an average of forty-four acres a year by the century's close. In total, 90 percent of the bay's original marshland, amounting to thousands of acres, has disappeared. Hardened coastline edges, pollution, and sea-level rise all contribute to ongoing habitat loss, threatening both animal and human populations.[45]

By making the land less porous, the already significant risk of flooding steadily increased. By 1951, the American Red Cross had organized a flood relief fund in Brooklyn and Queens to "help over 26,000 families rendered homeless by water infiltration."[46]

Meanwhile, national flooding disasters during the mid-twentieth century increased pressure on the federal government to shoulder responsibility for flood prevention and disaster response through infrastructure and federal aid. As the Army Corps of Engineers undertook massive efforts to levee and dam rivers out of floodplains, scholars warned that converting floodplains into developable land would inadvertently intensify risk.[47]

Environmental planning scholar Raymond J. Burby called this phenomenon a "safe development paradox" because "in trying to make hazardous areas safer, the federal government in fact substantially increased the potential for catastrophic property damage and economic loss."[48] To address this issue, the government created the National Flood Insurance Program (NFIP) in 1968, requiring jurisdictions to regulate flood zones to discourage further risky development.[49] However, over time, subsidized insurance rates, low participation, and relentless development pressures led to further paradoxical impacts. The long-embattled NFIP program has often been accused of encouraging floodplain development by diffusing the risk.[50]

In 1983, for the first time, the New York City building codes responded to the NFIP program requirements by passing an amendment to designate flood-hazard areas.[51] After striving for centuries to construct a city resilient to both conflagration *and* saturation, New York City initiated a practice of building in response not only to fire hazards but also to flood risks. However, the adoption of flood zones and mandated insurance policies came too late to dissuade development or significantly impact the building stock.

The same year, the Federal Emergency Management Agency (FEMA) drew its first floodplain maps of New York City, which became the standard reference for flood-resistant construction and NFIP mandatory coverage. Thirty years later, a disastrous flood would bring renewed attention to the city's codes, building-material patterns, and designated flood zones.

FLUCTUATING RISK

In 2012, Hurricane Sandy slammed into New York City, bringing with it the highest water levels the city had seen in three centuries. Although Hurricane Sandy was one of over twenty-two historical storm tide events recorded in New York City, its destruction was unparalleled, laying bare the vulnerabilities of the contemporary city.

Sandy left a path of wreckage that overwhelmingly impacted Type V structures and neighborhoods in the formerly "undetermined areas" of 1916 zoning maps. Of all buildings affected by Sandy, only 20 percent were single-story, Type V buildings. Yet this same subset accounted for an alarming 73 percent of the storm's structural damage, likely comprising the majority of 5.25 million cubic yards of storm debris.[52] A full 99 percent of the "red tag" buildings—those damaged beyond repair—were Type V construction.[53]

Studies estimated that the small remaining wetlands in New York prevented $625 million in flood damage during Hurricane Sandy and that neighborhoods protected by marshes experienced 16 percent less damage compared to those bordered by rigid bulkheads.[54] The transformation and decline of the Jamaica Bay ecosystem, coupled with the formal designation of ambiguous marshland as Type V zones within building codes, exacerbated the vulnerability of extensive coastal neighborhoods. This interplay of ecological degradation and regulatory decisions heightened material risk factors at the community level.

Sandy inflicted significant structural damage, disrupting infrastructures ranging from housing and transportation to health and recreation facilities. The storm caused immediate, visible destruction and also led to gradually developing problems like mold outbreaks, which local officials described as a public health crisis.[55] Efforts to assess the damage, plan for future disaster mitigation, utilize federal aid, and rebuild required extensive coordination.

While planning for recovery, several insightful recommendations focused on enhancing coastal ecosystems. National rebuilding strategy reports emphasized the integration of green infrastructure to improve coastal storm-surge protection.[56] Additionally, FEMA reviewed their floodplain designations within the region along with city and national building codes. The federal government allocated funding to support these initiatives.[57]

However, the rebuilding outcomes show that old floodplain building habits are hard to break. The city quickly reconstructed the same problematic structures in the same locations without substantially increasing coastal wetland ecosystems, redrawing flood zones, or reducing the concentration of Type V construction in the outwash floodplain. By 2022, New York City had spent 99 percent of the $3 billion in federal funds to rebuild single-family housing, but only 13 percent of the roughly $1.9 million federal and city budget for coastal resilience projects was used.[58]

When the hurricane landed in 2012, FEMA had not updated New York's flood-risk zone maps since their initial drafting in 1983. In Kings, Queens, and Bronx Counties, the 1983 maps predicted only 40–79 percent of the hurricane's flood area, resulting in thousands of damaged structures without mandatory flood insurance.[59]

FEMA responded quickly with recommendations. They released preliminary revised floodplain maps in 2013 along with suggestions to revise the flood-resistance requirements within building codes. Their proposed revision to the hundred-year floodplain included the Sandy inundation areas and nearly doubled the number of structures that would be required to purchase flood insurance.[60] However, the city's own Office of Recovery and Resilience challenged the validity of FEMA's science, claiming that FEMA's revised map "overstated the base flood elevation by more than 2 feet in many areas across New York City and misrepresented the special flood hazard area by 35 percent."[61] FEMA eventually withdrew its proposal and released another revision in 2018 that reverted to flood boundaries almost identical to those drawn in 1983.

In the midst of this debate, the executive director of the Association of State Floodplain Managers commented, "There is a lot of talking in [the city's] appeal about how aggressive New York City is being in terms of climate change. Yet they are almost regressing to old data and old methods, and not wanting to look at sea-level rise and climate change."[62]

Had FEMA expanded the designated floodplain, it would have significantly enlarged the areas of influence for new flood-resistant building codes and flood insurance requirements. The flux zone—the contested area between the 2013 expanded proposal and the 2018 reduced map—remains dominated by fragile wood-frame construction (plate 7).[63] However, fears of the increased cost burden triggered by flood insurance and construction mandates outweighed the urgent need for enhanced protection, echoing post-disaster compromises and short-sighted decisions that long plagued American urban development.

Even if future extensions of flood zones occur, the pace of updating construction will remain slow. Unlike many coastal areas, a staggering 80 percent of New York's at-risk properties were built before the 1983 flood maps and requirements were established, compared to just 20 percent nationally.[64] Only new or significantly modified structures will need to adhere to flood-resistance codes, regardless of where the line lands.

This slow march toward progress, constrained by historical inertia and regulatory lag, underscores a broader narrative of urban material development—one where the urgency of adaptation is continually overshadowed by the weight of past decisions and the immediate pressures of the present.

TYPE V ABSORPTION

> Build your house in a wetland, and you've got a hobby for the rest of your life.
>
> ED PERRY, QUOTED IN "CAUTION: BUILDING IN A WETLAND CAN BE HAZARDOUS TO YOUR HOUSE," *NATIONAL WILDLIFE MAGAZINE*, 1998

Like New York's coastal *infra*structure, wood *micro*structures became more susceptible to water infiltration as twentieth-century construction trends evolved. This material vulnerability manifested through persistent mold issues in the weeks, months, and years following Hurricane Sandy. Residents described symptoms as "Sandy Cough," "Coney Cough," or "Rockaway Cough," attributing them to mold infestation.[65]

Far Rockaway resident Nicole Harper and her four-year-old daughter Darcy struggled to eradicate mold in their wood-frame home in 2013. Darcy, who has asthma, faced ongoing health challenges while Nicole drained most of her savings on remediation efforts. Despite this, inspections repeatedly uncovered mold throughout their eighty-seven-year-old home, noting its "porous studs."[66] A 2018 survey of almost four thousand New York residents found that the presence of mold or dampness in their homes after the hurricane doubled the likelihood of lower respiratory symptoms.[67]

Within the hurricane's inundation zone, neighborhoods dominated by Type V, wood-frame construction reported 50 percent more mold violations than neighborhoods with fewer Type V structures.[68] These coastal neighborhoods defy typical predictors of maintenance issues and mold violations across the city. They are not characterized by high poverty or high rental occupancy.[69] Yet residents struggle to combat mold hidden within wood-cavity walls, behind gypsum board, and within the wood framing itself. Most wood-frame homes in these areas were built before the city designated flood zones or required mold-resistant material at lower elevations.

When building with wood, managing exposure to moisture has always been a crucial architectural consideration. Understanding the specific properties of Type V construction and its evolution over time provides essential context to New York's contemporary issues.

In Type V construction, exterior walls typically consist of three layers: the structure, sheathing, and finish. Structural lumber may be referred to as studs, joists, or rafters, based on their use in walls, floors, or roofs. Early twentieth-century homes in New York likely used two-by-four or, occasionally, two-by-six lumber to build exterior framing. Next, a middle layer, called sheathing, is applied to create a substrate for the exterior finish layer. Traditionally, one-inch-thick wood boards were used for sheathing on floors, roofs, and exterior walls. Some older homes omitted exterior wall sheathing entirely, applying the finish layer directly to the studs.

The finish layer in early Type V construction often consisted of thin wood boards referred to as wood cladding or wood siding. This method of construction is sometimes called "layered construction" or "cavity wall construction" due to the interior gaps left between the structural framing.

Many historical architectural accounts describe the sensitive relationship between the architectural use of wood and its propensity for water absorption. The ancient Roman architect Vitruvius summarized the relationship between building materials and water, stating: "Bodies which contain a greater proportion of water than is necessary to balance the other elements, are speedily corrupted, and lose their virtues and properties. Hence bodies are much injured by damp winds and atmospheres."[70]

Vitruvius detailed the application and properties of particular wood species, noting the weather resistance of charred olive wood and the microstructure of oak. He observed that oak, "lacking the voids afforded by a looser structure . . . lasts into eternity when it is buried in earthworks."[71] This ancient recognition of species distinction is echoed in more contemporary accounts of wood-frame construction. As mentioned earlier, early New York building codes specified the use of locust in basement sill plates.

Permeability, porosity, and natural chemical composition control wood resistance to biodeterioration. These factors vary widely among species and depend on the growth conditions of the tree. The Department of Housing and Urban Development (HUD) estimates that early twentieth-century homebuilders used seventeen common wood species.[72] In the year 1909, New York codes referenced structural span guidelines for hemlock, spruce, white pine, oak, chestnut, and yellow pine.[73]

Today's building and structural codes describe only five common species of framing lumber in prescriptive structural tables: Douglas fir, hem fir, southern yellow pine, spruce pine fir, and southern pine (see fig. 2.5). Some of the most water- and pest-resistant species, like cedar, cypress, and redwood, have disappeared from common use.[74]

Kit homes sold by the Sears, Roebuck and Co. provide a record of early twentieth-century Type V materials and sensitivity to wood properties. The Sears "standard built" construction did not specify a species or lumber grade and applied wood cladding directly to two-by-four wall studs. The upgraded "honor-built" system also used two-by-four studs but specified that the lumber be "high quality framing lumber (virgin growth, dense grain, from the Pacific Northwest, Douglas-Fir and Hemlock)," and added 13/16-inch sheathing boards between the studs and cladding.[75]

In contemporary construction, builders remain sensitive to wood species choice. In 2000, three researchers from Louisiana State University surveyed over five hundred homebuilders nationwide, revealing that nearly 75 percent of respondents believed wide growth rings compromised lumber quality, attributing this to the rapid growth of contemporary farmed lumber.

Builders expressed species preferences, many claiming that southern yellow pine often warps and speculating that it's either grown or kiln-dried too quickly. Conversely, northern species, like spruce and fir, with their shorter growing seasons and tighter growth rings, were preferred for their stability.[76] In the decades since this survey, climate changes have shifted species zones further north, and the country has grown more reliant on younger trees of southern species for lumber production (plate 20).[77]

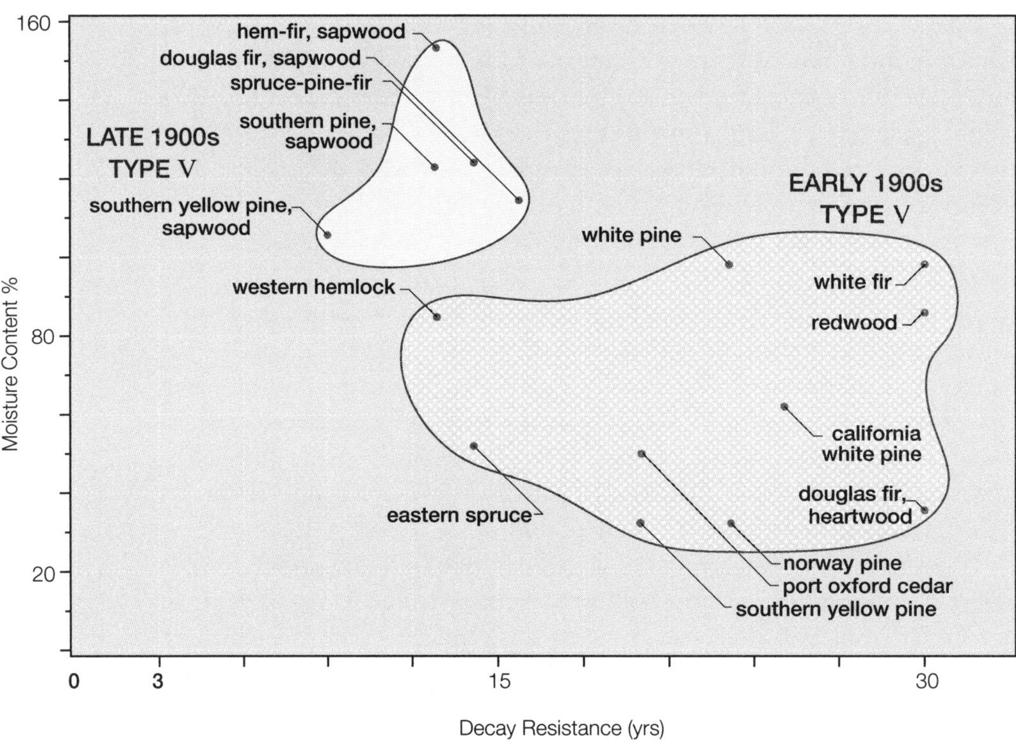

FIGURE 2.5 *Moisture content and decay resistance of wood species common in early and late twentieth-century construction.*

Along with changes in lumber species, the density of framing lumber also transformed over time. A tree's heartwood, the darker, denser, and more water- and decay-resistant portion, expands later in the tree's life.[78] Today's framing lumber is primarily composed of younger sapwood harvested from small, fast-growing, cultivated species.[79]

Unlike old-growth forest environments, cultivated trees grow without competing for access to sunlight and water resources. The cross section of farmed lumber reveals wide sapwood growth rings due to rapid summer growth, contrasting with the tight growth rings of old-growth heartwood (fig. 2.6). Less dense wood offers less strength, dimensional stability, and moisture resistance.[80]

Additionally, the advent of dimensional lumber and balloon-frame construction in Chicago led to a reduction in standard lumber sizes. Whether measuring by size or density, today's wood studs and joists make up a more fragile kit of parts with chemical and physical properties more susceptible to mold and decay.[81]

The layers comprising Type V home construction—the sheathing and cladding surrounding wood studs—also evolved over the twentieth century. Plywood technology was patented in the United States in the late

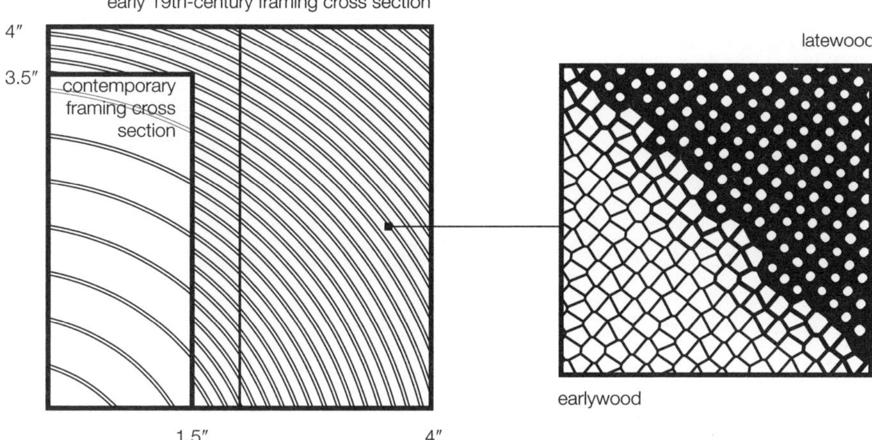

FIGURE 2.6 *Evolution of American lumber size and density, from large old-growth posts with tight growth rings ("heartwood") to smaller, younger, farmed-lumber sections ("sapwood").*

1800s, but the industry skyrocketed after the Second World War, fueled by the postwar housing boom and advent of waterproof adhesives. Plywood replaced solid wood boards that traditionally formed the outer sheathing, above floor joists and beyond the wall's wood studs. The uniformity and scale of plywood sheets markedly accelerated the construction of outer walls and floors compared to the labor-intensive onsite assembly of individual wood boards.

In the 1970s, the manufactured wood industry introduced an even more lightweight, low-cost form of sheathing called Oriented Strand Board (OSB). OSB panels, available in the same sizes as plywood, are made by laminating small wood strands rather than the veneer sheets used in plywood.[82] This innovation further streamlined manufacturing while maintaining construction efficiency.

Moisture can cause wood to expand and contract. It can lead to deterioration, and, when combined with exposed wood glucose (sugars), it can foster mold growth. Building scientist Joseph Lstiburek summarizes the association between mold and the material properties of contemporary wood products:[83]

> We once cut trees into timbers and large boards. With timbers and board lumber, we had few mold problems because mold could not burrow into the timbers and board lumber and access the carbon in the wood fiber. . . . But we don't build much out of timbers and board lumber anymore. Instead of cutting the tree, we peel the tree and smush the layers together under heat and pressure. We cook the raw wood meat to tenderize it and make plywood. The plywood goes out to the job site slightly brownish in color because

> we've caramelized the wood sugars—we made mold candy.... As we have moved down the process stream from timber, board lumber, plywood, OSB, hardboard, particleboard, to paper laminates—each step of the processing has made the products more water and mold sensitive.[84]

Engineered wood products, while more susceptible to degradation and health risks, offer environmental efficiencies by utilizing scrap material and farmed lumber. Building scientists like Lstiburek do not argue for overhauling the wood industry; instead, they emphasize the importance of controlling the microclimates where wood is used through careful detailing.

One of the most challenging microclimates in wood construction is within the framed wall itself. Before the 1930s, wood-framed walls were often uninsulated, allowing inner wall cavities to absorb moisture but also to dry quickly due to sufficient air and moisture permeability across layers. However, in the 1930s, the introduction of interior wall insulation disrupted this balance. Insulation prevented airflow and trapped moisture, producing saturated outer cladding and peeling exterior paint. Builders of the time often warned that "insulation draws water," highlighting the unintended consequence of building technology development.[85]

The construction industry embarked on a long process to test and refine air and vapor barriers, as well as flashing details at doors and windows, to address the challenge of wall-cavity moisture and insulation. Over time, wall barrier technology evolved from tar paper to plastic wrap and eventually to synthetic building wraps.[86] By 2008, New York City building codes mandated exterior wall weather-proofing, specifying that "the exterior wall envelope shall include flashing ... and a water-resistive barrier behind the exterior veneer."[87]

While contemporary waterproofing techniques are highly effective at keeping water out, they are also inherently less permeable and breathable than the original uninsulated Type V construction. Particularly in the case of a flood or storm, contemporary building technology inconveniently traps more moisture inside the wall cavity.

The majority of New York's existing Type V construction was built beyond the city's moraine ridge between 1920 and 1970. During this period, Type V materials and technologies underwent dramatic changes. Innovations often solved one problem, such as improving insulation or introducing affordable OSB sheathing, only to create new issues, like preventing evaporation or increasing mold risk. As large-scale ecological risks escalated in New York, small-scale building technologies also became more vulnerable.

Today, Type V construction increasingly relies on protective layers and treatments designed to mitigate these inherent vulnerabilities, perpetuating the cycle of unintended consequences. The remainder of this essay will explore the final stage of building code evolution in New York and the wood preservation strategies that underpin the city's hopes for resilience in its Type V neighborhoods.

TYPE V TOXINS

> You will observe with Concern how long a useful Truth may be known, and exist, before it is generally receiv'd and practis'd on.
>
> BENJAMIN FRANKLIN, LETTER ON LEAD POISONING TO BENJAMIN VAUGHAN, 1786

In the wake of Hurricane Sandy, New York City touted its updated building codes while rebuilding with the latest flood-resistant construction mandates. However, the new codes still permitted large quantities of Type V construction within moisture-rich landscapes, relying on chemical preservation as the default mode of protection. This raises questions about the historical effectiveness of such preservation methods.

One of the most prominent twentieth-century techniques for wood preservation was lead paint. The enduring legacy of lead paint serves as a cautionary tale for today's flood-resistant building code strategies. Lead paint was once considered the gold standard for moisture protection in Type V construction, especially in wood-clad homes with extensive exposed wood siding.[88]

The dangers of lead poisoning were known and documented as far back as the Roman Empire.[89] By the late nineteenth century, doctors were already warning against the specific dangers of lead paint to children.[90] In 1904, Australian doctor J. Lockhart Gibson published "A Plea for Painted Railings and Painted Walls of Rooms as the Source of Lead Poisoning Among Queensland Children."

In 1922, Greece, Sweden, Great Britain, Belgium, Poland, parts of Australia, and Tunisia banned the use of interior lead paint.[91] By this time, New York City had completed its revised building and zoning codes, solidifying its emphasis on single-family, Type V housing in coastal outwash plains while development expanded rapidly. Despite the known risks, New York continued to use lead paint for an additional forty years as it erected 70 percent of its current building stock, including over 25,000 Type V structures. Although the United States recognized the toxicity of lead, regulators opted to set "acceptable limits" to exposure rather than banning its use outright.[92]

New York City officially prohibited lead paint in 1960, yet many suspect its use persisted until the national ban in 1978.[93] The simultaneous removal of lead from US gasoline by 1976 significantly reduced elevated blood lead levels in children due to environmental exposure.[94] However, lead-contaminated building materials produced a more enduring health hazard. Lead is bioaccumulating, meaning it does not degrade over time.[95]

According to a 1996 study by the Environmental Protection Agency (EPA) and HUD, exterior paint contains higher lead concentrations than interior paint, making wood exterior siding an amplified threat. HUD reports, "49 billion square feet or 44 percent of all painted exterior surfaces in the United States are covered with lead-based paint. On average, each private housing unit with lead-based paint has approximately 601 square feet of the lead paint on the interior and 869 square feet on the exterior."[96]

After years of accepting trace amounts of lead in human blood as safe, the CDC now acknowledges that no level of lead is safe in the human body.[97] Lead is a likely carcinogen, causing detrimental effects on the cardiovascular, kidney, immune, blood, and reproductive systems, as well as developmental delays, learning and behavioral problems, and brain and nervous system damage.[98] Additionally, "at the community level, lead exposure is associated with increased crime and homicide rates, as well as decreased income."[99]

As recently as 2004, over three thousand children in New York City were diagnosed with lead poisoning. In 2007, the CDC declared that poor children were eight times more likely to suffer from lead poisoning. Current estimates place the cost to remediate all remaining household lead hazards in the United States between $1.2 billion and $11.0 billion, but the remediation could save between $181 billion and $269 billion in healthcare, lost earnings, tax revenue, decreased criminal activity, and education costs.[100] If the United States or New York had followed the cautious approach of Australian or European regulators and fully banned lead paint in 1920, the portion of the city's building stock carrying risks of exposure would have decreased from 70 to just 13 percent.

The regulation of lead in the United States offers crucial lessons for today's building codes. The European Union operates according to the precautionary principle, a guideline that "enables decision-makers to adopt precautionary measures when scientific evidence about an environmental or human health hazard is uncertain and the stakes are high."[101] In stark contrast, the lead crisis exemplifies the United States' historical risk acceptance approach to chemical preservation, which carries the potential for enormous, unanticipated fallout. In the case of lead, the lack of precaution meant that "in effect, children [were] used as biological monitors for environmental lead."[102] Lead is just one of many toxins found in building materials—including formaldehyde, asbestos, and arsenic—managed according to "acceptable limits" and later restricted after avoidable impacts on human health.[103]

The analysis of lead also informs our understanding and potential caution regarding urban material patterns. Recent health data from New York reveals a correlation between the concentration of Type V housing and the risk of toxic exposure through elevated blood lead levels (BLL). Similar to the analysis of mold in Sandy's flooded regions, elevated BLL levels are more closely tied to dense Type V construction in New York than typical social vulnerability predictors—like high rental and high poverty rates—often associated with lead concerns (plate 8).[104]

Despite these lessons, the city now risks repeating past missteps by continuing to encourage chemical treatments in urban floodplain materials. Current regulations codify requirements for water-resistant treatments in flood zones, including areas with dense Type V construction. These measures further infuse risk within already saturated urban material landscapes.

Today's regulation of wood chemical preservatives varies internationally and across different states, recalling the divergent approaches to lead paint bans in the twentieth century. These distinctions are most evident in the different standards for treated wood waste, especially whether materials recommended by new flood-resistant construction codes are considered hazardous waste.

Since the 1830s, the wood products industry has impregnated wood with chemical preservatives. The most prevalent biocide and insecticide treatments have included creosote, pentachlorophenol (PCP), and chromated copper arsenate (CCA). These chemical preservatives and coal tar products have been used in construction to prevent microorganism growth and insect attack.[105] Although the United States now restricts PCP and CCA, both were once common in residential construction in the latter half of the twentieth century.[106]

Arsenic, chromium, and copper can leach from treated wood products, dispersing into groundwater systems. Exposure to arsenic and chromium can damage the human larynx, liver, and immune and nervous systems, and cause liver and kidney cancers. High concentrations of copper exposure can cause liver and kidney damage, muscle pain, and mental disorders such as Wilson's and Parkinson's diseases. However, recent research suggests that the concentrations of copper leached from wood is likely sufficiently small that it poses a greater risk to aquatic organisms than to human health.[107]

The United States curbed the use of PCP and arsenic-containing CCA in 2004 but did not entirely restrict their use.[108] By contrast, most European countries banned PCP and CCA entirely in the 1990s.[109] Copper treatment remains the standard, now highlighted in flood-resistant building codes and used internationally.

European and Australian standards encourage an alternative approach reminiscent of New York's 1899 codes related to *naturally* durable wood species. Australia publishes national hazard maps designating zones according to risks of fungal decay, natural decay above and below ground, termites, beetles, and marine organisms.[110] These hazard maps are then linked to recommended naturally durable wood species. Similarly, the European Committee for Standardization classifies the natural durability and service life for heartwood and sapwood of 20 softwood and 107 hardwood European wood species.[111]

The US approach to wood preservation remains heavily reliant on chemicals, and while naturally durable species are included as options in some codes, species detail is limited and often listed as secondary options. In several US local and national codes, treated wood is typically suggested for use in wet locations, but four species also appear consistently as naturally durable alternatives.

Since 2008, New York City's building codes have reintroduced language referencing naturally durable wood, specified as the heartwood of redwood, cedar, black locust, and black walnut.[112] The 2008 codes were also the city's first to reference FEMA's material standards for floodproof construction. FEMA lists common biocide-treated wood, including alkaline copper and copper azole, or decay-resistant lumber within its table of allowable materials. In fine-print notes below its allowable material table, FEMA defines decay-resistant lumber as the heartwood of redwood, cedar, and black locust.[113] The IBC follows the same pattern, requiring either preservative-treated or naturally durable wood in locations exposed to ground moisture. The IBC's list of naturally durable wood includes the heartwood of redwood, cedar, black walnut, and black locust.

The revived inclusion of naturally durable species in New York City and national model codes offers important alternatives to chemical treatment. However, specifying only four species without detailed hazard resistance is notably less thorough than international standards, which sometimes include over a hundred species tailored to specific hazard locations.

The United States hazard map for wood decay is developed by the American Wood Protection Association (AWPA), a private research entity. The AWPA primarily focuses on developing standards for chemically preserved wood and is sponsored by several prominent chemical companies, including American Chemex Corp. and Dolphin Bay Chemicals.[114] Unsurprisingly, the AWPA hazard map links to recommended chemical preservatives rather than naturally durable species.

Within the last decade, the AWPA established a task force to explore the possibility of providing a standardized list of naturally durable species to accompany its chemical treatment recommendations.[115] A 2011 AWPA publication points out the curious and inconsistent list of naturally durable species in some model building codes. The article notes that "the heartwood of redwood and eastern red cedar are listed [within building codes] as termite resistant as is, unaccountably, the sapwood of western red cedar."[116]

The same AWPA publication discusses the agency's conflicted considerations in weighing the creation of US standards for natural durability: "There are also valid arguments against AWPA standardization of naturally durable species. There is no doubt that doing so would require the expenditure of considerable time and effort by AWPA members and subcommittees. It would also provide an opportunity for materials that compete with treated wood to gain credibility and market share."[117] These deliberations within the AWPA highlight the intricate considerations involved in establishing building standards that are both effective and equitable. In this case, the key authors of these standards are driven primarily by market share, casting doubt on their commitment to human and ecological health and well-being.

The challenges associated with chemical preservation intersect with many of the other issues previously discussed in this essay, such as material toxicity, ecosystem and microsystem vulnerability, and public health. These interconnected concerns highlight the need for a holistic approach to building standards.

To ensure structural integrity while addressing broader societal and ecological impacts, greater input and scrutiny of building rules from diverse fields and perspectives is essential. Architects, well versed in the technical intricacies of these codes and generally free from conflicts of interest tied to product market share, are ideally positioned to champion more ecologically responsible guidelines. They can also translate these codes and their impacts to a broader population.

The challenge is not only one of collaboration and communication but also of cultural change, necessitating a shift in priorities when significant ecological and human health consequences are at stake. Currently, contrasting regulatory caution is evident in both production and disposal requirements for treated wood waste.

California currently regulates most treated wood as hazardous waste, stating: "Treated wood waste [TWW] has the potential to be a hazardous waste if it contains elevated levels of one or more of the following constituents: arsenic, chromium, copper, pentachlorophenol, and creosote. If TWW is not properly disposed of, the chemicals it contains can contaminate soil, surface water, and groundwater. This poses a risk to human health and the environment."[118]

Similarly, several European nations classify most chemically treated wood as hazardous waste.[119] US federal regulations only restrict the disposal of CCA-treated wood at a national level. The disposal of arsenic-treated wood in the United States is estimated at 18,400 metric tons annually, and the country's copper-treated wood waste is expected to increase to 20,900 tons by 2030.[120] In the late 1990s, European average treated wood waste was less than 20 percent of the American totals.[121] Since then, American-treated wood waste has seen a ninefold increase, while earlier regulatory restrictions limited European production.[122]

Even when federal requirements mandate contained wood disposal to prevent leaching into water sources or soil, the EPA has limited authority over state debris management. Disaster debris poses particular challenges due to the massive quantities of unsegregated, potentially hazardous waste.[123]

Hurricane Sandy left 5.25 million cubic yards of debris in its wake, with an estimated half comprising construction and demolition waste.[124] Applying statistics measured from disaster waste research in other locations nationally, arsenic-treated wood likely constituted between 200,000 to 580,000 cubic yards of Sandy's debris.[125] Additionally, most damaged residences likely contained lead paint, given their age. Doctors in affected neighborhoods saw a spike in lead levels in children's blood, consistent with the aftermath of other national hurricanes.[126] A Jersey City pediatrician reported more cases of elevated BLL in the storm's aftermath than she had seen in thirty years of practice.[127]

Meanwhile, chemical treatments are persistently applied to increasingly porous Type V wood, as national regulators fail to agree on hazardous waste protocols. The city resists extending flood zone designations, while privatized standards obstruct the expansion of naturally durable species in the guidelines. New York City's new "flood-resistant" codes endorse the use of treated wood in hurricane-prone areas in contact with water by design.[128] Today's flood zone material codes risk becoming tomorrow's crisis of ecological health and waste management. Although New York City has finally woven topographic logic into its material regulations, it has failed to keep porous materials out of sunken swampy grounds or to extend protections to hydrological ecosystems beyond the water's edge.

And so the 1805 householder's cautions quoted at the beginning of this essay echo through the centuries, underscoring persistent threats, short-sighted development, and superficial fixes that have spanned generations: "The Island of New York, as formed and situated by nature, was calculated to be a healthy place. [Yet] the manner in which it has been laid out, built upon, and altered, has in many particulars tended to make it unhealthy. . . . Thus surrounded by dangers, we sleep in the midst of them, or only adopt the same hackneyed and unavailing measures of precaution. We sweep the surface of our streets, then fold our arms, trust fortune, and shut our eyes."[129]

TYPE V PHILADELPHIA

Labor and Affordability

> If one were to design a building in brick or block, there would be a much greater chance of employing more minority people. Designing a building in materials that are more labor intensive obviously has other benefits as well.
>
> MAX BOND AND PAUL BROCHES, "SOCIAL CONTENT IN TEACHING AND DESIGN," 1981

MATERIAL OPPORTUNITY

On a cold January morning in 2021, Cherise Farris stood outside a construction site on Drexel University's campus in Philadelphia, reporting to the field office to ask for work. Farris, a Black woman completing her carpentry apprenticeship, felt intimidated by the process of seeking work in person in a predominantly white male industry. "You hear some people don't want women out there, some people don't like Black women, some people don't like Black people, period. . . . It's just like, I'm really [about] to go out here in front of all these white people? Because that's what it is, majority white people."[1] Cherise introduced herself in the field office that morning and returned to meet the foreman the next day and for three days following. Finally, by the fifth morning, the foreman told her to report for work on Monday.

Farris is in her thirties with four young children. She worked for years as a clerk at ShopRite, making $13 per hour. It wasn't enough to support

FIGURE 3.1 *Philadelphia's contemporary residential Type V and Types I–III construction (2022).*

her family. When she completed a carpentry apprenticeship program in 2018, she started at $18.35 per hour, a jump that Farris described as "freedom" in an interview for Juliana Feliciano Reyes's 2022 article on Philadelphia's building trade exclusion. Farris treated her children to Jamaican food and said "yes" to them more often. Now finished with her apprenticeship program, she earns $40.60 an hour.

Racist graffiti is common on the job site, as are comments from male colleagues complaining about diversity programs. Yet Charise feels fortunate and picks her battles. Her situation is unique. In the last nine years of census data, carpenters in Philadelphia have registered only 5 percent Black workers, and women haven't registered a single percentage point.[2] When describing her work, Farris says, "It's heaven. You can't ask for anything more."[3]

Within the story of America's Type V city, Philadelphia stands as a counterpoint, a tale defined by restriction and missed opportunities rather than compromise and unforeseen risks. Previous narratives in this book have broadened the scope of collective material risk beyond the threat of fire, encompassing health, ecology, durability, and economics. Yet this essay shifts the focus of material performance toward social systems, considering the characteristics of the community alongside the material, and examining not only measurable risks but also potential social benefits of building codes. In doing so, it reveals how political influence over building codes and construction policies has shaped both the physical fabric of urban life and the labor demographics of the community.

The evolution of Philadelphia's building codes is distinctly marked by the influence and resistance of labor unions. A strong craft community enabled labor-intensive construction methods to dominate the city's codes and structures, resisting Type V construction and fiercely guarding job access. Throughout most of Philadelphia's history, building code regulations served as a form of protection for highly skilled labor. This ancillary function of building codes is well known in the construction industry across the country. Building codes are the subject of significant lobbying by labor groups because employment opportunities are at stake as codes evolve.

Philadelphia was among the few early American cities to fully ban wood-frame construction, a regulatory step often hindered by uneven political will and labor shortages. Philadelphia's formidable skilled-labor faction provided both the impetus and the means to enforce a comprehensive noncombustible construction mandate. By resisting conversion to a Type V city for over a century, the city also bolstered employment. But instead of producing widespread economic benefits, Philadelphia fostered one of the most restrictive and contested construction cultures in the nation. In Philadelphia, the protected skilled-labor jobs were held by a suburban white male subset of the population for most of the twentieth century. In the end, the city eliminated both the will and capacity to maintain its brick mandate by excluding most of its urban population from essential blue-collar jobs.

Philadelphia's building codes did not create the unions' discriminatory labor practices. However, they did safeguard, strengthen, and secure an exclusive industry, ultimately to the detriment of the urban economy. Philadelphia offers a case study in the affiliation between union labor political strength, building codes, and affordability.

Sixty years ago, in 1963, Charles E. Stubs was another Black parent of four in Philadelphia with a similarly unusual opportunity as a bricklayer's apprentice. Stubs worked for a brick subcontractor that he claimed was the only one in the city to include a Black person in its apprenticeship program. When the NAACP organized a protest against racial exclusion in the construction industry, it began with bricks. Although Philadelphia's bricklayers union local no. 1 typically honored the picket lines, this time it ordered its members to cross, to show up for work or risk losing their union status. As an apprentice, Stubs would not yet be paid as much as a fully qualified skilled worker with journeyman status. However, he still faced union pressure to work, and his apprenticeship likely also represented "freedom" for Mr. Stubs and his family.

The protest site was Strawberry Mansion Junior High School, a public city school under construction in a Black neighborhood. The NAACP protested that not a single Black (nonapprentice) skilled worker had been hired at the site. Since 1953, the Philadelphia Commission on Human Relations (PCHR) had been investigating the building trades and negotiating plans to diversify. Despite these efforts, "the 7,300 combined members of the local plumbers, electricians, and steamfitters' unions included only one single black electrician" in the early sixties.[4]

Two weeks after the May 1963 civil rights protests in Birmingham, Alabama, and after years of attention to racist hiring practices in the building trades, newly elected NAACP branch president Cecil B. Moore decided to act. In June, he and the NAACP organized picketers to prevent a flatbed truck piled high with bricks from unloading when it arrived at the Strawberry Mansion Junior High School. Charles Stubs did not cross the picket line. Instead, he joined the sixty-six Black unskilled laborers on-site in protest of racial exclusion in Philadelphia's construction unions. Stubs later told the *Philadelphia Tribune* that it was worth the sacrifice. "I'm not going to cross a picket line that's fighting for my kids. If I don't ever work in this city again, it's worth the sacrifice for my children."[5]

Over the next two months, Philadelphia became a focal point of protest. Demonstrators marched to the mayor's home, staged a sit-in at city hall, and picketed construction sites at the Municipal Services Building and city school buildings. The protests captured national attention, sparking similar movements against exclusionary construction labor in Harlem and Brooklyn; Cleveland, Ohio; and Trenton, New Jersey.[6]

By 1965, President Lyndon B. Johnson had empowered the secretary of labor to spearhead an affirmative action program for all government contractors that resulted in the first Philadelphia Plan. This initiative directly addressed the stark racial exclusion prevalent in Philadelphia's construction trades and union apprenticeship programs. It mandated that contractors submit detailed plans, outlining goals and timetables for hiring minority workers in six specific trades, as a prerequisite for receiving government contracts. Though the plan was later extended to other cities, Philadelphia remained the symbolic center of the struggle for racial equity within the skilled labor unions.[7]

Philadelphia's building industry, its building regulations, and its affordable housing efforts formed the epicenter of a fight for equal job opportunities in the United States in the 1960s. Historian Thomas J. Sugrue described this battle as one that "emerged amid a great and unresolved contest over race, employment, and civil rights that played out on the streets, in the union halls, and the workplaces of the urban North."[8] The focus on Philadelphia construction reveals a city deeply influenced by a thriving craft community, bolstered by substantial government support.

Over the years, labor-intensive building requirements ensured steady employment for those constructing Philadelphia brick by brick. This laborious building fabric could have engendered decades of widespread economic opportunity and upward mobility. Instead, it perpetuated a white male monopoly on quality blue-collar jobs. In 1893, when the Bricklayers and Masons International Union released a nondiscrimination mandate, Philadelphia's local bricklayers union responded by refusing affiliation.[9]

By the time protesters took to the streets in the 1960s, public construction investment in the Philadelphia area amounted to more than $17 billion, with brick masonry comprising over 90 percent of Philadelphia buildings.[10] The bricklayers union local no. 1 was among the first to be scrutinized by the Commission on Human Relations for discriminatory practices, featuring prominently in hearings and debates throughout the drafting and revision of the Philadelphia Plan. However, the plan ultimately failed to include the bricklayers union in its targets for improvement, instead focusing on the "skilled mechanical trades" such as plumbers, pipe fitters, electricians, and sheet metal workers.[11]

While the plan attempted to dismantle a government-supported monopoly on *who* could build, it failed to adequately consider *what* the city builds. Today's building code evolution often suffers from the opposite form of myopia, ignoring labor implications of building-material debates or opposing any costly restrictions rather than seeking mutual benefits.

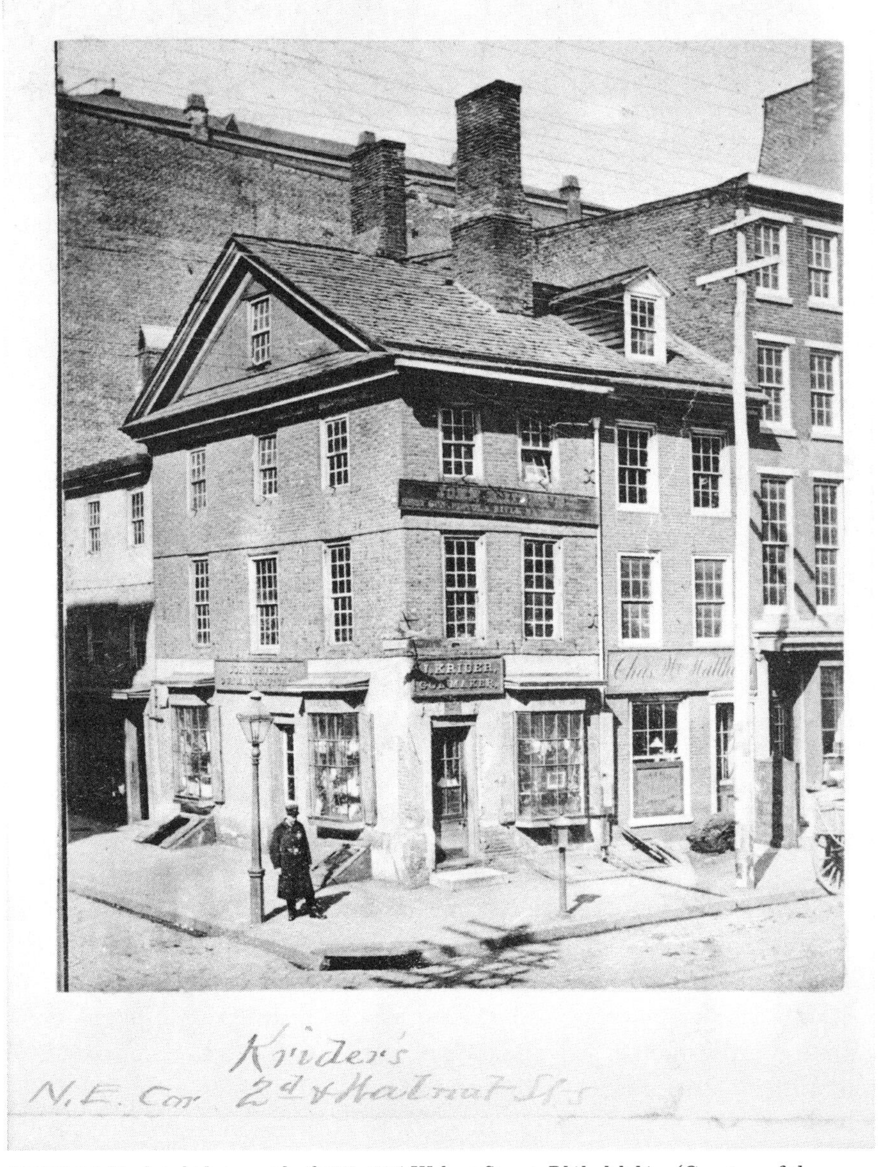

FIGURE 3.2 *Undated photograph of 133–135 Walnut Street, Philadelphia. (Courtesy of the Library of Congress, Historic American Building Survey)*

BRICKS AND LABOR

Philadelphia once supported one of the most mature building craft communities among American colonial cities. During its colonial construction, "more men were engaged in [building] trades than in any other group of similarly related skilled, urban crafts. . . . They were the most numerous element in the artisan group in the largest American late colonial city."[12]

As William Penn noted in 1684, "It is said that the people of Philadelphia used brick, made in their local yards, for sidewalk pavements and for building, and that even with the brick selling at $28 per thousand clamored at the kilns for them."[13] Consequently, the Philadelphia region was renowned by the nineteenth century as one of the great brickmaking centers.

In 1841, Philadelphia entirely banned framed construction within the city limits and authorized the removal of any existing frame buildings.[14] At this time, New York was only incrementally expanding its fire limits, moving between water boundaries as the city grew. It would be thirty years before Chicago burned on a massive scale and subsequently failed to institute a complete ban on framed construction within the city limits. Philadelphia's ability to enact an early and comprehensive investment in material longevity stemmed from the strength of its craft traditions, the political power of its building trades organizations, and the richness of regional clay deposits to support a robust brick industry.[15]

As the country grew and industrialization flourished, new construction drew enormous economic investment. In his acclaimed book on the rise and fall of union labor, historian David Montgomery stated, "In no other industrial country was so large a proportion of the working class made up of building workers.... Construction workers and coal miners together constituted half of the country's union members by the first decade of the twentieth century."[16]

However, this opportunity for work was not equally accessible. In 1899, W. E. B. Du Bois published *The Philadelphia Negro*, documenting the exclusion of Black workers from union and skilled-labor jobs. "Skilled labor" here refers to the higher-wage jobs that require specific training or apprenticeships, such as bricklayers, carpenters, plumbers, and electricians, among others. Within the skilled trades, a subset of mechanical trades includes electricians, plumbers, ironworkers, steam fitters, and sheet metal workers.[17] Construction also involves a large amount of work referred to as "unskilled labor," which includes demolition, material hauling, site preparation, cleanup, and assisting a skilled craftsperson. Unskilled laborers might still belong to a laborers' union but invariably earn lower wages. Du Bois stated that "special effort was made not to train Negroes for industry or allow them to enter" skilled-labor careers. If Black men arrived in Philadelphia already knowing a trade, they were forced to "either give them up and hire out as waiters or [unskilled] laborers, or they [became] job workmen and floating hands, catching a bit of carpentering here or a little brick-work or plastering there at reduced wages."[18]

Du Bois described the mechanisms of exclusion in Philadelphia. In some cases, the word "white" was actually listed as a qualification for admission into certain trade unions. But more often, the racism was less explicit. He noted that local unions "invariably failed to admit a colored applicant except under pressing circumstances. This is a most workable system and is adopted by nearly all trade unions. . . . Thus the carpenters, masons, painters, iron-workers, etc., have succeeded in keeping out nearly all Negro workmen by simply declining to work with nonunion men and refusing to let colored men join the union."[19]

By 1905, the city's building codes and ordinances directly protected organized labor by mandating union rates for public works projects. The codes state: "For salaries . . . foreman of bricklayers, one thousand four hundred (1,400) dollars; . . . foreman of carpenters, one thousand one hundred (1,100) dollars, . . . foreman of plumbers, one thousand dollars (1,000); . . . foreman of laborers, eight hundred and forty (840) dollars. . . . The union rate of wages [will] be paid to the bricklayers, carpenters, and painters."[20] The codification of wages for organized building labor and contract appropriation was not typical among city ordinances at the time, further revealing the strength and political power of labor unions in Philadelphia.[21]

During the Great Migration of Black Americans from the rural South to the urban Northeast (ca. 1910–1970), Philadelphia's Black population increased by 600,000, jumping from just 5 percent to 42 percent of the city's population today. By contrast, the white population decreased by 800,000 over the twentieth century and today makes up only 41 percent of the city's population.[22] Black men and women arriving during the early waves of northern migration found limited opportunities for employment. Du Bois described Black workers as "handicapped by a somewhat indefinite but existent and wide-reaching discrimination." In Philadelphia's Seventh Ward, 32,000 Black men over twenty-one were eligible for work at the turn of the twentieth century. Nearly 80 percent of those men were employed as laborers or servants, with only 7 percent in the skilled trades. Black women had access to more jobs, although almost exclusively in domestic service. While Black men and women were confined to the city's lowest-paying jobs, their housing costs steadily inflated. Discriminatory leasing, racially restrictive covenants, and a rapidly increasing population led to abnormally high rents for Philadelphia's Black population.[23]

In 1950, Black bricklayers nationwide made up only 10 percent of all bricklayers and a mere 4 percent of union apprentices, despite the national bricklayers union's constitutional prohibition of racial discrimination.[24] At the same time, the City of Philadelphia doubled down on its union labor investment through codes and policies. In 1956, the city's updated building ordinances reaffirmed its noncombustible building mandates, designating only four of sixty-six wards as "frame districts," for Type V construction. When Mayor James Tate took office in 1962, he amplified union political power by appointing union leaders to most city boards and commissions. Tate mandated the use of union labor for all public projects, declaring that "Philadelphia will be known as a Union Town."

FIGURE 3.3 *Dominic Ligato, "Cecil B. Moore in front of crowd" (1963). (Courtesy of the Special Collections Research Center, Temple University Libraries, Philadelphia)*

In total, federal, state, and local governments spent nearly "$17 billion on Philadelphia-area construction projects in the mid-1960s."[25]

By 1963, it seemed almost inevitable that the simmering outrage at inequitable access to publicly supported jobs would erupt. The city's codified, labor-safeguarding materials became the flashpoint, as the flatbed truck laden with bricks was barred from delivering to Strawberry Mansion Junior High School. Philadelphia bricks fueled and symbolized the city's frustration and demand for justice. One protestor exclaimed, "We're tired of carrying bricks: we want to lay them. We'll stay all day, all week, all year. . . . We want freedom NOW!"[26] Another protester asserted, "This is a false democracy when qualified colored people can't get a job building schools for their own kids."[27]

In 1963, the city's commission on human relations opened hearings with accusations of discriminatory practices by several trades, including the bricklayers, sheet metal workers, glaziers, plumbers, and plasterers unions. Notably, some of these trades, namely bricklayers and plasterers,

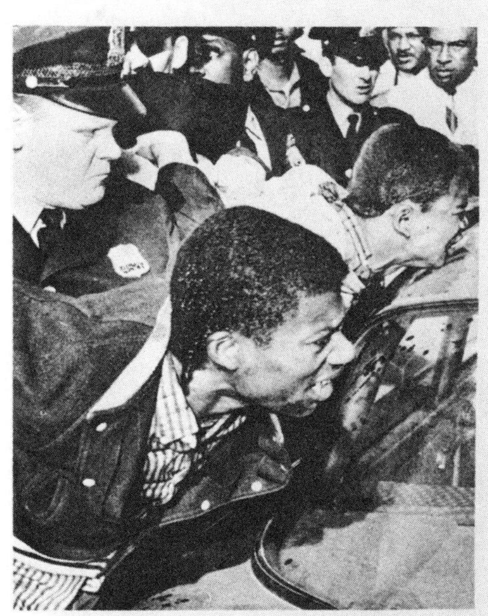

FIGURE 3.4 *Detail image of "Youth arrested and attacked by police . . ." from a "fact sheet" published for Thacher Longstreth's mayoral campaign against Frank Rizzo (1971). (Courtesy of the Historical Society of Pennsylvania, Thelma McDaniel Collection)*

were virtually guaranteed employment on many city construction projects due to fireproofing requirements within the building codes.

Joseph Schwartz, secretary of the American Federation of Labor and Congress of Industrial Organizations (AFL-CIO) commission on human relations, specifically criticized the bricklayers union when noting the lack of Black participation in board of education–sponsored apprentice training programs. Schwartz quoted a bricklayer instructor who claimed he would "face a $1,000 fine by my union if I teach them," pointing to Black students, "to lay one brick."[28] Schwartz urged the board of education to withdraw the use of school facilities for such exclusionary classes.[29]

John M. Doyle, president of the bricklayers union local no. 1, responded to Schwartz's accusations in a later Philadelphia Plan hearing, asking, "Does Joe Schwartz or his committee know that Bricklayers Union #1 has a colored apprentice boy? I should not call him a boy. He is married and has a family."[30]

Doyle estimated that local union no. 1 might have 75 Black members out of 1,300 total members (less than 6 percent). He explained that acceptance into the apprenticeship program required sponsorship from a union member with at least ten years of membership and letters from the applicant's clergyman and school. Doyle disputed the implication that union instructors were fined for training Black students, noting that the fine applied only if the student was not following the required sponsorship rules. However, Doyle did not respond directly when asked why the sponsorship rules could not be loosened, especially considering their potential to perpetuate existing demographic imbalances and the union's expressed desire for more apprentices.[31]

Conclusions from the 1963 public hearings mention ten construction trades by name, identifying them as either exhibiting a pattern of discrimination or "appearing not to be discriminatory." Despite the bricklayers union's prominent role in the hearings and ubiquity of bricks in the city's buildings, the union was notably absent from the list. Instead, the report stated that "numerous trades have either not been investigated at this time or the information gathered to date has been inconclusive."[32]

In hearings held in 1969 on the revision of the Philadelphia Plan, John B. Kelly Jr., president of one of the largest all-union masonry contractors in the area and member of the Philadelphia City Council, testified again about the lack of Black participation in the brick layers union apprenticeship program.

> Back in 1950, when I started my apprenticeship, we had no Negro apprentices whatsoever that I knew of, at least in our local. That's Local No. 1 here in Philadelphia. About ten years ago, the Bricklayers finally started accepting black apprentices. I'm not sure as to exactly how many or the percentage of them, but there has been an increasing number of them accepted each year, to my knowledge, up to the present time.[33]

The public hearings confirmed a historical lack of Black bricklayers and limited avenues for nonlegacy entry to apprenticeship programs. Despite vague claims of progress within the bricklayers union, Black membership remained at an estimated 6 percent. Armed with this knowledge, the insights of a bricklayers union head on the city council, and a cityscape dominated by brick masonry construction, the Philadelphia Plan still failed to include bricklayers among the six trades targeted for improvement.

The building trades named in the Philadelphia Plan included electricians, plumbers, ironworkers, steam fitters, and sheet metal workers. Two primary reasons were typically given for the choice of these trades: extremely low minority membership and high wages. Upon closer examination, neither argument convincingly justifies excusing such a prominent local union.

Secretary for Wage and Labor Standards Arthur Fletcher announced the first reason in his 1969 remarks at the signing of the Philadelphia Plan, stating that "the named trades have been singled out for special emphasis because in the past these trades, at least in Philadelphia, have been operating without significant minority participation."[34] A 1950s national report by the NAACP supported Fletcher's claims, noting that only 1 percent Black electricians and 3 percent Black plumbers were reported nationally, compared to 10 percent Black brick masons.[35]

However, the focus on national general trade statistics may have obscured the extent of local challenges and union exclusion in Philadelphia. Congressional debates at the time highlighted the importance of distinguishing between general trade participation and union membership.

> Even more discouraging are these figures, when they are broken down to consider only the construction industry unions. These unions account for five-eighths, or 1.3 million, of the 2 million union members in referral bargaining units. Of these 1.3 million, only 106,000—8.4 percent—are blacks and only 56,000—4.5 percent—are Spanish surnamed. Thus, these percentages are even lower than the aggregate figures I have previously noted. And of these 106,000 blacks, 81,000, or about 75 percent, are laborers. In the skilled occupations, the percentages are bleak.[36]

John Doyle's 1963 testimony revealed that Black bricklayers union membership was estimated at only 6 percent, far lower than the 10 percent national average for the trade and the 8.4 percent national average for Black union membership across trades.[37] Although Black membership in the bricklayers union slightly exceeded the 1–3 percent average Black membership in the mechanical trades, this incremental improvement must be viewed in the context of Philadelphia's population at the time (1960–1970), which was 26–33 percent Black.[38] Additionally, these numbers should be considered in relation to the scale of employment opportunities that the city incentivized or mandated through building codes. Historian Timothy Lombardo described the mechanical trades as "the highest-paid workers in the city's trade unions" but noted that "they represented only 4 percent of the city's union membership at the time."[39]

The high-wage argument is also cited as a reason for the Philadelphia Plan's focus on the mechanical trades. However, according to national union wage reports in 1967, bricklayers also ranked among the highest-paid trades.[40] National surveys reported that half of the bricklayers and boilermakers earned the highest hourly rates in the industry through labor-management agreements, compared with only two-fifths of the electricians and pipefitters and three-eighths of the plumbers surveyed. The average bricklayer wage was $4.17 per hour in 1960, compared to $2.88

for general laborers, the level at which most Black construction workers in Philadelphia found work.[41]

Plate 12 illustrates the spatial extent of the opportunities missed by Philadelphia's Black workers to participate in the construction of a predominantly brick city, both before and after the initiation of the Philadelphia Plan. Most of the city's building stock (light blue) was brick masonry built before the 1963 hearings began. Since 1963, brick masonry buildings (dark blue) have continued to dominate as the primary construction type.

Philadelphia missed an opportunity to further amplify the plan's impact by aligning its targets with the trades required by its building codes. Alternatively, a more pessimistic interpretation of the bricklayers union's omission is that Philadelphia deliberately excused the union from the plan's mandates, reflecting its strong political influence. Whether intentional or not, regulatory protection combined with a failure to reform magnified the ongoing marginalization of Black workers, limiting their access to the most lucrative and stable construction opportunities.

BUILDING CODES, LABOR, AND AFFORDABILITY: THE JOB-HOUSING FIT

Philadelphia's union labor debates unfolded against a national backdrop of civil rights protests over discrimination in construction labor, the dawn of affirmative action, and fervent calls to increase funding for affordable housing—each with significant implications for building codes and union control.

In the late 1940s, more than a decade before the halted brick delivery at Strawberry Mansion and the admission of the first Black apprentice in the local bricklayers union, the City of Philadelphia was drafting revised ordinances. The city reportedly clashed with unions and manufacturers, challenging the prohibition of wood-frame construction in the name of cost savings. A 1948 *Philadelphia Inquirer* article titled "Housing Costs Boosted by Multiplicity of Codes" lamented that proposed building code reforms were "barred by organized groups," sparking an "underground war." Organized labor groups were reportedly "anxious to protect the monopolies safe-guarded for them in existing municipal ordinances, state laws, and union-sponsored building regulations."[42]

The article contrasts the perspectives of code reformers advocating for affordable construction with those of unions focused on job protection: "Opponents of code revision are found both in labor and in business. . . . [Code reformers] believe the restrictions give labor groups a protection against new materials and methods which the latter feel would curtail manpower on building jobs. Because of the preferred status given these groups, proponents of code changes look for concerted opposition in modernizing local building laws."[43]

Revised city ordinances were eventually released in 1956, including a distinct title that covered building codes.[44] The revision allowed a few wood-frame districts at the city's periphery and portions of allowable wood-frame construction in detached dwellings.[45] Yet much of the bricklayers' codified monopoly remained throughout the duration of the Philadelphia Plan protests and hearings. It would be another thirty years before Philadelphia adopted regional and then national model codes with conditions allowing Type V construction according to site, size, and occupancy limitations.[46]

Philadelphia's debate in 1948 over Type V construction was driven by its significant impact on bricklayers and brick manufacturers. Leveraging building codes to protect union interests was not unusual. The same 1948 article highlighted the national scale of building code and labor conflicts, noting labor resistance to plumbing regulation changes in Chicago, building foundation code battles in Boston and several other cities, and electrical code debates in Milwaukee.

The chairman of the Joint Congressional Committee on Housing stated that "his committee's investigations have disclosed that efforts to change building codes have been jealously watched and combatted by some materials manufacturers and some local labor unions.... [New performance codes] will discourage some monopolies and they certainly should encourage home construction and decrease its cost."[47]

However, performance codes did not solve the issue of labor influence over building regulation. In Philadelphia, 1968 reports again point to the influence of union pressure on federal construction standards and spending. That year, HUD invested $44 million to rehabilitate 3,300 Philadelphia dwelling units. Later, HUD accused the local Philadelphia Housing Authority (PHA) of inefficient management of funds, reportedly accepting higher material standards to "appease local unions."[48]

When discussing building codes, housing affordability is often pitted against labor intensity.[49] However, this argument falters if affordability is viewed as a balance between housing and job access rather than merely as an abstract measure of upfront construction costs. Urban planning researchers Chris Bennet and Alex Karner describe this balance as "the extent to which housing price is well matched to local job quality"—or the "job-housing fit."[50]

The alignment between low-wage job access and low-cost housing is especially crucial, as it influences a spectrum of urban economic pressures, from transportation to public housing. Viewing affordability through the lens of a job-housing fit immediately transforms the way cities might approach building objectives: prioritizing job creation over compromising housing quality.

The construction industry constitutes a significant portion of blue-collar jobs targeted in a job-housing fit strategy. Historically, construction labor expenditures served as a primary means through which federal and local governments promoted economic stabilization. Consequently, the 1963 report by the City of Philadelphia's commission on human relations underscored a moral and legal imperative to ensure equitable access to well-paying jobs.

A 2009 report on construction labor diversity by the Philadelphia mayor's commission further highlights strong economic arguments for diversifying access to local jobs. The report notes the beneficial increase in taxes and expenditures as minorities and women ascend the income distribution ladder.[51] Philadelphia's construction jobs still comprise "11% of all blue-collar jobs, but 38.5% of blue-collar jobs paying wages above $20 per hour."[52] However, an estimated 80 percent of construction jobs are held by workers living outside the city limits, with only an estimated 3 percent held by Black city residents, 3 percent by Hispanic city residents, and a mere 0.4 percent by women.[53] Meanwhile, nearly half of all Black and Hispanic households in Philadelphia are burdened by rent or mortgage costs, and the problem is particularly acute among female caregivers.[54]

There is a stark mismatch between the demographics of *need* and *access* to blue-collar jobs that undermines housing affordability in Philadelphia. Exporting jobs outside the city perpetuates long-term cycles of economic loss. Affordable-housing scholars have long argued that reliable blue-collar jobs stabilize neighborhoods when residents have access to these local employment sources.[55] A recent report by the National Association of Home Builders quantified this economic stability by calculating the ongoing benefit of homebuilding *if* local workers are employed during construction. Investing in the local workforce generates a continuous economic influx from the recurring spending of income and taxes. Local workers building a hundred single-family houses will add an estimated $4.1 million to the economy annually as they spend their salaries. Similarly, a hundred rental apartments result in an annual $2.6 million of recurring spending. Conversely, when workers' salaries are immediately exported outside of the local area, the cycle of gains for local businesses, wages, and taxes is disrupted.[56]

In essence, the city and the unions found themselves at an impasse during the mid-twentieth century, primarily over building codes and labor protections. The city simultaneously pushed for lowering code standards to cut labor costs and also expanding the workforce, while the unions staunchly opposed these measures. A more integrated approach, considering both objectives simultaneously, might have paved the way for innovative solutions and mutual gains.

FIGURE 3.5 *The caption to this photo from "Unpublished Black History" reads: "The Rev. Jesse Jackson (background with hands raised) was only 27 on Sept. 22, 1969, when he led a rally of 4,000 people in Chicago calling for an end to discrimination in the construction trades." (Courtesy of Gary Settle/* New York Times*)*

CONSTRUCTION EMPLOYMENT DISCRIMINATION NATIONALLY

Labor access imbalance was not unique to Philadelphia or to bricklayers alone. Throughout the twentieth century, labor union discrimination was pervasive and well documented across the United States. In 1913, Booker T. Washington published an article titled "The Negro and Labor Unions," highlighting national prejudice. He posed a poignant question: "Shall the labor unions use their influence to deprive the black man of his opportunity to labor . . . [or] unite with those who want to give every man, regardless of color, race or creed, what Colonel Roosevelt calls the 'square deal' in the matters of labor?"

Washington also underscored the critical distinction between skilled and unskilled labor in construction, noting that lower-paying, more arduous unskilled labor became the default option for Black workers who were denied access to apprenticeship programs.[57]

The National Urban League later built upon Washington's argument, documenting widespread labor union discrimination nationwide. Their report describes frequent mislabeling of Black laborers as being wasteful or inefficient, only suited for work "with a wheelbarrow, as a hod carrier, in cleaning tracks" rather than positions requiring precision. The report criticized the lack of data supporting these claims and concluded that "the tragedy of human waste in industry is nowhere more outstanding than in the case of Negro employment."[58]

In 1918, W. E. B. Du Bois remarked on the "already astonishing" political power of unions at local, state, and national levels. He issued a call to action, stating:

> We might as well recognize that the time has come when we can no longer indiscriminately assume that the present labor movement is the movement for the uplift of labor. On the contrary, standing unshakably by the principles of collective bargaining, we must refuse to allow the men who are now using it for their selfish ends at the expense of the masses to be the exclusive mouthpiece of those masses.[59]

Despite widespread acknowledgment of pervasive labor discrimination, the federal government continued to shield and support construction unions throughout the mid- to late twentieth century. Herbert Hill, former NAACP labor director, lamented that the US government missed a crucial opportunity to mandate the elimination of union racial discrimination as a condition for its support. He described the impact of the Depression and the New Deal on the Black population as "catastrophic":

> Much of Roosevelt's New Deal was a variety of efforts to generate new employment. The New Deal sought to provide economic stabilization and security as well as emergency relief and new jobs through a series of laws and programs. In general, these efforts improved conditions for whites but had little impact on the status of Negro workers. Because the Federal Government failed to require or enforce equal racial access to government-created jobs, the ultimate effect of the New Deal employment programs was to widen the gap between the economic condition of black and white workers.[60]

The federal government also introduced regulation that provided uneven protection for different types of workers. In the 1930s, 70 percent of Black workers were employed in agricultural or domestic work—industries that were excluded from the protections provided by the National Recovery Administration established in 1933 and the Fair Labor Standards Act of 1938. The National Labor Relations Act of 1935 safeguarded employees' rights to organize but failed to address widespread union discrimination. Consequently, the New Deal era resulted in more jobs for white workers and further legal protection of exclusively white jobs.[61]

During World War II, the US government signed a series of "stabilization agreements" with many unions to ensure adequate wartime labor supply. Hill describes these agreements as "closed-shop contracts" with the AFL-affiliated unions that simultaneously denied membership and jobs to Black workers. As a result, government-sponsored work during the war became the primary source of employment at unusually high wages for white workers, while unemployment or underemployment was prevalent among Black workers in the building trades.[62] Hill's argument—that regulatory safeguards provided to unions, coupled with their exclusionary membership, exacerbated economic imbalances—also applies to Philadelphia's building codes.

The civil rights movement and national construction labor protests in the 1950s and 1960s illuminated the pervasive issue of racial discrimination across cities and trades. In 1963, the NAACP assessed progress in securing union membership and job access for Black workers. They estimated that at the current rate, it would take until 2094 for Black individuals to achieve equal participation in skilled-craft training and employment.[63]

Throughout the 1960s, civil rights efforts sustained pressure on workplace discrimination, leading to widespread protests across the United States. In 1967, a Department of Labor official noted: "The absence of nonwhites among construction trade workers has been a focal point for racial unrest and a prime symbol of the lack of equal employment opportunity."[64]

In 1969, the National Urban League meticulously documented the status of Black labor and union exclusion across American cities. The report paints a vivid picture of discrimination, spanning various geographies and trades. By 1969, Cleveland's paperhangers local no. 128 had not welcomed a Black member in twenty-seven years. In Pittsburgh, no Black painters had ever been admitted to the union. Buffalo unions barred Black workers, claiming that "they would not be welcome in the homes." In Alabama, despite Black plasterers forming the majority of the union, white workers were still given employment preference. White bricklayers in Atlanta would not work alongside Black masons. Only one Black bricklayer had been admitted to the local no. 9 union in Minneapolis. In Los Angeles, hod carriers were the only union with significant Black membership. Black carpenters in New York and Philadelphia were compelled to establish their own unions. In Denver, electricians, plumbers, and gas fitters unions outright refused to admit Black workers. New York's Union of Steam and Operating Engineers deemed Black membership "impractical," arguing that tenants would find it "repulsive" to see Black workers repairing equipment in office buildings and factories.[65]

Women across racial groups, particularly Black women, have long struggled to gain access to the construction industry. In 1989, legal scholar Sylvia A. Law wrote in the *Harvard Civil Rights Law Review* that "anecdotal evidence suggests that problems of sexual harassment are unusually acute in the construction field," citing several related court cases. She also noted that "construction workers are particularly threatened by, and hostile to, women of color."[66] When Law published her article, women made up only 1.5 percent of the construction workforce.

By the early-2020s, the US Bureau of Labor Statistics estimated that women constituted 10 percent of the roughly 12 million construction workers nationally.[67] Women have often allied with other marginalized groups to seek equal treatment in construction and other labor organizations.[68] Diversification strategies developed in response to the civil rights movement have also benefitted women and other underrepresented groups.

Despite some progress, the persistent exclusion and discrimination documented in the past continue to resonate in today's labor and construction industries, underscoring the need for ongoing attention to labor opportunities as a crucial aspect of urban material performance.

MAKING FEW GAINS

When protesters took to the streets in Philadelphia, Cleveland, New York, St. Louis, and other cities, they demanded equitable access to union jobs, challenging decades of recognized exclusion and ongoing government support. They called for measurement of progress rather than just policies and promises of future improvement. This movement led to the creation of the Philadelphia Plan, the first affirmative action requirement aimed at construction industry discrimination and exclusion.

The Philadelphia Building Trade Commission initially resisted the Philadelphia Plan by challenging its legality. The plan placed requirements on contractors bidding for public work rather than on unions directly. However, because contractors hired from union halls, restrictive apprenticeship programs and union membership demographics pushed them to hire nonunion labor to meet the plan's diversity targets. Nonunion hiring became a controversial side effect of the Philadelphia Plan, trapping it in debate and ultimately leading to resistance from the unions and a subsequent softening of the plan's requirements. Unions received federal funding to create diversity outreach programs, and the final revised Philadelphia Plan required only a "good faith effort" by contractors to meet hiring goals.

The US Department of Labor expanded its diversity programs nationwide. Over subsequent decades, diversity hiring goals, plans, and quotas remained central challenges, often positioning unions against community demands for recognizable progress. Today, government entities navigate this conflict by directing affirmative action programs toward contractors, emphasizing business ownership demographics rather than unions or workforce characteristics. For example, the City of Philadelphia aims to allocate at least 35 percent of city contracts to certified minority-owned, woman-owned, or disabled-owned businesses.[69] By concentrating on the composition of business ownership rather than the workforce, these programs sidestep union hiring conflicts. However, they may fall short in addressing the fundamental issue. As they now fail to incentivize or measure workforce impact, have these programs proven effective in Philadelphia and other major cities?

In 1971, *The New York Times* reported minimal improvement from affirmative action efforts in the 1970s, stating: "Despite 'outreach' programs. . . . and despite seemingly constant litigation, the number of black and other minority workers entering the construction industry remains a thin trickle."[70] In the decades that followed, cities increasingly recognized that structural inequities, housing segregation, and discriminatory union reputations built over decades presented significant cultural obstacles to reversing minority exclusion in the construction industry.

Awareness and acceptance into apprenticeship programs often hinge on kinship, friendship, or informal social networks. Consequently, residential segregation tends to limit these relationships across racial and ethnic lines. Additionally, the construction industry's reputation for racism and sexism creates a formidable psychological barrier to diversification. Philadelphia's 1963 commission on human relations report stated that extensive research from sociology, psychology, and economics shows that Black individuals "perceive the craft unions as conspiracies of exclusion so effective that all individual attempts to breach these barriers are destined to end in failure."[71]

A report from the last decade of the twentieth century indicates that the construction industry remained largely homogeneous. A comprehensive 1993 study by New York City's commission on human rights documented persistent racial and gender discrimination, as well as sexual harassment at union worksites. The report included testimonies from workers and government officials, revealing widespread discrimination against Black, Latino, and female workers, with Asian American workers particularly underrepresented in union membership.

Access to union membership without an apprenticeship was almost exclusively available to white males through personal connections. By contrast, four- or five-year apprenticeship programs remained the only entry route for women and persons of color. One worker explained, "The union will bring in a guy who happens to be their friend—he may be working in a pizza parlor all his life—and they put him to work. He doesn't have to know anything, and he can get paid full [journeyperson] scale. That mostly happens with the white guys."[72]

In 2020, Chicago Black United Communities, a long-standing South Side organization, staged a "no labor day" protest. This demonstration, which included unemployed Black Chicago residents, was a response to recent Department of Labor statistics revealing that apprenticeship programs in Illinois remain predominantly white.[73]

Ta-Nehisi Coates, award-winning author and journalist, contextualized the long-standing tension between Black residents and the Chicago unions, stating, "In Mitts' ward—and among many poor blacks—some unions rank only a couple of notches above the Ku Klux Klan. Black leaders in Chicago have repeatedly charged that the building-trades unions, traditionally controlled by whites, are keeping a grip on jobs."[74]

In Philadelphia, a recent mayor's advisory commission study and subsequent city disparity reports found that minority workers and women are still vastly underrepresented in public construction work. In 2018, Black construction workers logged only 9 percent of the top ten city-sponsored trade hours in Philadelphia, and women accounted for just 1 percent of this work.[75]

Analyzing the effects of affirmative action in specific cities since the 1960s is challenging due to limited workforce demographic data. The US Bureau of Labor Statistics provides only national and state-level demographic data by trade, while the US Equal Employment Opportunity Commission (EEOC) offers data by city, but only for the building construction industry in aggregate. Fortunately, the US Census Bureau began collecting occupation data as part of its Current Population Survey (CPS) in 2014. The CPS gathers monthly information from approximately sixty thousand households nationwide, enabling demographic analysis by occupation, trade, *and* city.[76] The surveys also ask respondents whether they are union members or represented by unions.

CPS surveys are limited by their sample size and their representation of workers who *live* in a particular geography instead of all who *work* in that geography. Additionally, census data may underreport undocumented immigrants living in the United States.[77] Undocumented workers likely constitute a substantial portion of the construction industry, recently estimated at 1.4 million workers, or 13 percent of all construction workers, by the Center for American Progress.[78] Notwithstanding these limitations, CPS data provides valuable and relatively new insights into detailed labor demographic trends.

In Philadelphia, CPS census data includes an average of 2,800 brick masons annually. Yet Black and other minority brick masons fail to register a single worker among the nearly 20,000 masons recorded over seven years of available data.[79]

Philadelphia carpenters show a slight improvement, with 26 percent Hispanic workers, 4 percent Black workers, and 2 percent women. In

2020, Philadelphia's Black residential population was the city's majority at 42 percent. Hispanic or Latino residents made up 15.2 percent, and women comprised 52 percent of the population.[80] However, the city's Black construction workforce accounts for only 15 percent overall, and women are scarcely represented in the local trades in CPS data. Extrapolating today's trade demographics across the city material map reveals a stark disconnect between those who live in Philadelphia and those who had the opportunity to build it (see plates 10 and 11).[81]

Across the case study cities in this book, CPS data consistently reveals the underrepresentation of minority construction workers, particularly Black, Asian, Indigenous American, and women workers (see table 3.1).[82] The trades listed in table 3.1 are chosen to highlight those most influenced by construction type and material choice. Black workers are typically better represented in lower-paying laborer jobs across cities. However, the overall percentage of Black construction workers is consistently far lower than the residential Black population within each city. Asian Americans, Indigenous Americans, and women are almost absent in CPS construction demographics.

The percentage of women in local building construction industries appears to be higher in data collected from the EEOC, which is self-reported by large private firms and those with substantial government contracts. This suggests that larger construction companies offer more employment opportunities for women. However, there is no indication of the specific roles women hold within these companies, so these opportunities may not be within the trades themselves.[83]

In some cases, low or no numbers are recorded in a particular city over the CPS reporting years since 2014. This may be due to a combination of the small sample size of CPS data and the construction workforce residing outside of the city. For instance, recent census data suggests that only 20 percent of regional construction workers live within Philadelphia's city limits.[84]

AFFIRMATIVE ACTION

In 1918, W. E. B. Du Bois warned that union discrimination posed a grave threat to American democracy. He placed his hope in "an appeal on one hand to the educated thinker of all classes—on the other hand to the mass of laborers."[85] A century later, this hope remains unfulfilled as architects and policymakers continue to constrain material regulation criteria to a narrow definition of health, safety, and welfare, focusing solely on material combustibility. This approach fails to consider the broader welfare interests that building regulations and material choices serve or hinder.

Civil rights activist Whitney Young, addressing the 1968 American Institute of Architects convention, condemned the profession's inaction. He declared, "You are not a profession that has distinguished itself by your social and civic contributions to the cause of civil rights, and I am sure this has not come to you as any shock. You are most distinguished by your thunderous silence and your complete irrelevance."[86]

Philadelphia's 1963 commission on human relations report contextualized this sentiment, asserting that any failure to act affirmatively is "an act of discrimination." The commission stated,

> History and experience. . . have amply demonstrated that traditional racial barriers are not eliminated by simple declarations of policy, nor by the passive removal of overtly exclusionary practices. The barriers to opportunity are overcome only through affirmative action which actually enables and causes qualified members of the excluded groups to pass through the traditional barriers and become established in those jobs from which they were so long excluded.[87]

Top-down regulatory attempts to correct construction discrimination since the 1960s protests and subsequent federal legislation have made little impact. More localized action, such as agreements between clients, community coalitions, and contractors, offers some optimistic potential but also suffers from a persistent lack of reliable information.

This essay advocates most strongly for greater synthetic design of regulatory, material, housing, and employment incentives. This requires better, more consistent and accessible data to restructure the objectives and assessments. Architects can play a crucial role in this process by prioritizing local labor opportunities through material specification and design choices.

A tool designed to facilitate this synthetic design process, known as a community benefit agreement (CBA), is gaining popularity. Private developers and community coalitions use CBAs to identify priorities and co-benefits, ranging from local workers' opportunities to protection against resident displacement.[88] Because CBAs begin with partnerships between community coalitions and developers, they can also disrupt social and psychological barriers to workforce diversity. Community groups can help connect the available local workforce with opportunities, addressing the often missing social connections that thwart government quota-based efforts. In 2016, Detroit became the first American city to pass a community benefit ordinance, requiring developers "to proactively engage with communities to identify community benefits and address potential negative impacts of development projects."[89]

	Average Salary	Annual Average Workers Surveyed	White	Hispanic or Latino	Black	Indigenous American*	Asian	Women
Philadelphia								
Brick Masons	$62,380	2,852	100%	0%	0%	0%	0%	0%
Carpenters	$58,510	16,528	68%	26%	5%	0%	0%	0%
Structural Iron and Steel	$66,750	1,314	16%	0%	65%	0%	19%	0%
Glaziers	$64,690	534	100%	0%	0%	0%	0%	0%
Cement Masons	$59,240	0						
Supervisors	$82,170	3,858	93%	7%	0%	0%	0%	0%
Laborers	$45,770	23,156	54%	25%	22%	0%	0%	0%
All Trades – CPS		112,277	68%	15%	15%	0%	2%	2%
All Craft Trades – EEOC		5,257	83%	6%	7%	0%	2%	29%
Resident Demographics		1,603,797	34%	15%	42%	0%	7%	53%
New York								
Brick Masons	$73,390	4,518	24%	60%	16%	0%	0%	0%
Carpenters	$61,680	52,735	43%	41%	11%	0%	5%	2%
Structural Iron and Steel	$89,650	1,395	55%	16%	29%	0%	0%	0%
Glaziers	$61,770	972	0%	23%	0%	0%	77%	0%
Cement Masons	$59,790	977	0%	69%	32%	0%	0%	0%
Supervisors	$98,880	15,395	66%	16%	14%	0%	4%	0%
Laborers	$53,200	95,538	29%	51%	15%	0%	5%	1%
All Trades – CPS		392,853	42%	44%	10%	0%	4%	2%
All Craft Trades – EEOC		13,213	66%	17%	10%	0%	5%	21%
Resident Demographics		8,804,190	32%	29%	24%	0%	14%	52%
Chicago								
Brick Masons	$92,010	3,291	63%	37%	0%	0%	0%	0%
Carpenters	$84,100	45,688	45%	41%	12%	0%	2%	1%
Structural Iron and Steel	$91,210	2,801	55%	31%	0%	0%	13%	0%
Glaziers	$68,670	0						
Cement Masons	$74,410	613	50%	50%	0%	0%	0%	0%
Supervisors	$88,940	6,065	40%	46%	14%	0%	0%	0%
Laborers	$69,370	40,551	42%	48%	9%	1%	0%	5%
All Trades – CPS		182,727	50%	39%	9%	0%	2%	4%
All Craft Trades – EEOC		12,043	71%	21%	6%	0%	2%	16%
Resident Demographics		2,746,388	33%	29%	30%	0%	7%	51%

	Average Salary	Annual Average Workers Surveyed	White	Hispanic or Latino	Black	Indigenous American*	Asian	Women
Seattle								
Brick Masons	$90,380	650	68%	0%	0%	0%	32%	0%
Carpenters	$64,780	17,820	61%	25%	5%	0%	7%	3%
Structural Iron and Steel	$93,740	484	51%	0%	0%	0%	49%	0%
Glaziers	$64,310	0						
Cement Masons	$77,940	479	100%	0%	0%	0%	0%	0%
Supervisors	$99,840	7,587	84%	9%	5%	3%	0%	0%
Laborers	$53,530	18,573	50%	34%	2%	6%	8%	12%
All Trades – CPS		87,826	53%	36%	3%	1%	6%	6%
All Craft Trades – EEOC		7,955	76%	11%	3%	1%	4%	17%
Resident Demographics		737,015	64%	7%	7%	0%	15%	49%
Tampa								
Brick Masons	$40,070	647	32%	28%	0%	0%	40%	0%
Carpenters	$39,080	11,883	63%	27%	10%	0%	0%	5%
Structural Iron and Steel	$39,280	467	100%	0%	0%	0%	0%	0%
Glaziers	$48,320	0						
Cement Masons	$38,060	0						
Supervisors	$58,610	4,960	78%	22%	0%	0%	0%	20%
Laborers	$32,700	18,849	67%	21%	11%	0%	0%	9%
All Trades – CPS		66,273	57%	29%	12%	0%	0%	7%
All Craft Trades – EEOC		3,309	72%	17%	7%	0%	0%	28%
Resident Demographics		384,959	45%	26%	24%	0%	4%	52%

* The term "Indigenous American" is substituted by the author for the U.S. Census demographic category, "American Indian."

TABLE 3.1 *Workforce salary (2022) and demographic averages (2014–2021) for construction trades impacted by building material choice and construction type. (Compiled by the author from the Census Bureau Current Population Survey)*

Municipalities can proactively create incentives and investments aimed at local labor participation as a mechanism to stabilize communities. The City of Philadelphia recently launched the Rebuild Philadelphia initiative with the express agenda "to serve as a model for diversity and economic inclusion by hiring local, ensuring that the contractors and workforce on

Rebuild projects are diverse, [and] improving access to the building trades for women and minorities."[90] This initiative was informed by local city council members "express[ing] the need to use the program as a way to increase opportunity for people of color and women in union construction." The Rebuild initiative aimed for 45 percent minority and women participation in its labor force, aligning more closely with the city's demographics.[91]

However, Rebuild and similar initiatives are hampered by a lack of reliable, accessible, and adequately detailed demographic union and trade data. Recent reporting on the Rebuild Philadelphia initiative alleged that unions inflated their minority participation numbers by "stuffing people of color into less meaningful roles and not utilizing as many as they could for higher-paying, skilled roles."[92]

In 2009, the Philadelphia mayor's office commissioned a report on construction industry diversity that also cited the lack of reliable data as one of the most significant obstacles to success in diversifying the unions. The report recommended that unions set diversity targets and collect and report data; in addition, contractors and project owners (public and private) should "insist that unions and subcontractors provide demographic information about their staff workers, especially their 'steady workforce' and documentation of their efforts to increase inclusion of minorities and women workers in all of their projects."[93]

Architects are among those responsible for creating a culture insistent on change. J. Max Bond Jr., a prominent architect in the late twentieth century and principal of Davis Brody Bond, demonstrated the potential to influence job access through design. Bond specified the use of brick for Harlem's Schomburg Center for Research in Black Culture after analyzing minority participation in construction trade unions in New York City. He chose labor-intensive construction material with relatively higher diversity and local union representation to maximize the benefit his project could have within the neighborhood. Bond described his efforts as follows:

> When we design a building, we look at the composition of the labor unions in the area and then try to design to make sure that, if it is in a Black or Hispanic community, people who live in the community have a better chance of working on its construction. For example, if one were to design a building completely out of aluminum products, very few minority people in America could work on the building, because the aluminum industry is one in which not many minorities are involved, from plant to fabrication to erection. If one were to design a building in brick or block, there would be a much greater chance of employing more minority

people. Designing a building in materials that are more labor intensive obviously has other benefits as well.[94]

Architect Lance Hosey later described Bond's approach as "material justice." Hosey argues that focusing on the social equity impacts of material selection can challenge common assumptions about sustainable design.[95] Despite Bond's demonstration of an architect's potential for social impact through material selection over four decades ago, architects and regulators seldom describe material design objectives in terms of local job opportunities. Furthermore, government affirmative action programs only impact government contracts and fail to incentivize the broader workforce. Designers, planners, owners, contractors, and community members can address the policy shortfall by advocating for inclusive construction investment. Several data sources provide a starting point and may help to build a culture of increased accountability.

The US Census's CPS enables demographic analysis by occupation, trade, city, and union membership.[96] This data was unavailable in 2009 when Philadelphia's report called for more reliable information. While imperfect, it provides a crucial benchmark for cities and trades to refine.

Two additional sources add further local specificity. Government disparity reports provide insights into construction demographics. Entities operating affirmative action programs are required to demonstrate "a significant statistical disparity between the number of qualified minority contractors willing and able to perform a particular service and the number of such contractors actually engaged by the locality or the locality's prime contractors, an inference of discriminatory exclusion."[97] These reports vary across municipalities and over time, often limiting their scope to government-sponsored work demographics. For instance, they might detail business ownership statistics such as woman-owned and minority-owned businesses hired for government contracts.

Philadelphia is one of the few cities to include the full construction workforce demographics by trade in their reports.[98] Regulators and building industry professionals across the country can promote uniform, detailed reporting in consistent, legible formats to facilitate broader, comparative use of this data.

The US Department of Labor maintains another important data source on apprenticeship program demographics by occupation, trade, and geography. The Registered Apprenticeship Partners Information Management Data System (RAPIDS) database does not distinguish *between* minority groups but does tabulate women and minority participation as two subsets within the total participants in each apprenticeship program. Updating this data to reflect census demographic categories would further enable use of this reference to predict the trajectories of specific trades within a municipal market.

In contemporary construction and building code regulation, developers often push to lower the demand for skilled labor by removing regulatory barriers to Type V construction. Reducing upfront costs is generally seen as the only path toward affordability, although it may sacrifice some well-accepted forms of urban resilience (fire protection, wind resistance) and this book's proposed additional considerations for well-being (durability, adaptive capacity, health). According to popular opinion, there are only two alternatives: affordable construction with lower labor skill and material quality, or robust construction with higher standards at the expense of affordability. However, these alternatives fail to consider the historical role of construction labor expenditures in economic stabilization.

Pitting affordability against material resilience creates a downward spiral. Restricted access to jobs increases pressure on housing affordability, which in turn pressures building officials to lower material standards, requiring less skilled labor and further restricting job opportunities. In Philadelphia, the strength of skilled labor among the population once provided the will and capacity for robust material mandates. Over time, unions constrained access to skilled labor until the city's population could no longer support or afford its brick building codes. This analysis posits an alternative, recognizing the interdependence among jobs, codes, and affordability.

Spatially and socially informed material choices have the power to transform design objectives and policy incentives, rewarding construction trades that champion inclusivity and fostering economic stability within local markets. This holistic form of assessment empowers policymakers and the public to consider the intricate contingencies across various dimensions of welfare and resilience. By evaluating building policies not only in terms of the obvious and upfront costs and risks but also through the potential benefits for urban communities, architects and policymakers can create a more equitable and enduring urban material landscape.

TYPE V TAMPA

Occupancy and Urban Vitality

When the material culture of a community is dislodged, displaced, or demolished, it is easy to forget the more abstract components of the defunct community that made it functional, active, and vital.

CHERYL R. RODRIGUEZ, "RECAPTURING LOST IMAGES: NARRATIVES OF A BLACK BUSINESS ENCLAVE," 2010

IN THE LATE NINETEENTH CENTURY, Henry Brumwick settled his family in Tampa's Central Avenue neighborhood, one of the few areas in the city that welcomed Black residents. This community exemplified diversity in both its residents and its architecture, situated just outside the central city fire limits. Bustling masonry and wood-framed shops and restaurants lined Central Avenue between Cass and Kay Streets. Home-laundry and pressing businesses scattered across twenty-nine acres of adjacent wood cottages on sandy, unpaved streets with clothing hung on lines between shared porches and outdoor yards. The local scrub palmetto trees that characterized the neighborhood prompted locals to call it "The Scrub."[1]

Henry Brumwick opened a successful shoemaking shop, earning enough to ensure the education of his daughters, Iola and Mamie.[2] Their Central Avenue neighborhood was a beacon of opportunity in Tampa. Roughly twenty-eight irregularly shaped blocks were home to Black-owned businesses, cherished institutions, and tightly packed residences.[3] This vibrant community formed the backbone of social interaction for Tampa's Black population in the early twentieth century.

By the turn of the century, despite the constraints of Jim Crow segregation, Iola and Mamie were thriving in Central Avenue's bustling social and

FIGURE 4.1 *Tampa's contemporary residential Type V and Types I–III construction (2017).*

entrepreneurial environment. They may have visited the movie theater near Roosevelt Street or frequented one of the many in-home bakeries. They likely attended St. Peter Claver's Catholic School at the corner of Governor and Scott Streets or the Harlem Academy. Yet they also witnessed their community face numerous challenges.

In 1918, Tampa upgraded its building codes to mandate stricter material fireproofing for specific businesses and occupancies.[4] The wood-framed movie theater on Roosevelt Street no longer met assembly requirements. In-home bakeries and laundry facilities were banned from all-wood structures. Central Avenue gradually transitioned some buildings to brick construction to comply with the new codes. Neighbors pooled funds and labor to rebuild St. Peter Claver's Catholic School with stone masonry.[5]

Iola and Mamie grew up to become community leaders, joining civic groups that advocated for neighborhood improvements, such as removing dilapidated white-owned rental housing and constructing playgrounds and a new high school. Iola spoke of the community's collective efforts and sacrifices to invest in institutional buildings like schools and churches.[6]

Despite lacking the municipal support provided to white neighborhoods, Central Avenue residents shared resources and invested in building infrastructure. They navigated evolving municipal standards and supported many thriving businesses and public institutions. By adapting to new material and occupancy standards, they elevated the value of the community's buildings, and the variety of uses fostered social cohesion. In municipal codes, "occupancy" refers to different types of regulated uses, such as business, assembly, or residential use.

By the 1930s, many wood-frame residential neighborhoods populated Tampa, similarly situated outside the fire limits.[7] While occupancy requirements within building codes grew increasingly stringent throughout the city, plumbing access and zoning protections remained inconsistent and inadequate in some areas, including Central Avenue. When Tampa expanded water supply and sewer infrastructure, it reportedly prioritized dense areas and business centers. Yet the city failed to provide municipal water supply to Central Avenue, one of the most populated residential and commercial areas.

The Central Avenue neighborhood began with flexible and affordable construction and evolved to include multiple occupancy opportunities. It navigated regulatory shifts, championed improvements and investments, and contended with infrastructural and maintenance challenges that were prevalent throughout the city.

Despite its common challenges and uncommon successes, the City of Tampa methodically demolished the Central Avenue neighborhood beginning in the 1950s based on an argument citing building density and fire and health risks. It replaced Central Avenue with a freeway overpass

FIGURE 4.2 *Tilt of the Maroon and Gold parade, originally published in the* Florida Sentinel Bulletin. *(Courtesy of the Tampa Bay History Center Collection)*

and built public housing that was again demolished decades later. The city twice displaced Central Avenue residents and never recovered the area's thriving urban community, its buildings and business occupancies, or their embedded social value. Residents like Iola and Mamie Brumwick lost their family's livelihood and their community's physical, social, and economic investments. The building fabric that once enabled social agency and stood as a physical testament to community perseverance was erased.

The story of the Central Avenue neighborhood is, unfortunately, familiar. Cities across the United States razed Black business centers and hundreds of thousands of homes during federally sponsored "urban renewal" efforts of the mid-twentieth century. However, the regulations controlling the buildings, their material structure, and their occupancy are often overlooked actors in this narrative. In Central Avenue, as in many southern communities, material regulation first provoked the neighborhood's existence, then animated its use and limited its occupancy. In the end, the city weaponized building standards as justification for the neighborhood's demolition.

Looking back at Central Avenue's rise and fall, the link between building materials, occupancy codes, and a community's social and spatial life

FIGURE 4.3 *Children and staff in front of Tampa Urban League, Harlem Branch of the Tampa Public Library (1923). (Courtesy of Tampa-Hillsborough County Public Library System, Burgert Brothers Photographic Collection)*

becomes visible. In each of the previous case studies, America's large northern cities struggled to find and regulate a balanced material environment amid massive population influx throughout the late nineteenth and early twentieth centuries. However, smaller southern urban areas like Tampa were slower to develop and organize. As Tampa's building codes evolved, they shaped its spatial and social dynamics. Over time, like other cities around the country, Tampa used material codes as a mechanism to assert economic control over desirable land, particularly in Black communities.

Each of the previous essays expands the scope of collective risk and opportunities shaped by urban material codes. They show that urban material logic extends beyond the threat of fire to impact health and ecology, durability and economics, and labor opportunities. This essay highlights the role of building codes in relation to occupancy restrictions and sociospatial value. Through occupancy regulations, building material acts as a form of microzoning, informing spatial opportunity and social exchange. In Tampa, the intertwined evolution of the Central Avenue neighborhood and municipal material regulation show that building codes were connected to segregation, impacted community vitality, and assisted urban renewal.

MATERIAL SEGREGATION

> I remember the day when I used to go down on Central Avenue. You couldn't pay me to go down there in a pair of jeans and raggedy shoes. Man, people went home and dressed, because that's the only place people had to go, we thought a lot of it. You had night clubs, you had the theaters, you had the Blue room, you had all the activities, just about. And you would dress to go down there, you wouldn't see people sitting around any kind of way, everybody had pride, self-pride.
>
> BOBBY COLE, TAMPA RESIDENT, "RECAPTURING LOST IMAGES: NARRATIVES OF A BLACK BUSINESS ENCLAVE"

In 1870, developers began subdividing land surrounding Central Avenue, unrestricted by fire limit requirements or zoning.[8] By 1890, many newcomers established businesses along this burgeoning commercial corridor. The neighborhood was loosely bounded by industry and rail lines to the south and east. To the west, Central Avenue became the "pulsing heart" of a rapidly expanding Black community described by the *Tampa Journal* in 1887 as "industrious, thrifty, and progressive."[9]

Racially segregated communities and Type V construction emerged on the fringes of early southern American cities. Neighborhoods like Central Avenue developed during Reconstruction as Type V, wood-frame enclaves at the urban periphery. Historian David R. Goldfield, who writes about Black life in the postbellum South, notes that these communities arose just beyond the "areas controlled by fire codes that prevented erection of flimsy wooden structures."[10] During the Jim Crow era, Black and immigrant populations concentrated in these wood-frame border communities, one of the few affordable or available options. In this way, fire limits and racial covenants conspired to maintain southern cities segregated by material, race, and ethnicity. Tampa still demonstrates this southern American material phenomenon through associated patterns of Type V construction and some demographic concentrations (see plates 14 and 15).[11]

At the turn of the twentieth century, Central Avenue was celebrated for its predominantly owner-occupied homes and numerous community institutions, including churches and mutual aid societies. Historians describe this period of Central Avenue's growth as "heady times, with new and apparently major business concerns announcing themselves regularly."[12] Ms. Watts Sanderson, a local resident, expressed pride in Central

Avenue's thriving businesses during a 1916 interview with *Afro-American Monthly*:

> I think I'll start by saying this. I have listed here twenty-two businesses that were owned and operated by blacks on Central. I've got Saunders Central Blue Room Bar and Grill; 1310–1314 was the address. We had right next door the Palm Dinette. A little bit further down the street we had Rogers Hotel and also the Rogers Dining Room. We had the Cotton Club that was also a bar. We had Johnny Gray's Restaurant that was next to the Lincoln. We had Central Avenue Shoe Shine Parlor. We had Kid Mason and his slogan was "From Ice Cream to Hardware," and I want you to know that fit it. We had a recreation center named after him. Then right around the corner . . .[13]

Sanderson's description paints a vivid picture of the neighborhood's vibrant amenities, including dance halls, pool rooms, churches, barber shops, groceries, drug stores, doctors, law offices, and kindergartens. Social and commercial activity flourished along Central Avenue, spilling into adjacent residential blocks as corner restaurants, bakeries, shops, and home laundry and pressing businesses. The prominence of Black-owned businesses on Central Avenue even attracted the attention of Booker T. Washington, who visited and encouraged further economic self-determination through business ownership.

Business owners on Central Avenue assumed prominent leadership roles in local government and religious and civic organizations, fostering a strong sense of community. They established mutual aid initiatives, such as the Paul Laurence Dunbar Literary Society, which promoted literary discussions, encouraged scholarship, voiced community concerns to local government, and raised funds to add a library to the Harlem Academy neighborhood school.[14]

The Phyllis Wheatley Art Club, a women's group, aimed to "promote interest in Negro art and literature and assist in the uplift of the mental, physical, and moral life of Negro womanhood in Tampa." Many similar groups pursued community goals over time, such as establishing Tampa's first Black kindergarten and advocating for neighborhood improvements. The Afro-American Civic League, for instance, vowed to "have the disreputable white[-owned] houses removed from the Negro section of the city" while advocating for a playground and a new high school.[15]

The neighborhood's social history demonstrates a repeated pattern of achievement and mutual aid. Scholar Susan Greenbaum described this as "business, religious, and civic leaders mobiliz[ing] resources to achieve common goals, including organizing resistance to segregation and discriminatory laws."[16] Resilience and community solidarity continued to inspire and shape the identity of Central Avenue for many decades.

RESISTANCE AND RESTRICTIONS

As early as 1908, white businessmen and civic leaders began visibly resisting Black progress and political gains by forming the White Municipal Party. This political party openly declared its intention to "prevent the future operation of the Negro vote as a balance of power in municipal elections."[17] Consequently, Tampa's primary elections were restricted to White Municipal Party participation, excluding Black candidates and voters from the 1910 elections onward. All mayors elected until 1956 were members of the White Municipal Party. Central Avenue's residents and business owners had no effective government representation throughout this time, yet municipal regulation and investment decisions consistently impacted social and spatial opportunity for their neighborhood.[18]

During this period, Tampa city officials expanded fire limits and tightened building-material codes, occupancy standards, and minimum property standards. The 1918 city ordinances specified new building material requirements for certain businesses and occupancies, prohibiting bakeries and restaurants from operating in wood-frame buildings. Theaters over three stories, assembly buildings, libraries, markets, and churches required noncombustible structures. Large laundry stoves required masonry chimney exhaust, and all laundry businesses, including hand laundries, required a city license and fee.[19] By 1927, the Central Avenue neighborhood was included within the city's fire limits, prohibiting new wood-frame buildings in the area.[20]

While these material code upgrades were typical of a developing city responding to increases in density and public safety concerns, they significantly impacted Black and immigrant communities, who were excluded from political input. These communities relied on private businesses or institutions like those on Central Avenue for economic opportunity, but also for social interaction and recreational space, as segregation laws limited other alternatives. Additionally, limited borrowing opportunities for Black businesses and residents severely hampered their ability to invest in construction upgrades.[21]

An influential 1927 report titled "A Study of Negro Life in Tampa" by Arthur Raper details the living conditions of the Black community in Tampa and highlights the importance of Central Avenue's recreational amenities. The so-called Raper Report describes the recreational needs of Black Tampa residents as "accentuated by the congested conditions of their rent quarters." The small size of homes, unpaved streets, lack of garbage collection, and inadequate bathing facilities underscore the "need for a place away from home where [Black residents] can go."[22]

The report also notes that the City of Tampa invested "tens of thousands of dollars . . . for maintenance of [public] parks." However, these parks were largely inaccessible to the 23,000 Black Tampa residents in 1927, "except in the capacity of servants." There were no playgrounds at Black schools, no public pool or beach available to Black residents, and very few public bathrooms open to Black visitors, even at the city hall.[23]

Inequitable and segregated public infrastructure increased the Black community's reliance on gathering at Central Avenue. The Raper Report describes dance halls and motion picture venues as the primary recreation venues, emphasizing the significance of these businesses in the context of their physical infrastructure and building materials:

> The Central Theatre on Central Avenue is of brick construction and has a capacity of approximately 2,000. The Maceio Theatre is located on Central Avenue, corner Scott Street: brick and frame structure, seating capacity about 500. . . . The Lafayette Dancing Academy located on the corner of Harrison Street and Central Avenue is a two-story brick building: it has a capacity of 500 with an average attendance of 250. . . . [In summary,] commercial recreation and amusement for Negroes in Tampa is limited to that of [one] park, theatres, dance halls, and pool rooms.[24]

After Tampa's 1918 building code revisions, some businesses and recreational structures evolved from Type V frame to Type III masonry, but many businesses also disappeared from the maps at that time.[25] Assembly buildings such as dance halls, theaters, markets, and libraries required significant material investment to comply with new building codes, altering the accessibility and prevalence of these community recreational spaces.

The evolution of material and social space can be traced through historical maps. Tampa's 1915 Sanborn map (fig. 4.4a) shows gathering and community spaces in wood-frame buildings on Central Avenue, identified as poolhalls, saloons, restaurants, bakeries, and motion picture venues. It also shows small businesses occupying portions of wood-frame buildings within the neighborhood, including one at the corner of E. Scott and Lamar labeled "hand washing."

The 1931 map of the same area (fig. 4.4b) reveals that masonry commercial spaces replaced some of Central Avenue's wood-frame commercial buildings. The evolution of the maps reflects not only building material changes but also shifts in building uses, likely influenced by occupancy code changes and the prohibition of alcohol between 1915 and 1931. Motion

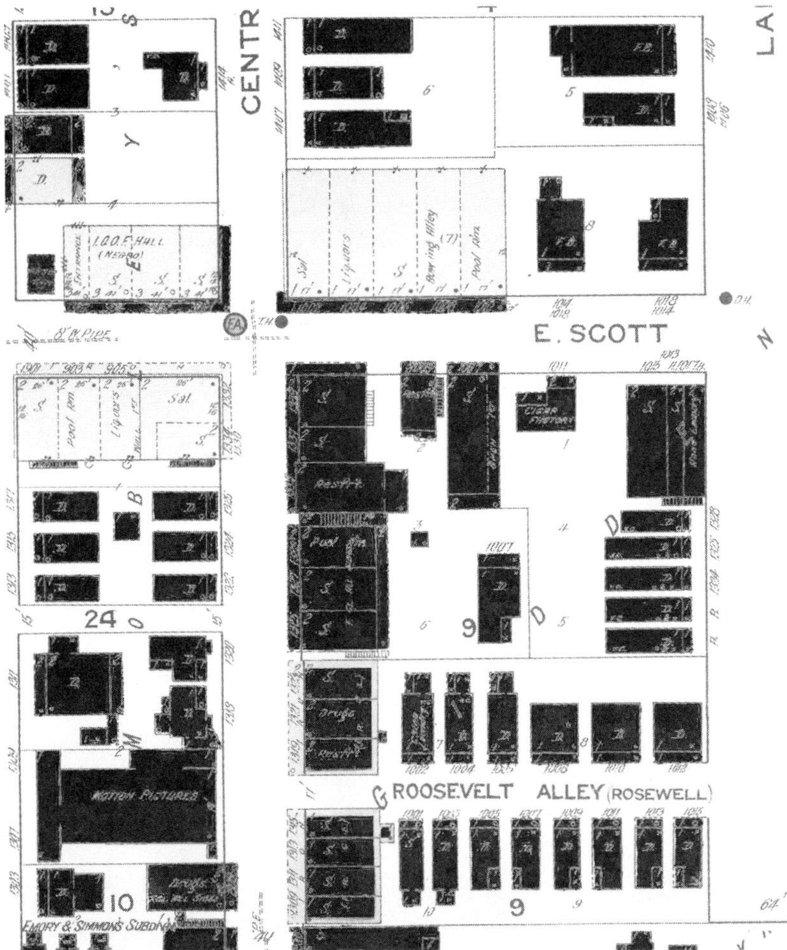

FIGURE 4.4 a & b *Wood-frame buildings are shown in black in the Sanborn maps (a) at Central Avenue and East Scott (1915); and (b) at Central Avenue and East Scott (1931). (Courtesy of Library of Congress, Geography and Map Division, Sanborn Maps Collection)*

picture venues, restaurants, pool rooms, and saloons noted within wood-frame buildings in 1915 had shifted to a generic *S*, for store or vacant office designation by 1931.[26]

Laundry facilities and bakeries also required new levels of robust material protection, likely beyond the reach of many small or residential businesses. For instance, the hand-washing business on the corner of Scott and Lamar in 1915 is labeled as a vacant building by 1931.[27] Regulatory changes and material restrictions impacted the viability of small businesses in the area.

A few blocks farther east, St. Peter Claver's Catholic Church and School also evolved with the city's shifting codes, showcasing a collective material investment in a community institution (fig. 4.5a and b). The church and

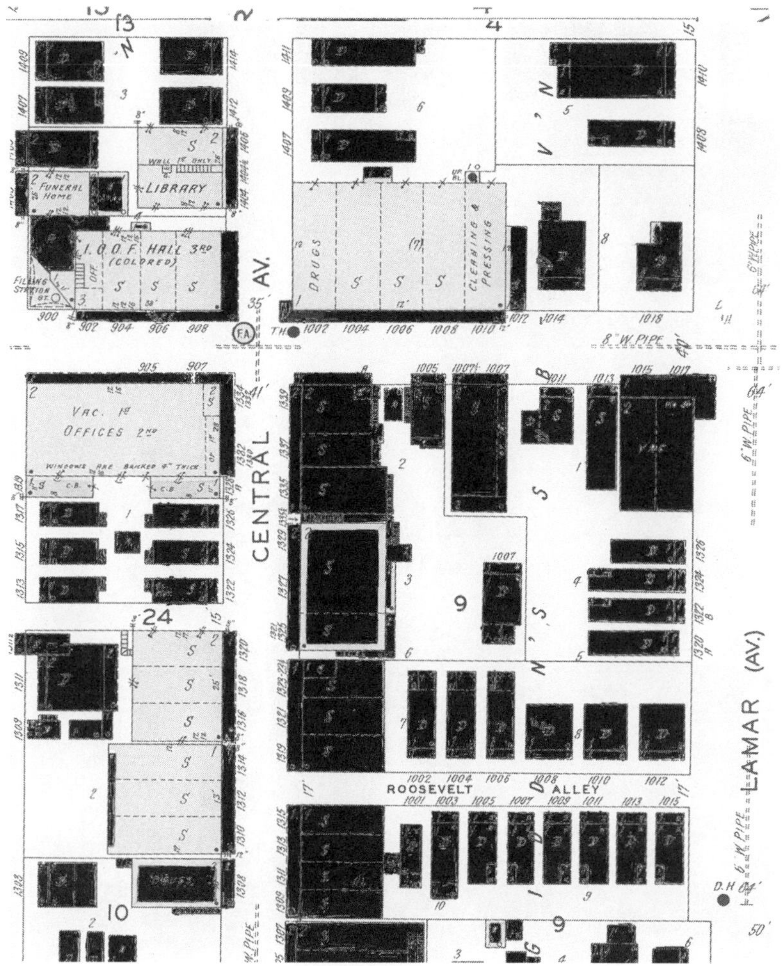

school transitioned from a small wood-frame building in 1915 to a new stone building by 1931 at the corner of Governor and East Scott.[28] This material upgrade likely required sustained effort and collective investment by community parishioners. In fact, St. Peter Claver's Catholic School had been built once before at a different location before settling at Governor and East Scott, where it stands today as one of the neighborhood's few remaining buildings.

The first St. Peter's Catholic School suffered the same fate as one of the prominent early Black schools in the area, Harlem Academy. Both were burned to the ground in racially motivated arson attacks in the late nineteenth century, and the community quickly rebuilt them. Historians Canter Brown and Larry Rivers described this rebuilding: "The

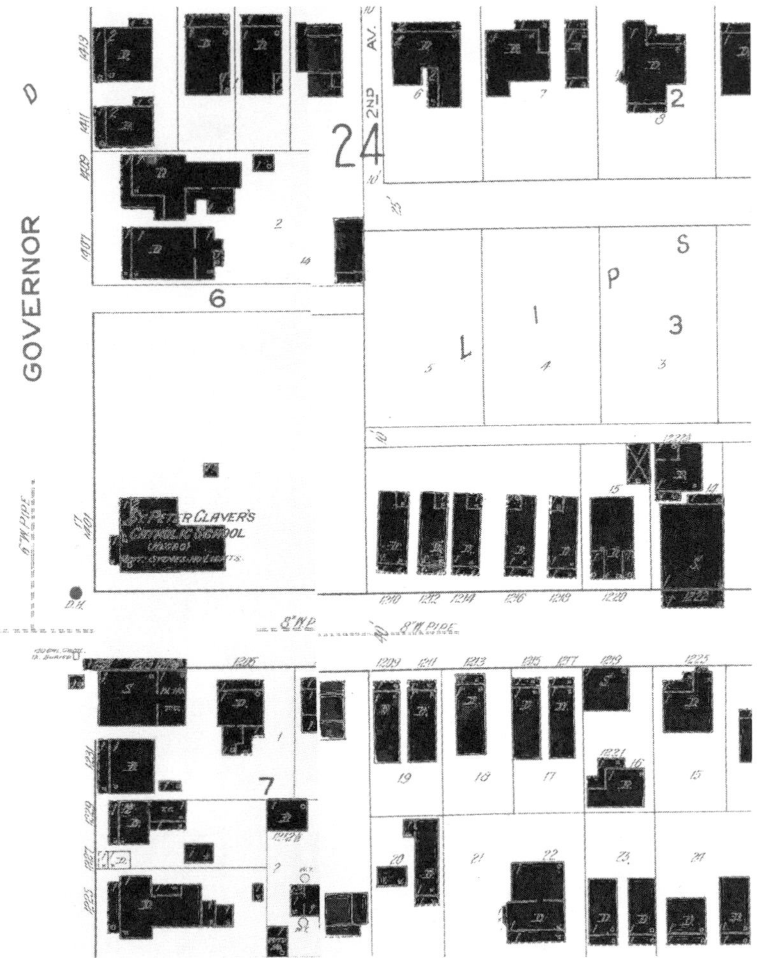

FIGURE 4.5 a & b *Wood-frame buildings are shown in black in the Sanborn maps at (a) Governor Avenue and East Scott (1915); and (b) Governor Avenue and East Scott (1931). (Courtesy of Library of Congress, Geography and Map Division, Sanborn Maps Collection)*

community's determination to rebuild its schools in the face of racist arson spoke volumes about its cohesiveness, sense of purpose, and forward-thinking."[29] The Black Tampa community not only managed to rebuild but did so using stone and brick masonry, increasing the material longevity and protection of critical social assets. Iola Brumwick, the shoemaker's daughter and civic leader, recalled the arson attacks and collective efforts to build educational infrastructure:

> We watched our achievement representing years of hard work and self-denial go up in flames and smoke and our hearts were heavy indeed. . . . The ministers of the Negro churches came to the rescue—they tendered the use of the church buildings, and the offer

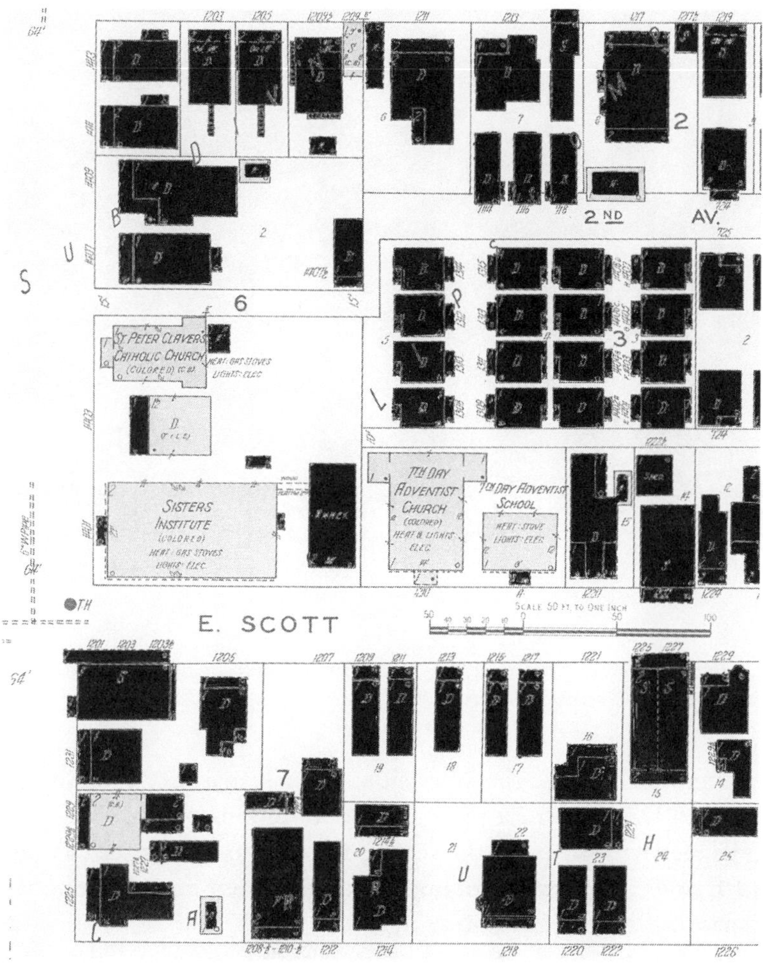

was accepted by the school board. This arrangement continued three years, until funds had been raised and a new building was erected.[30]

MATERIAL, OCCUPANCY, AND URBAN VITALITY

Despite the challenges and setbacks brought by changing material standards, the resilient community of Central Avenue adapted by producing a diverse stock of building materials. This urban fabric facilitated varied uses, enabling both flexibility and affordability across its spectrum.

Figure 4.6 presents a speculative view of Central Avenue in 1915, revealing a rich cross section of spatial, social, and economic opportunities

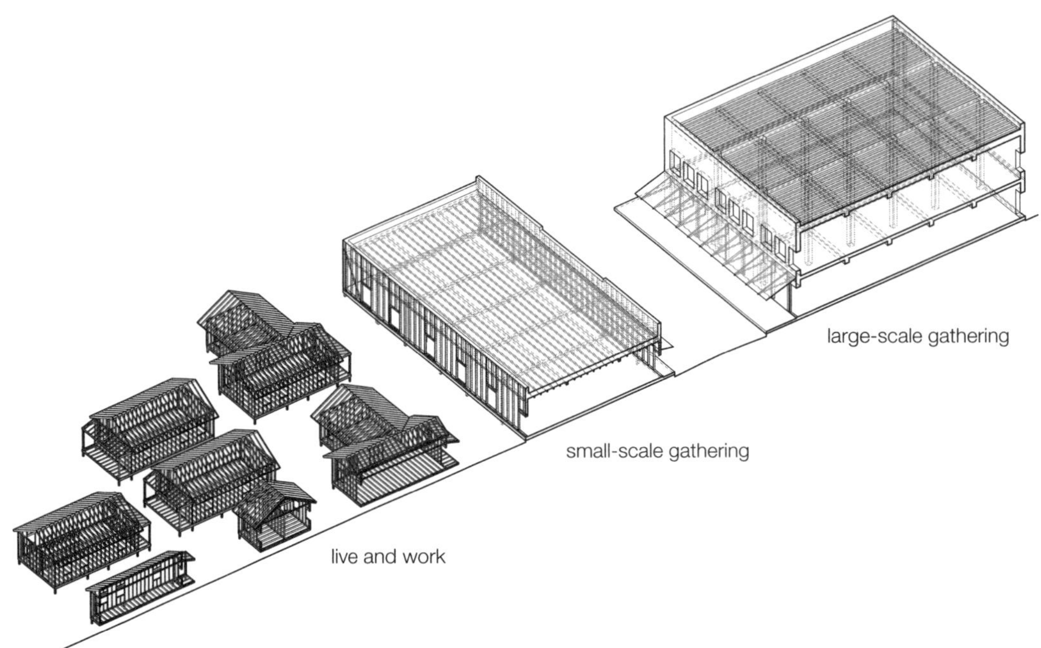

FIGURE 4.6 *Diagrammatic section through Tampa's Central Avenue derived from Sanborn maps and Burgert Brothers Photographic Collection, Tampa-Hillsborough County Public Library System.*

within a single block.[31] On the west side, a brick masonry building at Harrison housed five storefront restaurants and saloons on the first floor, with a large dance hall spanning the second floor. Across the street, a one-story, wood-frame commercial building contained seven more storefronts, providing space for small-scale gatherings.

In 1915, both sides of the street were lined with restaurants. However, by 1918, new codes restricted restaurants to the brick side, while the wood storefronts transitioned to businesses with less stringent requirements, such as drugstores, clothing stores, or barber shops.

The residential cottages displayed subtle variations in size and bedroom counts, from shotgun floor plans to L shapes that allowed small bedrooms to line one side of the house. Many families took in tenants for extra rental income, with the L-shaped design offering flexible layout options. Historical maps indicate that some residences had terra-cotta or masonry chimneys, suggesting the operation of laundry stoves was permitted in these homes.[32]

Material codes in Tampa, and across the United States, intricately shape opportunities and limitations for social gatherings and economic enterprises based on individual property characteristics. Municipal zoning ordinances are often seen as the primary drivers of land use and are subject to much public scrutiny.[33] However, both building and zoning regulations directly influence an urban neighborhood's social, economic, and spatial character. Building material, in particular, acts as a form of microzoning,

FIGURE 4.7 *Looking north on Lula from Long Emory (1951). (Courtesy of Tampa-Hillsborough County Public Library System, Burgert Brothers Photographic Collection)*

exerting fine-grain control over occupancy. Even if a zoning district permits expansive uses, the building material can further restrict or enable occupancies.

The material character of the Central Avenue neighborhood facilitated multiple scales of social interaction and various possible home-business and residential configurations. Semipublic spaces included shared residential yards surrounded by individual porches (fig. 4.7) and community spaces scattered throughout the neighborhood, such as mutual aid societies, churches, and social clubs. Many of these cultural institutions served as substitutes for public institutions that were unavailable due to segregation restrictions and municipal underinvestment. For instance, the Urban League Club at one time functioned as the neighborhood's public library (see fig. 4.3).

The gradient of building materials in the Central Avenue neighborhood, along with their associated allowable occupancies, fostered urban vitality. Jane Jacobs famously attributed urban vitality to building stock of varied ages.[34] In New York, varied building ages will naturally produce multiple phases of building material development and, therefore, diversity of allowable uses.[35] In Jacobs's New York, and in Tampa's Central Avenue, it was arguably the mixture of masonry and frame buildings, not only the buildings' ages, that further extended the business diversity and affordability range in the district.

Central Avenue's neighborhood emerged due to the absence of construction regulations outside city fire limits. This flexibility was preserved through a range of building materials and associated occupancies. Today, these features—versatile scales of commercial and residential space, variable occupancies, and multiple degrees of public interaction—are recognized as essential ingredients for thriving urban vitality. Varied sizes within commercial rental markets encourage the success of small businesses by lowering the threshold for entrepreneurial entry. Similarly, degrees of public interaction throughout a neighborhood can foster cohesive communities. However, the role of occupancy standards in enabling or restricting historical and contemporary urban social and spatial hybrids is often overlooked.

The material character of today's cities continues to invisibly shape social interaction and spatial function across the United States. For example, a three-story Type V building without sprinklers can be a barber shop but not a bakery, restaurant, or art gallery according to the 2021 US IBC.[36] Codes further restrict occupancy based on building size, the properties of walls separating each functional space, and limitations on mixed occupancy such as live-work.[37]

Planners, architects, and community groups must consider these occupancy opportunities and limitations based on construction materials and advocate for codes that encourage spatial hybrids and flexible occupancy. Understanding the implications of occupancy codes can influence material priorities within city plans to ensure varied spatial, social, and programmatic diversity.

PLANNED VULNERABILITY

In 1918, Tampa's ordinances aimed to bolster fire-protection standards, yet these rules are also notable for what they failed to protect. The Central Avenue neighborhood remained beyond the designated fire limits in 1918. The ordinance imposed no restrictions on the density of Type V housing, save for a broad stipulation of 90 percent maximum lot coverage. Water-closet requirements were minimal, largely left to the discretion of building inspectors: "Every tenement house hereafter erected shall be provided with as many water-closets, improved privy sinks, or other similar receptacles as the Building Inspector or the Department of Health may require, but in no case shall there be less than one for every fifteen occupants."[38]

From 1900 to 1925, Tampa's Black population surged by nearly twenty thousand residents. Segregation laws forced Black neighborhoods to become more densely populated than other city areas. Consequently, the Central Avenue neighborhood expanded inward, forming a fractal-like pattern of increasingly fine-grained subdivisions. Among the eight Tampa neighborhoods accessible to Black residents during segregation, Central Avenue was the largest: by 1927 it housed over 8,000 residents at a density of roughly 275 residents per acre.[39] Today, one can find a comparable residential density in a mid- to high-rise building in some of the country's larger metropolitan areas.

Sanborn maps illustrate the increasingly crowded housing development in the Central Avenue neighborhood. By 1935, an area previously divided into two lots north of Scott Street had been subdivided into sixteen small wood-frame residences (see fig. 4.5a and b). At that time, federal lending policies restricted lending to Black Americans, resulting in 86 percent of Black Tampa residents living in rental housing by 1941.[40] This high rental rate meant that housing quality and safety depended heavily on the city's regulations, building inspectors' attention, and landlord upkeep. As previously mentioned, building codes required indoor plumbing only as the "Building Inspector or Department of Health may require." This combination of limited neighborhood options and discretionary plumbing requirements meant that residents often paid more in rent while receiving less in landlord investment and municipal infrastructure.

In 1927, the Committee on Fire Prevention and Engineering Standards of the National Board of Fire Underwriters reported on Tampa's water supply infrastructure and conflagration risks. They made specific recommendations to improve protection and water supply within a "Congested Value District" in the city center. This report highlighted the lack of access to plumbing supply in the Central Avenue residential blocks. The criteria for infrastructural improvement—building density, wood-frame construction, and commercial activity—were all present in Central Avenue (fig. 4.8). However, the report did not mention the business activity or density of the neighborhood, nor did it acknowledge the conflagration risk or propose increases to the water supply. The report did note significant issues affecting Central Avenue: the lack of indoor plumbing, landlord accountability, and city quality control.

The Fire Underwriters stated that "the building laws are comprehensive and generally in accord with the National Board Building Code requirements. Their value, however, is materially reduced by laxity in enforcement, which apparently is due to inadequate inspection force. The fire limits as last amended are of sufficient extent, but the permission of frame construction therein is a weakening feature."[41]

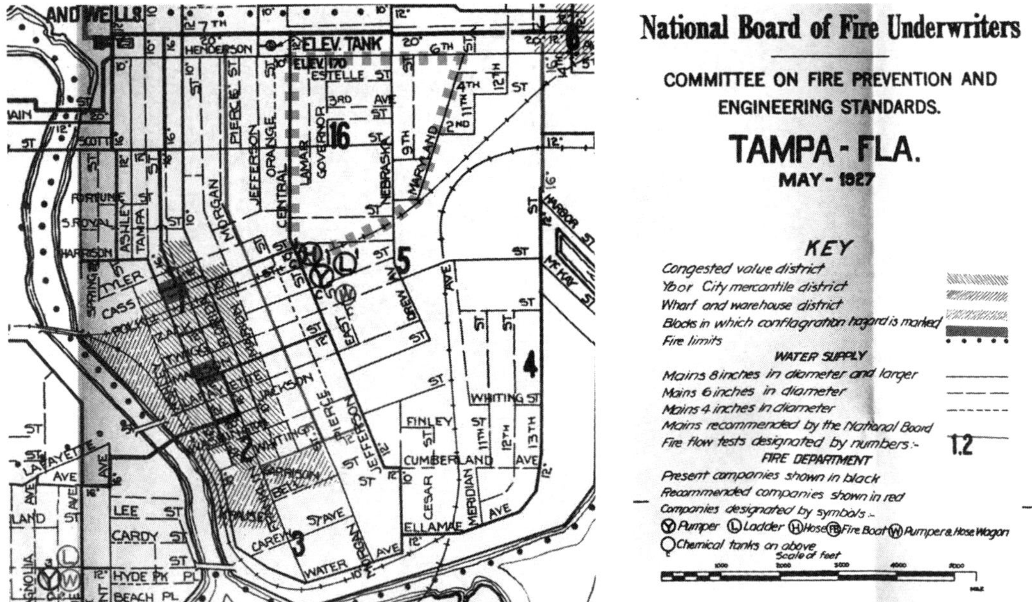

FIGURE 4.8 *National Board of Fire Underwriters Water Supply Map (1927). The dashed gray outline added by the author is the Central Avenue neighborhood. (Courtesy of the Thomas G. Carpenter Library, University of North Florida, George W. Simons Jr. Planning Collection)*

The neglect of Tampa's Black community extended far beyond building material regulations and water infrastructure. Within two years of the fire underwriter's report that failed to highlight any conflagration risks in Central Avenue, two other reports exposed a range of municipal funding disparities in Tampa. The Raper Report, "A Study of Negro Life in Tampa," detailed recreation access imbalances mentioned earlier and public health underinvestment. The two primary hospitals available to Black Tampa residents, the Clara Frye Hospital and Venezuela Small Sanatorium, occupied two-story frame structures accommodating only twenty-eight patients. "These two institutions, [along] with the Tubercular Sanitarium and County Farm, constitute[d] the entire hospital facilities for Negroes in Tampa." The Clara Frye Hospital received an annual city appropriation of $5,800 per year, while "not any of the [city's] $1,250,000 hospital bond money [was] available for a Negro hospital."[42]

A second report, published by Columbia University in 1926, surveyed Tampa schools. Despite Black students comprising half of the city's school population, only 6 percent of the school building budget was directed to Black schools. The report also highlighted spending disparities, with one district spending 60 cents and another 30 cents per Black student for every dollar spent on white students. Teachers at white schools earned an average of $32.50 per week, while those at Black schools earned only $13.79 weekly.[43] The report did not denounce or even draw attention to these imbalances. Instead, it focused on recommending upgrades and improvements for white schools. The first recommendation for Black pupils appeared sixty-five pages into the report, noting: "The only satisfactory buildings for the colored children are the Blanche Street School and the Lomax School. The Harlem Academy building will be used for a considerable period but the prospect is that its use for school purposes will be discontinued through the pressure of commercial growth in this district."[44]

These reports reveal that Tampa's investment in and protection of its Black community were grossly inadequate. Discrepancies in municipal spending on education, health, and recreation forced the community to rely heavily on the social and economic infrastructures housed within Central Avenue's buildings.

The Columbia report on Tampa schools also illuminates the impact of economic development pressures on building assessments and maintenance plans. The report did not include Harlem Academy in its list of satisfactory school buildings, and since its use was expected to be overwhelmed by development pressure, no maintenance or improvements were recommended. In other words, the City of Tampa made its priorities and vision for this district clear as early as 1926, planning minimal maintenance and upgrades within this district to make way for future alternative development.

The Central Avenue neighborhood held immense social and physical value for its residents, combining a stable spatial and social center with flexible gathering, business, and living spaces. The buildings of Central Avenue, its long-time residents, and the associated businesses and institutions were essential to this community. They embodied hard-earned opportunities and mutual support. However, the neighborhood's proximity to the city center made this land desirable for other groups, turning Central Avenue into a sought-after development opportunity.

IMAGES OF RACE, MATERIAL, AND RISK

Rather than investing in the preservation and improvement of Central Avenue's physical and social resources, Tampa City officials by midcentury began advocating for its demolition. Ironically, the city cited building material risks—enabled by its own under regulation, uneven enforcement, and inadequate water infrastructure—as a primary argument for "slum clearance."

In 1945, the city published a comprehensive plan referring to the Central Avenue neighborhood, which it called "The Scrub," as "a cancerous infection ripe for a major operation to transform it into something economically sound and worthwhile from a civic standpoint."[45] The report suggested converting the area into "an inspiring, spirit rousing group of government structures—a Civic Center!" The comprehensive plan even included an architectural drawing of the proposed new campus of government buildings.[46]

Soon after, the federal government passed the Housing Act of 1949, establishing and enabling a policy of "slum clearance" with funding mechanisms to support public housing replacement. In 1951, Tampa released another city planning report describing plans to redevelop the Central Avenue neighborhood because it was "located virtually in the center of the city" and was "an economic burden to all the taxpayers."[47]

That same year, the Tampa Housing Authority released a pamphlet entitled "Good and Bad Housing," arguing for the removal of "The Scrub" (Central Avenue neighborhood), which it described as the "worst slum area."[48] Contrary to the underspending documented in earlier reports, the pamphlet claimed that "slums" demanded an outsized investment in firefighting, health, and police infrastructure.

These actions and reports show that Tampa's priorities lay in redevelopment rather than in supporting and improving the existing community. The city's plans for Central Avenue were driven by economic interests, disregarding the social and cultural significance of the neighborhood to its residents.

The pamphlet's graphics employ visual rhetorical strategies similar to urban renewal reports in cities across the country, using imagery to reinforce the link between race, material, and risk.[49] The cover illustration depicts wood-frame, Type V homes in disrepair, with cracks, loose shutters, failing stairs, and a lone slouched figure with his back to the viewer. By contrast, the pamphlet's back cover features an illustration of well-maintained Type III multifamily housing on a lush lot, featuring a white woman facing forward, walking her bicycle (fig. 4.9).

The pamphlet includes a hypothetical bill addressed to Mr. and Mrs. Tampa Taxpayer. The bill lists costs for fires and fire alarm response times; epidemics of typhus, tuberculosis, and syphilis; and police arrests among the expenses incurred in The Scrub. Headlines such as "You Pay and Pay," "Everybody Pays," and "Costs Could Be Cut" accompany the bill, attributing high costs to the presence of the Central Avenue neighborhood and justifying the push for "slum clearance."

The report also prominently features images of fire and descriptions of the cost of firefighting infrastructure, citing The Scrub's wood-frame structures, lack of plumbing, and small lot sizes.

> Slums are Tampa's most expensive liability. They are Tampa's most expensive responsibility. . . . Slums cost as much or more than the entire amount the City collects in taxes. The net taxation of the City of Tampa is less than $3,000,000. The City appropriates $490,000 for its Fire Department; $645,000 for its Police Department;

> $629,500 for Health and Sanitation; $2,500,000 for Hospitals. These appropriations total $4,264,500. . . . [The slums'] cost is as great or greater than the total city tax bill. . . . They are like kindling tucked under the foundations of the community, an inviting pyromaniac's paradise. Slum homes are of dry unpainted wood. They are close together. They are cluttered inside and outside with rubbish.[50]

Black residents, including barefoot children, are pictured in rear yards with hanging clotheslines and a chair on the roof (fig. 4.10). The image caption states, "Sixteen for One is the price tag on slums." Another caption reads, "A CRIME SPOT in Tampa Scrub." Later in the pamphlet, the focus shifts to proposed solutions with clear racial and material associations. One image shows a white man fumigating a home with a caption reading, "HEALTH BATTLE in slums is costly." Another photo depicts stacked concrete blocks on a construction site, labeled, "NEW, BETTER public housing is started here" (fig. 4.11). Finally, an image featuring a neatly dressed white child outside of stucco, Type III housing is captioned, "HAPPY HOMES, happy children are the products of Tampa's public housing program" (see fig. 4.10).

By the end, the pamphlet reveals its driving motivation, stating, "Under local direction, some most distasteful conditions will be remedied and more room close to the heart of Tampa will be made available to private enterprise. . . . We congratulate Mr. [Mayor] Hixon and members of his committee on their humanitarian interest and foresight."[51]

Each of the report's arguments is either misleading or illustrates the consequences of municipal priorities and regulations. The pamphlet's claim that this neighborhood incurs all city costs related to fire, health, and sanitation is misleading when compared with previously mentioned external reports documenting underfunding in each category. It criticizes unpainted wood, despite wood construction's prevalence throughout the city at the time. It mentions the tight proximity of homes, an issue stemming from the lack of land-use regulation and lax enforcement over time. It also states that the houses are "cluttered inside and outside with rubbish," a problem exacerbated by the limited living options and inadequate sanitation services in a segregated city. This narrative not only obscured the true causes of the neighborhood's struggles but also facilitated the displacement of its residents in the name of progress and, notably, building material updates.

Recent articles by African studies scholar Cheryl Rodriguez acknowledge that the Central Avenue community was struggling and note where the responsibilities lay: "With the passage of time, the old buildings that housed a variety of businesses began to deteriorate. Yet more devastating than those remediable problems associated with dilapidated buildings

FIGURE 4.9 a & b *Tampa Housing Authority's "Good and Bad Housing" (a) front and (b) back cover, published by the Housing Authority of City of Tampa (1951). (Courtesy of the Thomas G. Carpenter Library, University of North Florida, George W. Simons Jr. Planning Collection)*

FIGURE 4.10 a & b *Tampa Housing Authority's publication "Good and Bad Housing" (1951) associated material with race and cost. (Courtesy of the Thomas G. Carpenter Library, University of North Florida, George W. Simons Jr. Planning Collection)*

FIGURE 4.11 *"Good and Bad Housing" (1951) highlights piles of concrete blocks on its construction site for "NEW, BETTER public housing." (Courtesy of the Thomas G. Carpenter Library, University of North Florida, George W. Simons Jr. Planning Collection)*

were the multiple social ills that accompany poverty, racial unrest, and opportunistic political decisions."[52]

MATERIAL DOUBLE STANDARDS

Central Avenue was not the only neighborhood in the city dense with wood-frame buildings. In fact, in 1940, 94 percent of all residential homes in Tampa were wood-frame.[53] Figures 4.12a and b compare the Central Avenue neighborhood, razed in 1954, with a neighborhood left intact just to the northeast in historic Ybor. Ybor was home to a large immigrant population and redlined within the same district as Central Avenue. Both neighborhoods were within the city's expanding fire limits by 1931 and were primarily of wood-frame construction.

Contrary to the arguments in "Good and Bad Housing," building material did not uniquely endanger Central Avenue. In fact, Central Avenue had more brick masonry than Ybor. Discrepancies between the two maps include home size and density, back-alley access to properties, and, most notably, water supply. This discrepancy suggests a double standard in determining material risk and reinforces the municipal responsibility for Central Avenue's vulnerability. Additionally, contemporary city data shows that storm- and wastewater lines were slow to reach wood-frame neighborhoods across Tampa, meaning health and sanitation challenges were shared across many similarly constructed neighborhoods. (See plate 16.)

The "Good and Bad Housing" report also cites property disrepair. However, one property owner, Mr. Grubstein, challenged the city's right to claim eminent domain of his well-maintained property based on "slum clearance" arguments. The courts ruled in favor of the Urban Renewal Agency of the City of Tampa, allowing them to include well-kept homes in the demolition area if necessary to meet the project's overall goals. During the case, the city presented the following arguments for demolition, noting that the project's purpose was economic gain.

> The area is made up of many small subdivisions, poorly planned and platted. . . . This slum area is a breeding place of disease and crime, and constitutes a menace to the health, safety, morals and general welfare of the City of Tampa and requires a disproportionate expenditure of public funds to preserve the public health and prevent crime, fire, accidents, and to supply public services to the residents of the area; that the tax income to the City, County and State is low and out of proportion to the amounts of public funds required to be expended in servicing the area; that nationally, where slums have been eradicated and the area redeveloped for the best purposes, the tax income accruing has been approximately seven times greater than when the area was a slum.[54]

In summary, the City of Tampa assessed the Central Avenue neighborhood according to a material double standard. The differences between Central Avenue and other wood-frame areas rested on exaggerated claims, planned infrastructural underinvestment, and potential economic gain. Residents like Iola and Mamie had long been advocating for stricter oversight of white-owned rental housing and greater investment in educational and civic infrastructure in the neighborhood. Yet evidence of intentional low maintenance due to economic development pressure appears as early as the 1927 school assessment. The "Good and Bad Housing" pamphlet associates material vulnerability with race and financial loss in its visual and written arguments. Finally, the legal case for "slum clearance" of a well-maintained owner-occupied home cites tax income incentives as justification for demolition.

FIGURE 4.12 a & b *Sanborn maps (1931) note building material and water-supply line locations for (a) the Central Avenue neighborhood and (b) Ybor. (Courtesy of Library of Congress, Geography and Map Division, Sanborn Maps Collection. Graphic highlights of Types I–III buildings and water-supply line sizes added by author.)*

In 1954, the first third of Central Avenue's residential blocks, those sometimes referred to as The Scrub, were razed and replaced by five hundred concrete masonry public housing units in the former Central Avenue neighborhood called Central Park Village.[55] By 1958, the president of the Home Builders Association, A. R. Ragsdale, sent a letter to Mayor Nick Nuccio thanking him for "allowing private industry to attempt to solve the acute housing problem before us" and "affording the opportunity to promote private enterprise."[56] Ragsdale enclosed a FHA pamphlet on urban renewal and associated federal funding.

Soon after the demolition of Central Avenue's residential blocks, Tampa claimed eminent domain in the neighborhood for a second time, demolishing the Central Avenue businesses to construct a highway.[57]

The new public housing development did not include opportunities for resident participation in the planning process or business occupancies. In 1958, Mayor Nick Nuccio received another letter, this time from Robert Saunders, president of the Florida NAACP, requesting the opportunity for community participation in the regulation and relocation efforts impacting Black neighborhoods.

> The Negro citizens will be called (along with others) to give up property for the innovation. It then becomes essential that this group should be represented in the initial and at all levels of planning. It is our understanding that a "Workable Plan" has already been submitted to the Federal Housing Authority; yet, we know of no Negro in

> the community who has been consulted concerning the plan, nor has there been any indication that Negro citizens have been or will be consulted on this or any plan for the City of Tampa. . . . We must be informed as to the kinds of codes, zoning regulations, and ordinances, etc., that are being contemplated for the specific areas. . . . We do not want to be planned for, but to be planned with.[58]

In 2007, the housing on this site, this time the Central Park Village, was again demolished to make way for new mixed-use multifamily housing owned by the Tampa Housing Authority. The latest development in the former Central Avenue neighborhood is called the Encore district to honor Central Avenue's vibrant music traditions. Four of Encore's mixed-use buildings were completed and occupied between 2012 and 2018, and further plans for neighborhood development remain to produce an overall dramatic increase in density.[59] Encore is set to include "2,030 residential units, 50,000 square feet of commercial retail space and 59,000 square feet of office space."[60]

However, like many dense, mixed-use, affordable developments in the United States, Encore lacks the flexible live-work spaces that once allowed Central Avenue residents to grow into their businesses. This limitation is not due to Tampa's zoning, which permits commercial, office, and residential uses in this area.[61] Instead, live-work limitations typically stem from either the intensity of housing needs, tax-credit financial constraints, investor unfamiliarity, or the economics of building-code requirements.[62] Contemporary building codes may inadvertently restrict flexible live-work housing by imposing stringent egress, ventilation, and material fire-protection requirements for the nonresidential uses that are often more demanding and costly than the requirements for purely residential units.[63]

As of March 2024, residents lamented that most of the ground-floor retail space sat empty. Unlike other neighborhoods bustling with shops, services, grocery stores, restaurants, and pubs, this new development has seen businesses come and go, leaving behind only a lone pizza parlor and a barber shop.[64] Today's Encore development offers a range of purely commercial spaces but lacks the built-in flexibility and low overhead of live-work units akin to the home businesses that once thrived on Central Avenue. Encore also fails to provide commercial spaces tailored for start-ups, such as incubator retail spaces or market stall–sized rentals. The only planned small-overhead workspace is a co-working area within a future luxury condo building and hotel.[65]

Encore exemplifies contemporary mixed-use construction, aiming to revive some of the neighborhood's past vibrancy. While its affordable housing offers various unit sizes, more intentional planning for adaptive potential and diverse uses within individual units is needed to re-create the entrepreneurial capacity and flexibility of the former building fabric.

MATERIAL CODES, OCCUPANCY, AND THE IMPORTANCE OF SPATIAL HYBRIDS

Reflecting on Tampa's history, one discovers a sociospatial value embedded in its building materials. Central Avenue once showcased the success of diverse material and occupancy options in fostering urban vitality. Initially, stringent material regulations posed challenges to Central Avenue's social and commercial growth. However, the community adapted portions of its building stock to meet evolving codes, ultimately reinforcing the value and potential longevity of community assets such as churches, schools, and recreational facilities built to higher standards.

By the middle of the twentieth century, Central Avenue featured a variety of building materials and corresponding social occupancies, creating flexible uses, spatial hybrids, and a vibrant community. Within a single block, one found brick masonry commercial and assembly spaces, wood-framed residential and commercial spaces, and live-work occupancies. These material and spatial combinations offered business opportunities ranging from a large masonry movie theater to small masonry chimneys for home laundry businesses. Masonry dance halls, churches, and restaurants stood alongside wood-frame barber shops, drugstores, and homes. Smaller commercial spaces along the street sat beneath large assembly spaces above. Homes ranged from pure shotgun configurations to L shapes with potential for extra bedrooms and boarding income. Residential front porches formed small, semipublic courtyards, punctuated by corner restaurants or shops. Commercial front awnings faced the larger public street, concentrating commercial, social, and cultural amenities.

Building occupancy is regulated by building codes at a finer scale than zoning ordinance land-use restrictions. These codes translate each building's material construction into opportunities or limitations in use. Contemporary building codes, housing demands, and economic pressures often result in limited spatial and use configurations in mixed-use housing, impacting both affordability and flexibility for commercial and residential spaces.

Cities investing in developments like Encore can incentivize not only mixed-use but also spatial and occupancy flexibility *within* units themselves, like the variations and flexibility once found in Central Avenue. By promoting design standards that encourage flexibility, cities can create more dynamic and resilient urban environments that better meet the diverse and evolving needs of their residents.

In addition to lessons on the importance of design with respect to occupancy codes and flexible uses, Tampa's history reveals how building material regulation intertwined with racial segregation, spatial opportunity, and political weaponization. Building codes in Tampa physically translated political power into the material landscape. The Central Avenue community first formed outside the boundaries of rigid material fire standards. However, unlike other nearby Type V neighborhoods, it suffered from municipal neglect, poor land-use planning, inadequate infrastructure, and overcrowding. Tampa withheld water access and sewer sanitation and denied this community adequate public health, recreational, and educational infrastructure.

Ultimately, Tampa used building material as a pretext for demolition, citing the neighborhood's density and lack of plumbing, an argument paradoxically based on evidence of its own neglect. When Central Avenue was razed, Tampa destroyed both physical and social infrastructure, displacing community bonds.

Building codes likely played a substantial role in urban renewal across the country, through uneven assessment of material standards and propaganda promoting associations between material risk and race. However, racialized material regulation and assessment are only occasionally documented in urban renewal histories and scholarship.

Carlos Moreno, a resident of Tulsa, Oklahoma, and a member of the city advisory board, recently wrote about Tulsa's immediate redrafting of its fire limits following the Tulsa Massacre. Moreno described the simultaneous change in building policy as a blatant attempt to discourage rebuilding.[66] Scholars at the University of Virginia documented an urban renewal assessment report's omission of many well-maintained, owner-occupied properties when Charlottesville justified the demolition of its Black business district, Vinegar Hill. Charlottesville's fire limits protected its white neighborhoods, and the association between race and material is still visible in the city today. The City of Charlottesville used visual techniques similar to Tampa's "urban renewal" advocacy to associate health and race with building materials in publications promoting the razing of Black neighborhoods.[67]

Portions of Tampa's urban fabric still loosely reflect the associations between its material and demographic patterns. Building materials influence occupancy limitations, meaning any link between race, ethnicity, and material patterns also translates into segregation of spatial opportunities. Tampa and other American cities can enhance equity and urban vitality by further analyzing current building material patterns and designing intentional futures that broaden material and spatial opportunity.

TYPE V SEATTLE

Adaptive Capacity and Lifespan

Seattle's troubles were America's troubles.

MATHEW KLINGLE, *EMERALD CITY: AN ENVIRONMENTAL HISTORY OF SEATTLE*

BETWEEN 1940 AND 1945, DURING the fervor of wartime production, the Boeing Corporation in Seattle swelled from a modest four thousand to over fifty thousand employees. Above its sprawling Plant II factory, covering nearly two million square feet, the company constructed a fifty-three-home suburb. These stick-frame, painted plywood residences, complete with generous yards, were dubbed "Wonderland" by the workers below. "Consum[ing] an estimated one million board feet of Pacific Northwest lumber" and over five hundred tons of steel, these homes echoed the character of local single-family neighborhoods, even featuring greenhouses and a gas station.[1]

Yet Wonderland was no ordinary suburb. It was an elaborate decoy, designed to camouflage Boeing's critical wartime operations. This faux neighborhood, with burlap trees and rubber cars, housed only US Army lookouts armed with antiaircraft weapons. Though many city residents were aware of its existence, they spoke of it discreetly to protect the safety of the workers and vital war equipment below.[2] Wonderland replicated established building typologies. It was also a harbinger of things to come.

The concept of Wonderland emerged after the devastating attack on Pearl Harbor Naval Base, which claimed over 2,400 American lives and destroyed nearly twenty naval vessels and three hundred aircraft.[3] The Army Corps of Engineers quickly recognized other potential vulnerabilities along

0

5 mi

Type V

Types I - III

FIGURE 5.1 *Seattle's contemporary residential Type V and Types I–III construction (2019).*

FIGURE 5.2 *Boeing Plant II, "Wonderland," Seattle (1942). (© Boeing Corporation)*

the West Coast, including naval bases and aircraft production facilities. Fortunately, the City of Seattle had on staff a "Director of Camouflage," William J. Baine Sr., who collaborated with the military to devise a plan.[4]

Baine and the Army Corps of Engineers enlisted John Stewart Detlie, an architect and Hollywood art director, to lead the design effort for Plant II.[5] Detlie distilled the essence of Seattle's urban fabric, deploying archetypes of the city's housing stock with remarkable speed. Wonderland's homes crystallized the housing priorities and types of that era. Wonderland also exposes a long-standing culture of building in the Pacific Northwest, one dominated by industrial priorities to suit immediate needs.

Boeing's wartime surge was not Seattle's first rapid industrial expansion. This city was shaped by cycles of boom-and-bust, and long relied on local wood resources to fuel decades of urgent, short-term construction projects. In this context, Wonderland may not be as extraordinary as it first appears. It was merely one of many provisional construction efforts in the history of the Emerald City.

The urban code narratives from previous essays reveal that while the Midwest, East Coast, and South were landscapes tamed for cultivation with structures built for flexibility and, occasionally, longevity, cities of the West Coast tell different stories. Seattle's narrative shows that the West Coast was not tamed, it was extracted, and the primary form of constructed adaptation was planned obsolescence.

Historian E. M. Gibson contrasts the early East Coast family- and church-centered priorities and the development of the West Coast under capitalist growth priorities. Gibson states, "The difference is important because capitalistic institutions tend to stress materialism and short-term goals in resource use; family [and] church tend to pursue, in addition to materialism, long-term and less tangible goals."[6]

Seattle's history of opportunism underpins both its temporary building mentality and its dependence on the forests of the American Northwest. Each era of boom-and-bust reveals recurring trends of extreme necessity, risk tolerance, and bold innovation.

Decades after Wonderland's demise, Seattle remains a city predominantly built with wood-frame construction. Type V construction accounts for 97 percent of Seattle's single-family housing, 90 percent of its multifamily housing, and 57 percent of commercial buildings.[7] While the prevalence of wood construction is often lauded as an ecologically friendly building practice, Seattle's building history raises questions about rapid building replacement and the true benefit of light-wood-frame construction. The cycles of building and resource-use in Seattle reveal the ecological impacts of boomtown building across America.

As J. B. Jackson once observed, "There has emerged over the last century, particularly over the last half-century, a vast number of structures designed and built to last for a period measured in a few years if not in months."[8] To understand the ecological impact of the Type V city, it is essential to learn from Seattle's boomtown history—from its growth and its multistory "Wonderlands" of ephemeral frames—for in constructing the urban vernacular, America is now following Seattle's lead.

AN INEXHAUSTIBLE WOOD FRAME

Seattle's foundational material infrastructure established it as a major metropolis and perpetuated its boom-and-bust cycles for over a century.[9] The city's initial prosperity was fueled by a resource rush for the "green gold" of Pacific Northwest forests, which supported construction from California to Alaska. Seattle's shorelines provided easy access to timber and deep-water transportation, making it cheap to process and export lumber to rapidly growing cities like San Francisco during the 1850s gold rush. As one of many early Northwest mill towns, Seattle soon distinguished itself by successfully transitioning into a railroad hub.

FIGURE 5.3 *Darius Kinsey, "Horses hauling spruce log." (Courtesy of the Library of Congress Prints and Photographs Division)*

In 1865, Seattle residents believed their lumber resources were inexhaustible. Asa Shinn Mercer, just twenty-five and already the first president of the Territorial University of Washington, wrote a pamphlet to encourage more westward emigration from the East Coast. The book was verbosely titled *Washington Territory: The Great North-West: Her material resources and claims to emigration: A plain statement of things as they exist.*[10] Within it, Mercer boasted of the annual manufacture of "a hundred and thirty million feet of lumber, twenty-two and a half million laths, a half million shingles, a hundred thousand feet of piles, and about two thousand spars, as well as a large number of ship knees."[11] He claimed that lumber production would only slow "when the mountains and the valleys surrounding the Sound are destroyed by some great calamity of nature."[12]

Unrestrained capital growth accompanied Seattle's resource abundance. People moved west for work but lacked the construction expertise or community support typical of the early East Coast settlements. Early Seattle was built almost entirely with wood-frame construction; buildings were very often erected hastily and without concern for craftsmanship.[13] New arrivals "urgently needed shelter [and] were slow to believe there was only one way to build; nor were they convinced that a simpler way was dangerously flimsy. . . . A speed-minded and economy-minded people were willing to be satisfied with 'lower' standards."[14] Historian Earl Pomeroy describes early Seattle structures as follows:

> Much of the early Western city seemed temporary, expendable—composed of jerry-built houses that could not have lasted long even without the fires that from time to time swept over it. Where the climate permitted, and also where it did not, builders often used burlap and paper for partitions and substituted them for wooden siding. A decision to use masonry tended to represent a judgment that the city would last as much longer as the difference in time between laying brick and stretching cloth, as well as a judgment that the rates of return on trade had fallen to the point where a man might not easily recover costs between fires.[15]

Fires in nineteenth-century Seattle were common, often caused by oil lamps or lumber-mill fuel. Several factors exacerbated the danger of urban fires beyond the usual risks posed by the predominance of wood buildings. First, northwestern softwood, especially if not fully dried, is more resin-rich and flammable than denser midwestern hardwoods. In the Northwest, Douglas fir was used for framing, while most roofs were clad in split cedar shingles.[16] Second, early settlers banded together in the face of conflicts with Indigenous Americans. They relied on dense construction in the city center, further intensifying the danger of rapidly spreading fires.[17] Finally, muddy streets and sidewalks were covered with wooden boards that acted as a fuse, spreading fire from building to building. It was not only Seattle's buildings that posed a fire risk but the entire urban infrastructure.

Despite these hazards, Seattle continued to grow, adapting as unforeseen challenges arose. Seattle's first settlement boom also brought social issues, particularly a significant gender ratio imbalance. Most of the work-hungry population moving west consisted of young men. By 1864, Seattle's population was so overwhelmingly male that Asa Mercer—the same young university president, now acting on behalf of the municipality—undertook two famous expeditions east to "import" young women.

Flora Engle, one of the young women who traveled to Seattle with Mercer, recounted: "His plan was to interest the government in his undertaking in view of the fact that he would endeavor to import, if the word may be so used, to the Northwest a goodly number of the numerous widows and orphans of the soldiers of the Civil War, for the express purpose of furnishing wives to the many unmarried men of that region."[18]

Mercer's voyages brought two successive groups, comprised mostly of women who went on to make significant contributions to Seattle's development. The stories of the "Mercer girls" and the cycles of fire and frequent reconstruction demonstrate the tenacity of a growing settlement.[19] They also reveal a picture of a transient population occupying a point of arrival and, perhaps, tolerating the conditions of temporary habitation rather than envisioning a permanent metropolis.

RESISTANCE VERSUS SUPPRESSION

As Seattle's population surged in the last two decades of the nineteenth century, wood construction was slowly interspersed with masonry. Local architects and historians Jeffrey Karl Oschner and Dennis Alan Andersen described these years of growth: "Seattle grew outward as well as upward, and the areas which emerged as Seattle's new residential neighborhoods in the early 1890s began to take the built form that they would have throughout the twentieth century. In many ways, the 1880s and 1890s became the defining decades for the character of urban Seattle."[20]

As late as 1884, more than a decade after the Great Chicago Fire and forty years beyond Philadelphia's brick mandate, only a few prominent buildings in downtown Seattle were built of brick outer walls, and all maintained wood interiors.[21] Most institutional buildings were still constructed with wood frames, often including decorative wood carving at the facade to mimic masonry detailing.[22] In some instances, buildings designed for brick construction were forced to change plans due to material shortages. The *Seattle Post-Intelligencer* reported on a Methodist church and the commercial Squire Building on South Second Street, both of which underwent redesigns during construction due to lack of available brick.[23]

The late 1880s and 1890s marked a period of profound transformation in Seattle's architectural landscape, driven by two nearly simultaneous events. In June 1889, a large, devastating fire razed much of downtown Seattle. Just months later, in September, several railroad lines consolidated, designating Seattle as their western terminus.[24] With clear signs of growth potential and a chance to rebuild, Seattle found itself in a position similar to Chicago two decades earlier. However, Seattle had the advantage of more established national building codes to guide its decision-making and reconstruction.

In the wake of the 1889 fire, Seattle revised its building codes, publishing the new ordinances in the *Seattle Post-Intelligencer* in July 1889. These revisions appeared alongside articles highlighting increasing capacity for brick construction. One article noted: "There has been a local impetus,

FIGURE 5.4 *"The view of Elliott Bay from First Hill in 1885." (Courtesy of Museum of History and Industry, Seattle, Robert Roblee Collection of William N. Bell Family Materials, 2008.54.16)*

since the fire, in the local brick market; and the present indications are that it may e'er long equal the demand for lumber."[25] Despite this, Seattle's revised codes permitted more wood usage than other contemporary American cities at the time.

Unlike most other growing cities that adopted stringent fireproof construction standards, Seattle's postfire ordinance took a different approach. It mandated masonry exterior walls within the fire limits but permitted the use of lumber for floors and load-bearing interior partitions.[26] By contrast, Chicago's 1872 ordinance, enacted after its great fire, required masonry walls and interior load-bearing partitions within the fire limits.[27]

Seattle's limited material resources hindered its ability to adopt fireproof construction. Despite efforts to boost local brick production, brick remained costly and scarce until after 1900, and materials like steel, cast iron, and terra-cotta were even harder to procure. Further complicating matters, rapid rebuilding was crucial to cement Seattle's status as the Northwest's leading metropolis.[28] Imposing stringent reconstruction standards that called for scarce, expensive materials risked jeopardizing the city's economic future. Thus, Seattle maintained lower standards within fire limits, accepting continued conflagration risks to facilitate capacity for rapid growth.

In addition to its relative material leniency, Seattle's 1889 ordinance also did not differentiate buildings by degrees of fireproofing or building height and failed to protect stairs or elevator shafts.[29] The 1889 Seattle fire commissioners criticized the rebuilding effort as "hastily constructed with no thought of being fire-proof or even slow-burning construction."[30]

Reflecting on Seattle's reconstruction, Daniel Turbeville's 1985 dissertation on urban geography states: "Upon reflection it is presumptuous to think that a city surrounded by the greatest forests on the continent, populated by people with two centuries of woodworking experience, and whose major industry was the cutting, processing, and shipment of timber, would turn overnight to unfamiliar, expensive, and unavailable building materials, no matter how great a tragedy might have suggested such a change."[31]

Seattle shifted its focus from material fire resistance to a robust fire-suppression infrastructure. By widening streets, regrading the business district's topography, procuring additional steam engines, and establishing neighborhood firehouses, the city compensated for its lack of resistant materials.[32]

By 1920, Seattle building codes had undergone several revisions, largely aligning with those of other American cities to meet insurance standards. However, one might argue that these changes came too late. The permissive 1889 codes had already facilitated postfire construction, and it was not until 1920 that housing districts outside of the fire limits were included in building material regulation of any kind.

Seattle's willingness to balance material risk-mitigation with growth priorities continues to shape its approach to building infrastructure today. Seattle's contemporary codes enhance affordability by reducing fire-resistance standards while carefully tuning firefighting capacity to suit multifamily zoning districts.

In the 1980s, nearly a century after the 1889 codes were drafted, Seattle revised its city codes again, stretching regional model code regulations by increasing the allowable height and density for multistory wood-frame construction. The city began experimenting with typologies that combined taller multistory Type V over Type I construction, initially only in areas equipped with ladder and engine firehouses. Seattle dubbed its new form of hybrid construction "five-over-one" and gradually expanded its use throughout the city (plate 18). Forty years later, five-over-one regulation would spread to national model codes and cities across the country.

POISED FOR CHANGE

The preference for rebuilding rather than constructing buildings for longevity emerged from the earliest days of Seattle settlement. Arthur Denny, a well-known Seattle pioneer and namesake for the Denny Triangle, or Denny Regrade neighborhood, described the moment that he and other early pioneers "vacated [their] log cabins as speedily as possible" to build frame homes as soon as mills began cutting lumber.[33] As the city developed, a combination of unskilled labor, frequent fires, and plentiful resources led to the acceptance of a "build-burn-rebuild" cycle of construction.[34] This approach prioritized immediate needs and economic growth without regard for long-term durability and fire resistance. Industry-driven rapid building and ready access to lumber produced a short-term metropolis on the West Coast.

In "The Westward Moving House," J. B. Jackson describes the shift in building priorities, starting with homesteads centered around family, church, and community in early New England settlements. His protagonist, Nehemiah, lived in an eighteenth-century home, which was

> a frame of oak which he laboriously constructed with the simplest of tools . . . a heavy and intricate piece of carpentry unlike anything we see in contemporary construction. . . . Such frames not only carried the whole weight of the building but were also mortised and tenoned together so they withstood any horizontal thrust of the elements. . . . Thus Nehemiah's house was built to last, built to be inflexible, built to carry a load, and not built for easy alteration or enlargement. Like his theology, perhaps.[35]

By contrast, Nehemiah's son, Pliny, moved to Illinois and built a balloon-frame house designed for adaptation.

> The most significant of all of Pliny's creations was his house . . . and it should be designed so that if the need arose it could easily be sold. . . . After reading several useful handbooks on building, Pliny and Matilda decided that their home should be a place which could be added to in the future as the family grew and as they put aside more money; they planned for rooms which could be used as bedrooms now and later as storerooms, they planned for sliding doors which could divide a room in two. A house with a flexible plan, a house designed so sensibly that it could be used by one family and then sold to another—a house, in short, that adjusted itself willingly to that outward thrust which Nehemiah's house had resisted so stoutly—was in itself a totally new concept.[36]

By the mid-nineteenth century, American construction was densifying and moving west, placing increasing emphasis on adaptability. In rapidly swelling Manhattan, flexibility manifested in the varied use of interior spaces. As immigrant populations surged in New York, their economic capacities and needs evolved. Brick tenements, despite facing health and

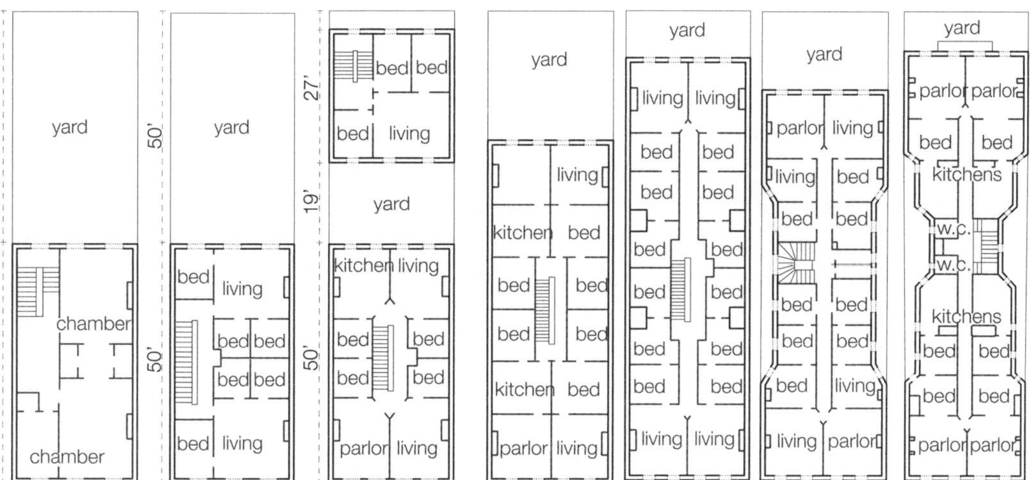

FIGURE 5.5 *From Jacob Riis,* The Battle with the Slum *(1902). Each plan demonstrates the flexibility of occupancy patterns in each stage of tenement design as they shifted to comply with reform laws introducing greater access to light and air shafts. (Redrawn by the author)*

siting challenges, offered a degree of spatial flexibility captured in Jacob Riis's famous documentation of tenement life. Riis's plans and room labels (abbreviated and enlarged for legibility in figure 5.5) blur the lines between units, reflecting mutable boundaries within the narrow confines of a tenement building.[37] This adaptability suited the diverse and changing needs of the city's burgeoning population.

The adaptability of New York City tenements was a key factor in their enduring utility. Partitions bisecting the cross-sectional width of these buildings were typically non-structural, meaning both the layout and the material logic allowed for changes over time. A single floor of a tenement building was often divided into four quadrants, used as workspaces, living spaces, or further subdivided to house multiple families. Early tenements became the testing ground for the limits of healthy living in New York, as previously discussed. Despite the challenges of overcrowding, these adaptable structures remained a staple of the city, evolving with their occupants and ensuring their continued relevance in the urban landscape.

As settlers moved west to the Rocky Mountains and beyond, they utilized an increasingly adaptable approach to wood-frame construction, through methods that were well suited to the stages of westward settlement. Incremental construction and spatial flexibility were essential to meet the demands of a rapidly changing environment.

Historian John Stillgoe, in his description of nineteenth-century American farmhouses, highlights the continuous alteration of homes over time: "Frequently . . . husbandmen added to [the houses] and modified them again and again as families grew, needs changed, and old timbers gave way. The typical American farmhouse is not always one structure, but is sometimes composed of several substructures behind a stylish façade."[38] This ongoing modification addressed the occupants' need to adapt to new circumstances and resources.

Solon Robinson designed house plans within his nineteenth-century pattern book as balloon frames, meant to be modified as families settled and grew. Robinson's widely published plans were accompanied by a narrative construction sequence:

> Now, suppose a family just arrived at the "new location." . . . First, they need some immediate shelter. Two hands in two days, can put up the room 13 by 13, marked wash room (a) in the plan, with a lean-to roof, the sides covered with wide 3/4 inch boards, feather-edged together, with a rough floor, which with a rough shed to cook under, will serve for bed room and parlor while the house is building. Next add the room marked kitchen (b), a good sized farmer's kitchen, 16 by 24. Board up the sides the same way and finish off inside complete.[39]

Robinson's description of the home's growth continues until it includes a pantry, storeroom, and bedrooms. The family builds the home in stages as they accumulate resources. According to Robinson, they can accomplish this feat without outside help. His designs offer a picture of flexibility and self-reliance upon arrival on the western farm. A phased, time-based approach to habitation ensured the possibility of adaptation while maintaining the self-sufficiency that long characterized American Type V construction.

In early Seattle, construction methods reflected the spirit of westward improvisation, though not adaptability, while residential needs mirrored the transient nature of East Coast arrival spaces. With a high percentage of the urban population consisting of single men seeking work in the lumberyards, Seattle's early housing development was characterized by short-term boarding needs. Most of the men were East Coast transplants. Referring to its transplanted population, Pomeroy refers to early Seattle as "the most Eastern part of America" next to the East Coast itself.[40]

Seattle's early residential buildings reflected the city's lopsided demographics. The 1888 Seattle Sanborn map, drawn just months before the fire, shows a district filled with wood-frame multifamily housing labeled "furnished rooms" or "boarding" (fig. 5.7). Pomeroy describes these early temporary quarters of the Far West:

> Most of the Western states are still predominantly male today. . . . When they married, the early city dwellers . . . still lived more than

> other Americans in transient style, many of them in rented quarters, hotels and apartments, rather than in their own houses. The phenomenon of hotel-living in the early Far West was marked enough to inspire frequent attempts to explain it. Some traced it simply to the costs of rent, servants, and fuel. . . . Whether as cause or as effect, the low incidence of the traditional family household in Western cities made it appear that life there was unstable, poised for change.[41]

Seattle's boarding houses and hotels were tightly packed wood-frame structures, separated by only five- to six-foot side yards and sixteen-foot alleys. Much of this early urban fabric was destroyed in the Great Seattle Fire. During the rebuilding, fire officials criticized the postfire ordinance for continuing to allow interior wood partitions. But the ordinance *did* include a mitigating requirement that partitions must connect from the foundation all the way through the roof, similar to the building's outer walls or party walls.[42] As a result, Seattle's postfire buildings typically featured structural, permanent interior partitions extending vertically through the entire building. This requirement aimed to enhance fire safety, yet it had unintended consequences.

Inflexible interior partitions were a significant deviation from the buildings in Chicago or New York, where nonstructural interiors could be altered from floor to floor, allowing for layout adjustments within a building, over time.[43] In effect, Seattle's postfire material leniency not only compromised fire safety; it also eliminated the spatial flexibility that had become a hallmark of western American settlement. This tradeoff likely escaped notice by a population of single men needing only short-term furnished boarding.

America's early construction practices showcased the importance of adaptability, whether accommodating newly arrived immigrant populations or farmers moving west. As American cities aged over the subsequent century, a building's adaptive capacity often determined whether it matured along with the city or faced demolition and replacement.

A recent study by the Athena Sustainable Materials Institute found that functional obsolescence—meaning a building's lack of suitability for new uses—was as frequent a reason for demolition as physical degradation.[44] This highlights a crucial point: building to last means building to adapt, and the longevity and energy implications of spatial versatility are significant.

Seattle's legacy of provisional building practices, while rooted in the history of America's Far West, failed to embrace the traditions of flexibility and adaptation. Moreover, its emphasis on immediate gains and acceptance of potential limited lifespans have now set a precedent for broader national construction trends. The proliferation of urban construction driven by shortsighted objectives poses an environmental threat. It

FRONT VIEW OF COTTAGE.—FIG. 11.

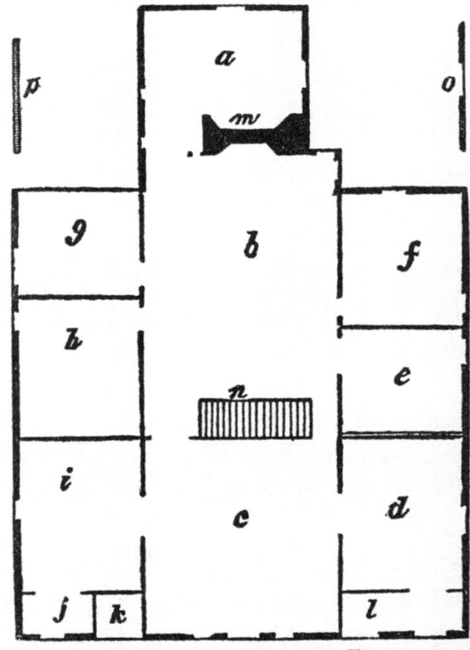

GROUND PLAN OF COTTAGE.—FIG. 12.

Description.—*a,* Wash-room, 13x13; *b,* kitchen, 16x24; *c,* parlor, 16x16; *d, f, h, i,* bed-rooms, 10x12; *e,* store-room, 8x10; *g,* pantry, 8x10 *j, l,* clothes press; *k,* entry; *m,* fire-place; *n,* stairway; *o,* wood-house; *p,* garden gate; the pump should be in the wash room.

FIGURE 5.6 *Plan of a Western Prairie Cottage by Solon Robinson, in* Pioneer and Agriculturist: Selected Writings 1803–1880.

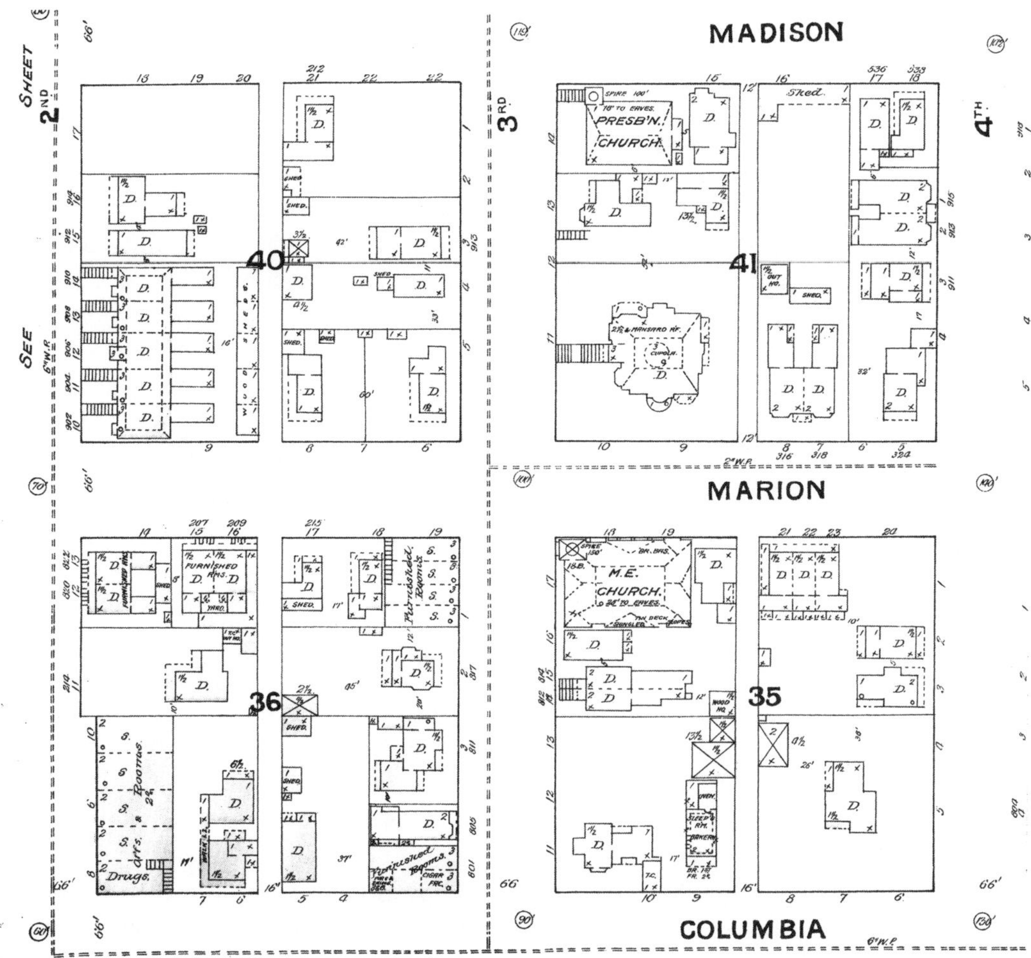

FIGURE 5.7 *Sanborn fire insurance map from Seattle, King County, Washington (1888). (Courtesy of Library of Congress, Geography and Map Division, Sanborn Maps Collection)*

threatens to undermine contemporary goals for low-carbon and sustainable urban infrastructures. It challenges cities as they continue to evolve. It demands a balance of immediate needs with long-term building priorities and remains a critical issue for designers and policymakers.

THE ENVIRONMENTAL COST OF IMPERMANENCE

The 1960s ushered in intense social and environmental movements across the United States. By the 1970s, the country was also grappling with a national energy crisis, which influenced building standards and legislation aimed at energy conservation.[45] By 1974, Seattle's building codes began including insulation requirements to conserve energy.[46] Recent contemporary legislation, such as the Inflation Reduction Act of 2022, continues this trend, focusing environmental action within the building industry on reducing energy use.[47]

However, in the intervening years, ecologically sensitive design goals expanded to include strategies such as material efficiency, occupant health, carbon and energy costs during construction and operation, water efficiency, walkable sites, building lifespans, and much more. These environmentally sensitive design approaches are described in broad terms like "sustainable," "green," or, more recently, "resilient" design. Yet each movement has consistently struggled to move beyond a less-harm approach. Importantly, these building strategies focus on minimizing the harm of an expansion economy rather than questioning the growth itself.[48] By focusing on development, not adaptation, on accumulation, not longevity, this growth-insistent approach sharply contrasts with the arguments for safety and welfare underpinning regulatory logic a century earlier.

However, some notable exceptions in the late twentieth century recognized the importance of adaptable, long-lifespan buildings as a strategy preferable to even the most efficient new construction. In 1994, Stewart Brand published *How Buildings Learn*, claiming that "age plus adaptivity is what makes a building come to be loved. The building learns from its occupants and they learn from it."[49] At the same time, a transcontinental group of architects and city planners identified adaptive capacity in buildings as a crucial feature of the environmental movement. They called this approach the Open Building movement. Open Building groups in the Netherlands, Japan, and the United States in the 1990s prioritized long structural spans and concentrated mechanical, electrical, and plumbing services to enable flexible interior layouts and exterior facades, designed to anticipate change over time.[50]

The Open Building movement is enjoying renewed interest among architects in the Netherlands and gaining attention in the United Kingdom.[51] Two projects embracing Open Building principles of adaptation and self-direction by occupants recently won high-level world architecture prizes. Superlofts Houthavens, by Marc Koehler Architects, was awarded the director's special prize at the World Architecture Festival. This two-story, loft-like system allows occupants to choose from among façade modules and build custom units within a two-story shell.

The 2017 Mies van der Rohe prize was awarded to a restoration of deFlat, one of the Netherlands' largest 1960s housing blocks, allowing users to customize the level of refurbishment of individual homes, improving affordability and choice.[52] In the United Kingdom, a similar scheme, called a "naked house," provides buyers with only the basic shell of a house

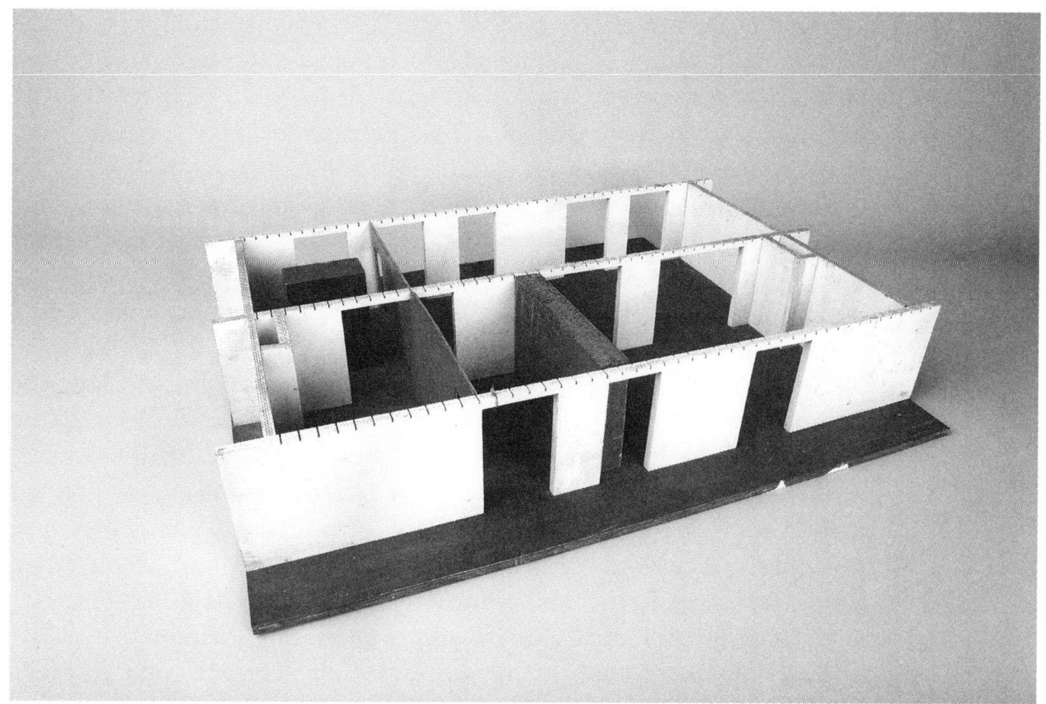

FIGURE 5.8 *Model of fixed support walls with flexible interior partitions developed by SAR Architects, the collaborative research group invested in the Open Building concept in the Netherlands (1969–1972). (Courtesy of Nieuwe Instituut Museum for Architecture, Design and Digital Culture)*

for 20–40 percent below the typical market value, along with DIY training, to promote lower-barrier entry into home ownership.[53]

When the structural shell is considered a vehicle for future flexibility, material strategies prioritize longer open spans within durable outer walls and nonstructural interior partitions. Among the current categories within building codes, Types III and IV, sometimes called ordinary and heavy-timber construction, may lend themselves to this form of building at certain scales and densities.

However, much of the American discourse on environmentally sensitive architecture overlooks planning for future adaptation, instead focusing on operational energy innovations and first-cost "score-cards" through LEED and other elective codes. These elective codes primarily focus on energy-related accounting and mitigation of negative impacts without tempering expansion and growth or generating co-benefits.

In his history of obsolescence in architecture, Daniel Abramson describes the energy-reduction version of environmental protection as a support mechanism for economic growth. He states: "Sustainability is promoted as an economic growth machine to support capitalist accumulation.

Ecobranding proves effective marketing. . . . Technology and administration are architectural sustainability's foci, not politics, transferring onto nature and away from the social. Not coincidentally, the neoliberal deregulation of capital flows and accumulation accompanies sustainability's hyperregulation of environments both built and natural."[54]

Abramson's observations align with the contemporary marketing of Type V construction. As lumber associations and developers advocate for wood-friendly code changes in the name of low-carbon construction, considerations of social implications, adaptive capacity, local material species, and longevity are conspicuously absent.

Current measures of carbon impact and building energy footprints may fall short in projecting building lifespans due to logistical challenges. It is difficult to establish definitive measurements or pinpoint specific attributes that determine a building's longevity. The lack of data on the reasons for building demolition further limits our ability to predict building lifespans. Nonetheless, American construction trends toward planned obsolescence with little discourse, analysis, or incentive focused on building longevity. Meanwhile, international climate efforts increasingly emphasize building material repurposing and embodied carbon.[55] Understanding correlations between building lifespans and building materials is essential to shift American construction sustainability objectives toward social dynamics, resource intelligence, and longevity goals.

It's important to first understand which lifespan data can be reliably measured and which is subject to speculation. The lifespan of building assemblies—the pieces and parts that make up a building—can be projected. Manufacturer warranties and home-inspection literature point to frequent maintenance needs for outer barriers like paints and sealants. The Type V city, its durability, and the economic implications of short material lifespans were described previously, in Chicago's narrative. Diligent maintenance, including the replacement of building seals and paints, can extend the life of a more vulnerable material assembly. Building age and demolition data can also be relied upon to study building lifespan, but the reasons for short lifespans and demolition often remain speculative. As previously noted, while physical degradation might be assumed as a primary cause for building demolition, functional obsolescence or lack of adaptive capacity can prematurely shorten the life of an otherwise sound building.[56]

The previously mentioned Athena study on building demolition was sponsored by a public-private partnership between the Canadian Forest Service and the Canadian lumber industry.[57] The authors conducted a letter-based survey, querying individuals in Minnesota on the reason for demolition permits. Overall, functional and structural obsolescence were equally cited as reasons for building demolition, leading the authors to argue that the adaptability of wood construction is an important advantage.

However, more wood buildings in the study were demolished due to lack of maintenance compared to other construction types.[58] These findings highlight the importance of adaptability *and* maintenance and durability in contemporary construction. The study also outlines a useful methodology for further demolition analysis across cities, which could provide valuable insights for design prioritizing embodied impacts.

Building age and demolition permits can provide an initial snapshot of construction-type longevity estimates. This data must be treated as an estimate, since many factors impact building age, including changing material trends over time and wood construction bans implemented in the early twentieth century in many cities. Since Seattle resisted most material limitations on residential construction throughout its history, its residential building ages offer a particularly reliable picture of longevity and replacement rates in an American city. Following an initial longevity estimate, a closer examination of the reasons for shorter lifespan construction related both to disrepair and to lack of adaptability can be conducted.

Average building ages across this book's five case study cities—Chicago, New York, Philadelphia, Tampa, and Seattle—reveal several important trends in urban material behavior. First, all city buildings tend to last a long time: on average they stand for sixty-three years, far exceeding the thirty-year mortgage and 27.5-year depreciation rate driving contemporary construction as well as the forty-year national average building age.[59]

Second, data across these cities reveals that wood buildings are, on average, fourteen years younger than those made of brick, stone, or concrete. In Seattle, this gap is even more pronounced. Seattle's wood buildings are typically twenty-seven years younger than its brick and stone structures, both in the city's overall building data and in demolition records.[60]

Considering the alignment of building age and demolition data and the city's history of wood origins and lenient regulation, Seattle offers an important comparison of building material and longevity. To study the environmental impact of this gap, one can translate the twenty-seven-year age difference to an estimated difference in building replacement rate. In other words, according to Seattle's data, wood buildings are replaced, on average, every fifty-one years, while concrete, steel, or masonry buildings are replaced every seventy-nine years. This significant difference in replacement rates greatly impacts the embodied energy and embodied carbon footprint of each system.

Embodied energy and embodied carbon are terms used to describe the average total energy or total carbon used (and sequestered) during production, construction, and disposal of materials. To consider the impact of lifespan on embodied energy, table 5.1 compares building code–defined assemblies within each construction type.[61] The table shows in megajoules (MJ) the estimated embodied energy per square foot of occupiable space

	values / ft² of occupiable floor area			
	Type I/II Avg. age = 79 yrs.	**Type III** Avg. age = 79 yrs.	**Type IV** Avg. age = *insufficient data in Seattle; using 79 yrs based on other cities	**Type V** Avg. age = 51 yrs.
Upfront Embodied Energy [MJ]	328	203	284	202
Lifespan Embodied Energy **over 80 years** [MJ]	332	205	287*	**316**
Upfront Embodied Carbon [kg CO2]	27	15	20	11
Lifespan Embodied Carbon **over 80 years** [kg CO2]	27	15	20*	**17**

TABLE 5.1 *Upfront and age-adjusted rates of embodied energy (in megajoules) and embodied carbon (in kilograms) per occupiable square foot, considering common wall, floor, and roof structures for each construction type.*

for each construction type. While embodied energy data is difficult to measure with certainty, this targeted comparison facilitates the evaluation of codified default assemblies.[62] This table represents energy and carbon costs to produce the most common selection of wall, roof, and floor assemblies defined in prescriptive building codes, and includes added insulation to meet contemporary energy code standards.[63]

Wood-frame Type V offers upfront carbon and energy benefits, with wood's sequestration offsetting some of the production carbon intensity. However, when lifespan-adjusted embodied energy and carbon impacts are considered, Type V emerges as one of the most energy intensive construction systems. Even its carbon sequestration benefits fall short compared to Type III construction.

Seattle's building age averages indicate a more frequent replacement rate for wood construction that not only diminishes but sometimes inverts the energy benefit of a light-weight renewable resource. Over an eighty-year period, wood-frame, Type V construction rivals concrete and steel (Type I) as the most energy-intensive method when accounting for higher replacement rates.

The frequency of replacement has a profound impact on the overall embodied carbon and energy footprint of building materials. When factoring in Seattle's building longevity corrections, Type V construction no longer offers the most carbon benefit, despite its sequestration capabilities. Additionally, when applying these age corrections to the geography of Seattle's building stock, the energy investment shifts from its core to its periphery (plate 19), which contradicts the logic of its current neighborhood development corridors. These corridors, if not built to last, will become energy drains instead of neighborhood resources.

Construction Type III (brick masonry with wood infill) and Type IV (mass timber) offer the most advantageous combination of low-energy, low-carbon, long-lasting building stock. These types strike a balance between resource consumption, component durability, and other factors discussed in earlier essays. Moreover, masonry and mass-timber construction can be designed to promote flexible use over time.

Type IV construction—encompassing heavy-timber, cross-laminated timber (CLT), and engineered mass-timber—combines the renewable, carbon-sequestration benefits of wood with enhanced dimensional stability and longer spans.[64] Allowances for engineered mass timber are expanding in national building codes, underscoring the growing importance of Type IV construction in sustainable building practices.[65]

However, type IV construction comes with higher production costs, making it unlikely to achieve the same widespread, market-driven popularity as Type V construction without additional incentives and an economy promoting reuse. Similarly, brick masonry, or Type III construction, offers an optimal combination of low-energy footprint and longevity. However, this construction type incurs additional labor costs. Cities may need to consider incentives, balancing job creation to promote affordability. Cities may direct this form of material investment toward areas designated to meet higher standards for longevity and future adaptability.

Building age is closer to an educated guess than an absolute measure of replacement-rate distinctions between material assemblies. The lifespans of twentieth-century construction already raise concerns about the long-term energy impact of wood construction. Even more troubling is the potential for new multistory wood-frame buildings to introduce additional maintenance challenges, which could further exacerbate the historical age gap between different construction types.

FIVE-OVER-ONE

> The trend in construction during this century has been toward ever-lighter framing, at least in America, with the result that buildings look

and feel increasingly like movie sets: impressive to the eye, flimsy to the touch, and incapable of aging well.

STEWART BRAND, *HOW BUILDINGS LEARN*

Today's five-over-one midrise housing emerged during Seattle's economic boom, reflecting all the attributes of boomtown construction: limited flexibility, low upfront costs, and maintenance complexities. Five-over-one refers to five stories of wood frame (Type V) atop a single-story concrete podium (Type I). This design threatens to exacerbate the short lifespan issues inherent in Type V construction, due to the behavior of the outer walls and hidden challenges within.

In the 1980s, Seattle's chief building officer, William Justen, spearheaded efforts to adapt Seattle's local amendments to the national model codes in response to development pressure.[66] Local architect and journalist Mark Hinshaw noted the origins of the city's building code experiments.

> William Justen, who was trained as an engineer, discovered that Seattle was allowed by the State to adopt its own building code provisions. So he came up with the idea of a hybrid form of construction: 4–5 floors of wood frame sitting on top of 1–2 floors of

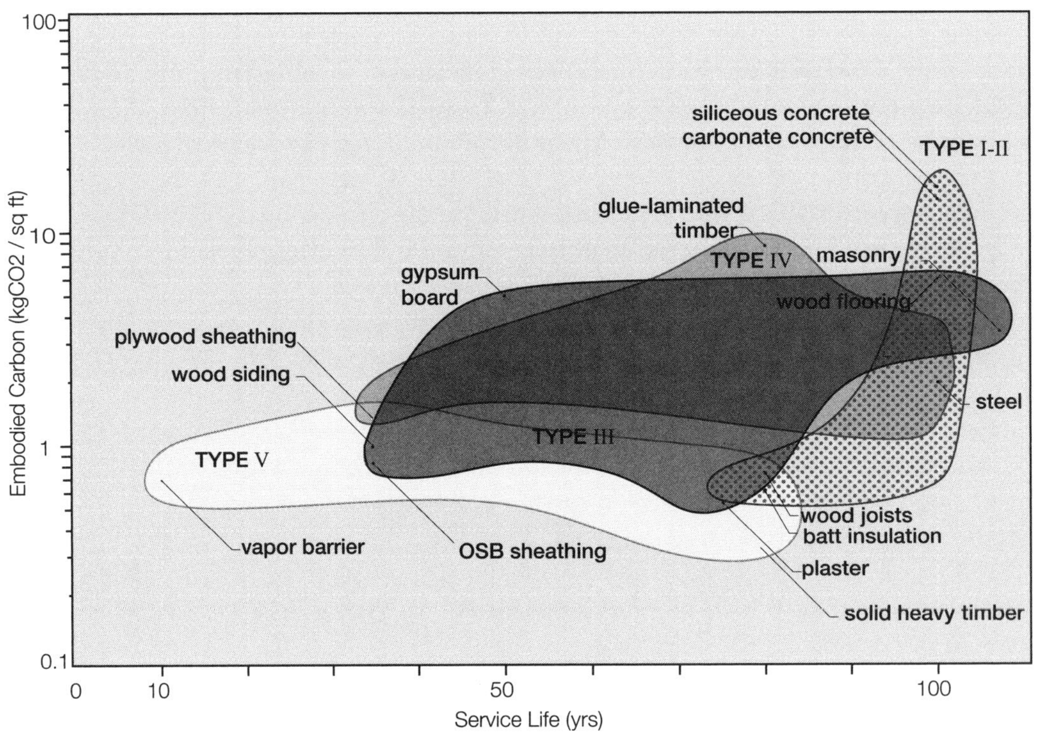

FIGURE 5.9 *Embodied carbon and the service life of construction type building components.*

FIGURE 5.10 *[Type] five-over-one construction.*

> concrete construction. He persuaded the City's Fire Marshal to try this out, despite his concerns about safety. Several buildings were built and there were no problems. So the code was changed to allow it throughout the city.[67]

Justen wrote an introduction to the 1979 building code ordinance for the Seattle City Council championing an approach that balanced a "reasonable degree of safety" with cost efficiency.

> The economic impacts of code changes have been evaluated, both long- and short-term, in working toward the goal of achieving a "reasonable" degree of safety, but avoiding the "safer is better" approach. . . . Many of the significant issues raised in this code proposal reflect several city-wide goals. The proposal takes advantage of all opportunities to lower construction costs and encourage the rehabilitation of existing buildings for both housing and other occupancies.[68]

Justen's regulatory innovation leveraged an existing provision within building codes, allowing a horizontal fire barrier to conceptually divide a building into two vertically stacked sections, each regulated separately in the eyes of the code. This horizontal separation was treated as the ground when calculating safety-related height limits above. Therefore, if three stories of wood frame were permitted at ground level, three stories were also allowed above a concrete podium first story. By 1991, Seattle began amending the regional model code to permit an additional story of Type V construction, up to four stories total. Within a decade, "tens of thousands of these [multistory wood-frame] buildings were built in Seattle."[69] In 2015, Seattle further increased its allowable residential construction limits to five stories of Type V construction, provided a sprinkler system was included.[70]

The five-over-one design swiftly became Seattle's architectural signature. Like Chicago's balloon frames a century earlier, five-over-one requires less skilled labor and significantly less upfront investment than more materially robust alternatives. This development not only transformed Seattle's building practices but also set a national precedent prioritizing cost-effective urban development.

In 2015, Seattle's innovation sparked a new national construction paradigm. The IBC adopted Seattle's multistory wood-frame experiment as a national compromise, expanding the permissible number of stories for vertical wood-frame construction.[71]

Affordability advantages quickly established five-over-one among the nation's most prevalent forms of multifamily housing. In recent decades, 74 percent of multifamily housing across the United States and 93 percent in the American West consists of multistory wood frame.[72] The market share for wood in rentals is higher than its share in owner-occupied buildings.[73] While occasional complaints arise that all new American apartments look alike, the country's building vernacular has quietly and rapidly shifted with little commentary by architects.[74]

Since the early 2010s, Seattle's housing growth rate has surged by 56 percent, far outpacing the national average.[75] Seattle owes its recent economic boom to the corporate success of Amazon, which contributed over $100 billion to the city's recent gross domestic production.[76] The influx of capital brought new jobs, spurred population growth, and increased housing pressure. True to its historical traditions, most of the jobs went to a male workforce favoring the rental housing market.[77] Unsurprisingly, the five-over-one design emerged as a panacea, enabling fast, affordable housing to serve both the booming demographic and the existing population striving to maintain affordable living within the city limits.

Jane Jacobs decried "cataclysmic money" for its short-sighted neglect of preservation. Stewart Brand expanded on this, warning that upward investment cycles can also be cataclysmic when "the financial pressure on every square foot is so great that the value of land overwhelms the value of existing buildings."[78]

Jane Jacobs and her contemporaries argued that cities should embrace a counter-logic reliant on slow investment and adaptation: "There should be more [money] in basic structure, less in finish, more in maintenance and adaptation."[79] The five-over-one design directly contradicts this advice. Much like Seattle's immovable postfire partitions, five-over-one buildings again limit spatial adaptive capacity through frequent structural partitions.

Figure 5.11 shows a contemporary five-over-one building plan and section in Seattle, compiled from rental agency information and common construction details. The spatial character of these buildings resembles the static, compressed nature of a hotel, suitable for temporary occupation. The building's light framing necessitates the structural use of each partition dividing apartments.

Five-over-one floor system spans are typically limited to fifteen to eighteen feet compared to the twenty-five to thirty feet customary for concrete construction. Plans also reveal a repetitive layout from apartment to apartment, with plumbing services anchoring each partition. Due to the inflexible divisions between apartments, there is little hope that this housing type will adapt as the needs of individuals or families change. On a broader scale, this inflexibility means these structures cannot be modified to meet evolving population needs as Seattle's industries and demographics shift, amplifying the risk of functional obsolescence.

Five-over-one faces an unfortunate confluence of functional and structural risk. The tragedy of the Great Chicago Fire revealed a fatal flaw in balloon-frame construction: continuous multistory vertical shafts between studs acted like thousands of small chimneys during the fire. In response, builders developed platform framing, where each story's floor caps the wall, limiting continuous air shafts and flame spread. While platform framing became standard practice in American home construction for over a century, it introduces expansion and contraction issues that are compounded with each successive platform level in a structure.

Wood's expansion and contraction is directional: minimal along the length of a timber but significant within its cross section. Each added floor platform introduces a cross section that will change in dimension by fractions of an inch. In platform-framed five-over-one buildings, the cumulative movement of five to six cross sections can amount to several inches over the height of the structure. Several inches of shifting and swelling can compromise exterior cladding and complicate connections to static elements such as vents and pipes.

Notably, in some regions, developers substitute light-gauge steel for its dimensional stability in market-rate housing while relying on wood

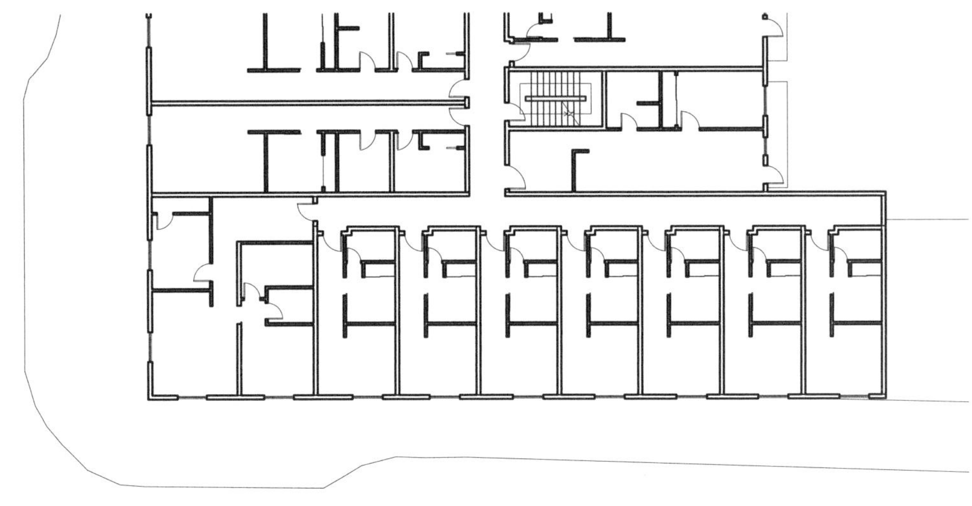

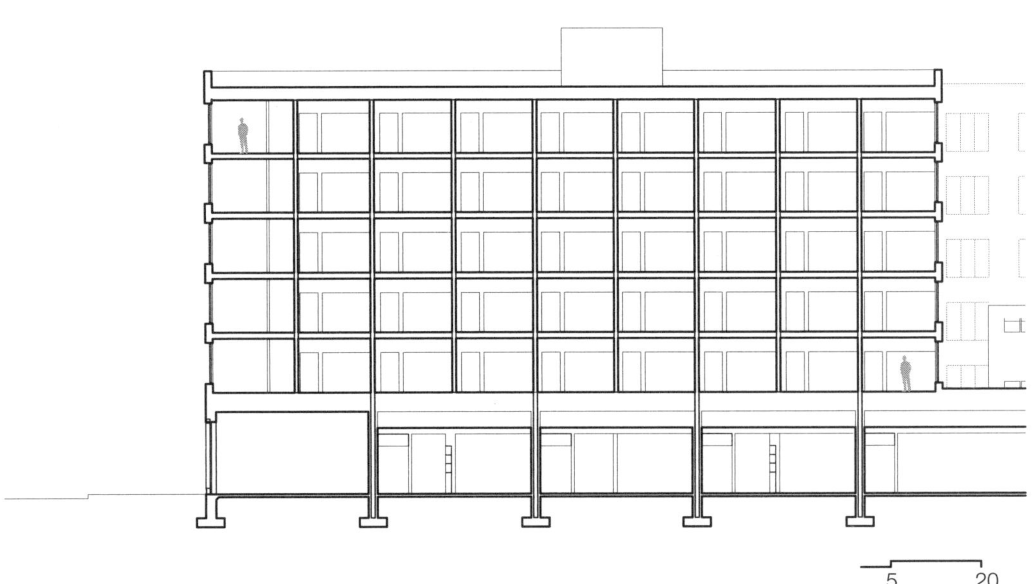

FIGURE 5.11 a & b *(a) Typical five-over-one Seattle block in plan and section; and (b) diagrammatic indication of frequent, difficult-to-move partitions that decrease flexibility of interior spaces.*

frame for affordable housing.[80] Although steel studs eliminate the risks of contraction and expansion, they exacerbate carbon and energy production costs without addressing the rigid inflexibility of this structural typology.

With apparent amnesia, the construction industry now recommends "modified balloon-frame construction" as a solution for expansion and contraction issues when framing wood studs over five to six stories. Modified

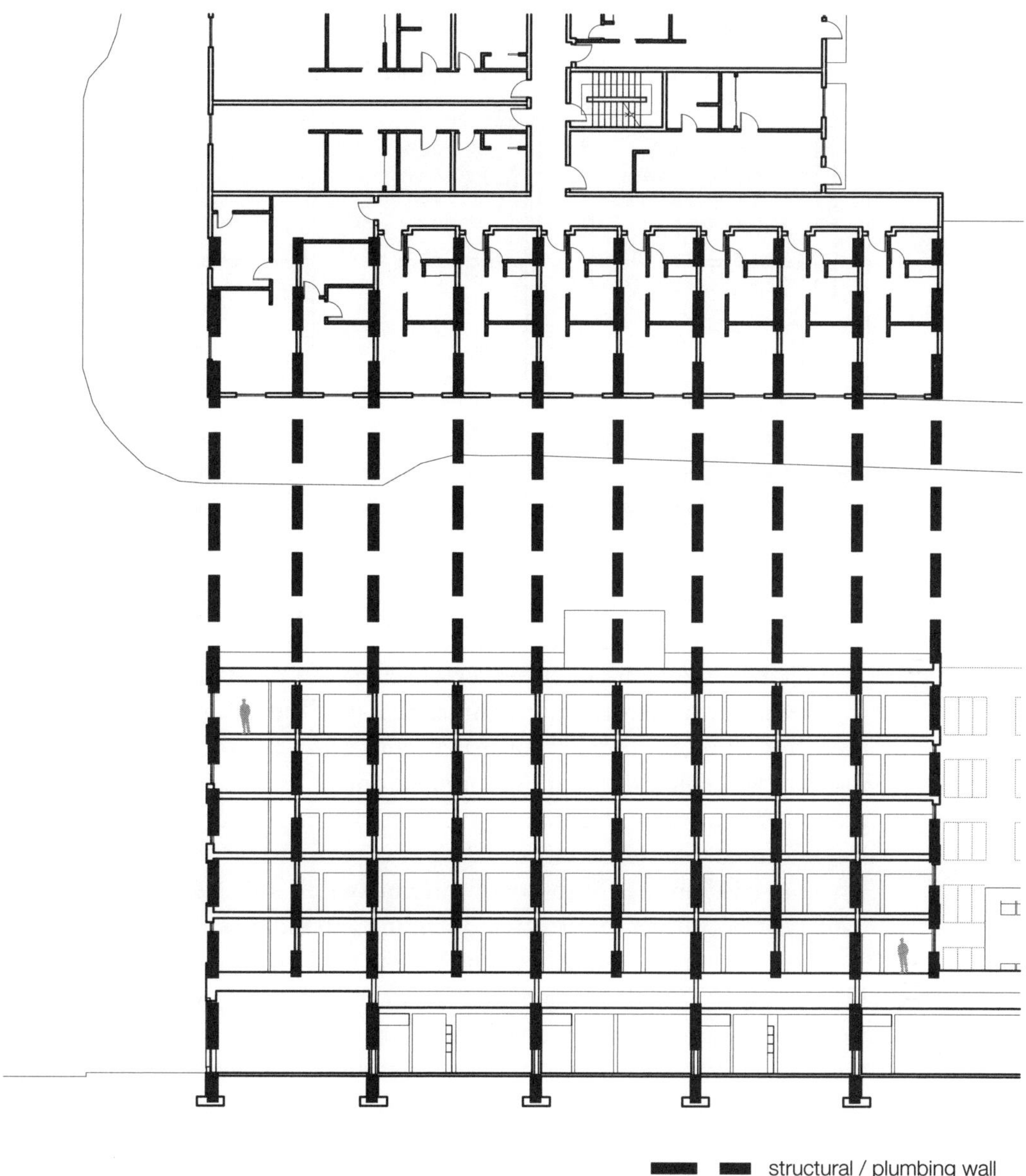

balloon framing minimizes the intervening platforms within the structure, using the continuous joists of prefire Chicago to mitigate movement problems. However, this method also requires the use of fire-blocking or specialized steel hangers to avoid vertical fire shafts, employing various techniques to curb the risk of fire spread from wall to floors and throughout the vertical structure (fig. 5.12). Although modified balloon framing improves durability in one respect, it also relies heavily on jobsite quality

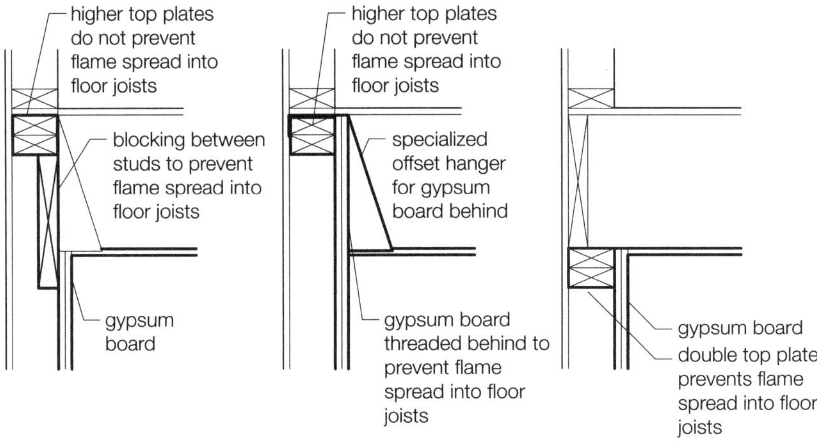

FIGURE 5.12 *Details of platform frame and two variations of modified balloon-frame construction.*

control to avoid significant danger, with any missed steps forever hidden from view after construction.

While the benefits of five-over-one include speed and minimal skill requirements, it also carries significant risks. This system relies on the execution of more complex construction to avoid significant maintenance issues or vulnerabilities that once ignited one of the greatest urban conflagrations in American history. In five-over-one, movement occurs where it is not wanted—within exterior walls and envelopes—but is hard to achieve where needed, in the flexibility of interior spaces. This new national standard may jeopardize the creation of enduring building stock.

Five-over-one construction mirrors the building traditions of the Far West so closely that it seems almost inevitable in a city like Seattle. In western cities, construction began with false fronts, fostering early building traditions reminiscent of movie sets. A century later, Boeing's Wonderland again reflected Seattle's provisional construction in response to industrial growth.

Seattle often catered to a limited, transient demographic through boarding houses built and replaced quickly. The city also crafted its own unique fire protection rules. Despite awareness of more stringent national standards, Seattle embraced lenient building practices while investing in firefighting capacity, navigating the tension between urgent housing needs and building risk. This strategy proved effective during the city's postfire rebuilding, and Seattle revisited it nearly a century later to address housing demands, adjusting its wood height allowances to match neighborhood engine-ladder capacities. Seattle's contemporary building trends echo its enduring preference for material convenience over safety measures or spatial flexibility.

Since the IBC codified five-over-one as a national standard in 2015, American cities must now question whether it aligns with the traditions and aspirations of nation-wide city building. Will it overcome limitations to meet energy standards, spatial needs, or the production of a stable city fabric over time? Jane Jacobs eloquently describes the value of urban buildings that age well. She states: "The economic value of new buildings is replaceable in cities. It is replaceable by the spending of more construction money. But the economic value of old buildings is irreplaceable at will. It is created by time. This economic requisite for diversity is a requisite that vital city neighborhoods can only inherit, and then sustain over the years."[81]

The five-over-one typology is still too young to accurately predict its lifespan across cities. However, it inherits and amplifies the durability challenges of its single-family Type V counterparts. The lifespan of some Type V protective barriers and sealants is designed to match a fiscal thirty-year investment period, but urban buildings typically endure much longer. Investing beyond the moment-of-sale price and toward longevity is in the best interest of cities, occupants, and ecologies. If the market drives investment toward fast, cheap, and inflexible construction, cities must counter by incentivizing enduring, adaptable investments.

MATERIAL ENVIRONMENTAL PARADOX

The pursuit of environmental protection in American construction is fraught with contradictions. One of the most perplexing challenges lies in the simultaneous and seemingly incompatible demands for affordability, renewable resource use, and longevity. Nearly a century after the construction of Wonderland on the northwest coast, America faces another crisis, this time driven by environmental threats. Yet the American response remains one of impermanence and illusion, where speed and affordability overshadow the aspirations for long-term material sustainability in urban environments.

As in 1941, light-wood framing once again serves as a convenient disguise, this time for the impression of sustainability. Wood is renewable, sequesters carbon during its growth, and retains that carbon when used in construction. When transformed into small, easy-to-assemble dimensional lumber and sheet material, it becomes both affordable and accessible to unskilled labor. However, Type V construction may not last sufficiently long to function as an appropriate enduring investment of funds or energy for urban construction. Compounding the issue, the Type V city is now morphing into a more vulnerable, less adaptable form of multifamily urban housing. Straying from the specificity of their regional material resources and traditions, cities across the country now adhere to national prescriptive standards, like five-over-one, which emerged from boomtown traditions. Cities embrace the affordability benefits while overlooking the risks of resource consumption and the likelihood of rapid replacement.

Seattle represents the culmination of the Type V city's evolution, marking the final stage of relevance for current construction typologies. As the ambitious western terminus of American settlement, Seattle resisted full compliance with eastern methods of city building. Over time, it pioneered new urban typologies utilizing modified balloon frames—the very assemblies that building-material codes aimed to eliminate—while pushing higher densities. Seattle developed the exception that upends the rules and undermined building-code logics focused entirely on fire resistance.

Today, the phenomenon of boomtown building is no longer confined to the American West or embattled in protests across Chicago streets. The traditions of short-term thinking and construction in the Type V city are more firmly entrenched in American building practices than ever before. However, the full-circle journey from balloon-frame cities to contemporary construction types and back to balloon frames presents a unique opportunity. Seattle and contemporary construction practices stretch building-material codes to their limits, disrupting the original paradigm. In doing so, they pave the way for a complete transformation of urban material performance and priorities.

CONCLUSION

> Folks who do systems analysis have a great belief in "leverage points." These are places within a complex system . . . where a small shift in one thing can produce big changes in everything. . . . We know from bitter experience that when we do discover the system's leverage points, hardly anybody will believe us.
>
> DONELLA MEADOWS, "PLACES TO INTERVENE IN A SYSTEM," 1997

TYPE V CITIES, A QUINTESSENTIALLY American phenomenon, are not merely the result of conflagration risk and affordability barriers. They reflect the cultural values and political priorities of the past century. American cities transitioned from delineating material fire resistance near urban centers to relying on fire suppression. Type V construction became a national norm, even in dense multistory buildings, typically accepted below a sixty-foot regulatory threshold.[1] Despite the relaxation of combustible materials limits, codes continue to regulate materials choices exclusively from a flammability perspective. Amid fire mandate debates, cities overlooked the relationships between materials and economies, ecologies, health, labor opportunities, social vitality, adaptive capacity, and building longevity.

As cities now embrace data-driven decision-making, they must also scrutinize what is measured or neglected and what outcomes are legible or obscured by urban rules. Understanding the historical context that shaped these decisions allows us to connect rules with pressures, priorities, and urban ideals.

Chicago workers invented and then fiercely defended the Type V city as a balloon-framed tool of social mobility. After the fire, Chicago's code compromise manifested as a geographic material boundary to balance the interests of business investment and the city's workers. The city then shifted from clear fire limits to a complex matrix of construction types that masked building material outcomes and fostered public indifference. Chicago investors and economists subsequently privatized urban risk assessment and valuation as they prioritized sprawling growth opportunities and racial segregation over building stock durability.

New York real estate developers preserved the Type V city. They erected wood-frame structures within unregulated wetlands through multiple stages of incremental development. Over time, the pressure to safeguard low-density development fortified the Type V city's position in New York's lower outwash plains. Operating in blind pursuit of real-estate expansion, New York's building codes ignored vulnerable ecosystems and filled the gaps in 1916 zoning ordinance's coastal "undetermined areas" with incentives for light-wood framing. Despite health risks and flood damage, policies reinforced Type V construction with flood insurance by socializing risk, creating a paradox of seemingly safe development. Building codes and flood regulations now tout resilience for Hurricane Sandy's most vulnerable building type by placing chemically infused Type V materials squarely in the path of future storm surges.

Philadelphia laborers resisted the Type V city, instead using building codes to narrowly channel government investment toward an exclusive construction workforce. The formidable political influence of labor unions codified material resilience in the nineteenth century through a unique brick mandate, only to later hinder its potential continuity. By excluding over half of the urban population from essential blue-collar jobs, the unions exacerbated material affordability challenges, ultimately undermining the city's will and capacity to uphold its brick mandate. Cities are now turning to another form of building regulation to address labor and other social equity impacts of buildings through requirements for proactive community engagement.

Tampa's Black community adapted the Type V city by gradually integrating diverse occupancies, opportunities, and material upgrades within a dense, racially segregated, and mutually supportive community. Tampa's Central Avenue showcased an unusual combination of material variety and density, shaped by the limits of segregation, lax regulatory oversight, and municipal underinvestment. The community's success underscores the importance of occupancy opportunities embedded within material codes to promote vitality in mixed-use development. Tampa's Type V city also demonstrates the role of material regulation in a southern city, first provoking postbellum settlement beyond the fire limits, then animating the neighborhood's use and limiting its occupancy, and ultimately justifying the neighborhood's demolition.

Seattle's boomtown population embraced the Type V city while often ignoring typical regulatory constraints. At the end of America's westward expansion, Seattle's residents prioritized short-term capacity over long-term stability. They favored the codification of inflexible interior partitions and enhanced firefighting capacity over reliance on scarce noncombustible resources. This preference persists today, as the city expands allowances for inflexible, short-span multistory wood-frame structures. Seattle's Type V city ultimately overturned the building codes' regulatory logic by reverting to balloon-frame construction to combat wood's expansion and contraction over five to six stories.

Type V construction emerged as a tool of American speculation and opportunistic expansion, serving as the lowest common denominator to facilitate widespread home ownership. Rather than uniformly protecting health, safety, or welfare as their authors claimed, building codes were used as a form of social and spatial priority-setting. These codes promoted growth but not preservation in Seattle; defended one business center while targeting another in Tampa; promoted white bricklayers but not Black laborers in Philadelphia; safeguarded development but not wetlands, the high ground but not the outwash plains, low density but not health, in New York; and they separated risk but privatized its assessment, protected business investment, worker housing, lenders, and insurers, but not all occupants, in Chicago.

In recent years, building codes have been used as mutable opportunities for innovation. In Seattle, they were more locally specific but less strategic, tuned to utilize local resource abundance but also to accept disposable, inflexible construction. As Seattle's experiments spread nationally, they reveal a national centuries-long struggle to balance conflicting ideals of opportunism and shared welfare. Is the future American urban material vernacular an unwavering acceptance of light-wood framing, reviving balloon-frame details while sacrificing intentional priorities?

Despite concerns about Seattle's building trends, its demonstration of local innovation remains significant. Additionally, international investment in repurposing building practices hints at future shifts in global construction priorities.[2] As American cities reconsider the influences and intentions shaping their building material goals, the preceding narratives reveal an alternative set of overlooked yet critical factors for evaluating risk and assigning value within the built environment. These factors can be distilled into three broad categories rooted in enduring American spatial values: adaptive capacity, environmental geographies, and socially generative potential.

ADAPTATIVE CAPACITY

American pursuit of short-term convenience and self-reliant opportunism has profoundly shaped its urban architecture. On one hand, city builders created an urban infrastructure of expendable utility, a logic now so ingrained in American culture that the market ignores the differential value of material durability. Yet early American building traditions also embraced a remarkable notion of architecture as a fluid process, inherently tied to the social evolution of a place and its inhabitants.

When Solon Robinson described the architecture of the American home within his pattern books, he emphasized the importance of adaptation over time, responding to resources, capacity, and the changing needs of inhabitants. In Tampa's Central Avenue, neighbors pooled resources to incrementally fortify spaces for social gatherings, leveraging the flexibility and accessibility of wood framing as both a starting point and an infill opportunity. As American cities expanded westward, their architecture and outlook became increasingly "poised for change."[3]

Building design for adaptive capacity remained a key objective in American architecture well beyond the frontier pattern books. Jane Jacobs championed the value of old buildings, advocating for "more [investment] in basic structure, less in finish, more in maintenance and adaptation."[4] Stuart Brand echoed this sentiment in the 1990s, noting that "the old factory, the plainest of buildings, keeps being revived. . . . Whereas 'architecture' may strive to be permanent, a 'building' is always building and rebuilding. The idea is crystalline, the fact fluid. Could the idea be revised to match the fact?"[5]

As current investment and policy focus relentlessly on operational energy efficiency, they risk underinvesting in longevity. On average, urban buildings in Seattle, New York, and Chicago are fifty to ninety years old.[6] How can cities tune these investments to last for the next several centuries?

Spatial adaptive capacity within buildings is essential to promote longevity. Yet adaptability, durability, and lifespan are currently absent as criteria in building codes and elective environmental codes. If urban markets are predicated on unwavering growth, planned obsolescence, and replacement, it is essential for city policies to develop alternative mechanisms to promote longevity and remove regulatory barriers that limit adaptive capacity.

Enacting a more adaptive, durable, and therefore longer-lasting urban architecture requires rethinking the spatial layering of material regulation at both the building and city scales. Contemporary adaptive architectures integrate flexible inhabitation and infill over time. Consider the benefits of the "naked house" and "open building" movements, as well as live-work occupancies. These models emphasize a stable structural shell with either variable use built into spaces and circulation, or, more capacious, less finished space, to be incrementally altered according to occupant needs and means over time. Construction Types III and IV, often brick masonry and heavy-timber construction, naturally align with adaptive design strategies at certain densities due to capacity for long structural spans, resistance to degradation over time, and the efficiency and flexibility of nonstructural wood infill.

This level of occupant and *occupancy* flexibility is unfamiliar within current American development and regulatory models, yet it aligns remarkably well with early American building traditions. Building for future adaptation has the potential to lower financial barriers to entry for home ownership or business startups. Robust building typologies offer several potential benefits, including labor-intensive construction to promote job opportunity, durable affordable housing solutions, and economic and environmental stability.

Contemporary building and zoning regulations often restrict the potential for flexible occupancy and incremental completion of unfinished housing units. Policymakers must consider: Under what circumstances is a municipality willing to issue a certificate of occupancy when some uses and finishes are to be further determined and completed by the occupant? Are cities prepared to incentivize live-work occupancies? And in which areas of the city might these mixed occupancies and densities flourish?

ENVIRONMENTAL GEOGRAPHIES

The resource and risk geographies of Type V construction are shifting even as national model codes drive increasingly uniform building strategies across the country. National uniformity diminishes the tendency for cities to consider local resource and environmental geographies. Meanwhile, resource geographies can influence and alter the risk and value propositions for building materials. For instance, consider the evolution of wood species and the implications of concrete aggregate geologies.

Throughout the twentieth century, the depletion of old-growth timber necessitated a shift in the lumber industry to farmed production. Porous sapwood lumber replaced dense heartwood boards, and the seventeen common wood species once used in construction dwindled to only four. The size of wood studs decreased, cavity walls shifted from breathable to tightly packed and wrapped, and the use of engineered wood increased the exposure of wood cellulose. This small-scale evolution of wood construction has large-scale consequences. By increasing the absorption of wood, the propensity for mold growth, and the need for additional biocide treatments, evolving production methods impact the health risks of Type V construction, particularly in areas prone to water infiltration.

The geographies of wood sourcing are also migrating. Most US lumber is currently sourced from Canada, where lumber production capacity faces expanding climate change–related challenges (plate 20).[7] Shorter cold seasons heighten the prevalence of beetle-kill infestations, increasing the risk of forest fires and mudslides that hamper lumber transportation infrastructure. Several Canadian mills consolidated in 2022 due to a lack of wood resources, while industry traders attribute skyrocketing prices to climate change.[8]

Scientists predict that climate change will continue to push growing-region geographies northward, increasing reliance on southern species for lumber production even as these species face rising threats from pest infiltrations.[9] As native forests migrate, lumber producers are moving south toward southern trees with longer summers and faster growth cycles. Southern United States mills reported an increased capacity of 4.5 million board feet of lumber from 2021 to 2022, while British Columbia, still the largest supplier of softwood, reduced capacity.[10] This growing dependence on more porous, rapid-growth, farmed lumber may result in less dimensional stability, further jeopardizing the longevity of Type V construction.

While the resource geographies of Type V construction are shifting, the resources for Type I and II construction remain more fixed, with building stock resources tied to the nation's geological deposits. Plate 20 illustrates the distribution of concrete aggregate resources, including carbonite deposits in the South and Midwest and siliceous rock concentrated on the coasts. The country's model codes (IBC) differentiate the fire resistance of siliceous versus carbonate aggregate concrete. Siliceous aggregate contains silica, primarily composed of granite and sandstone. It loses strength more quickly when exposed to high temperatures. By contrast, carbonate aggregate, consisting of dolomite and limestone, exhibits a higher capacity to maintain strength at high temperatures.[11] The codes require approximately an additional inch of material thickness using siliceous concrete for every wall, beam, or column to meet fire-resistance requirements. Transporting aggregate beyond a thirty-minute travel radius is both costly and energy-intensive, meaning the availability of regional resources could significantly influence the investment in Types I and II materials across North America.[12]

While the codes strive for uniformity, the practical realities of sourcing and transporting building materials reveal a more complex picture. Regional variations in material availability and properties necessitate tailored approaches to construction that can optimize both cost and performance. For instance, the proximity of certain aggregates or lumber types can significantly influence the economic and environmental impact of construction projects. Recognizing and leveraging these regional differences can lead to more efficient use of resources, reduced transportation costs, and enhanced structural resilience, ultimately fostering a more sustainable and adaptable built environment.

At the city scale, regulations can also tune requirements to local environments. In New York, environmental indeterminacy led to the default use of Type V construction, starting in Manhattan with sinking tenement rear yards and industrial sites occupying the former Collect Pond and extending to the hardened outwash plains surrounding Jamaica Bay. The city's focus on protecting real estate expansion resulted in an illogical mismatch between environmental and material vulnerability. Federal flood management pressures eventually forced flood zone strategies into building code requirements. Flood-resistant building requirements function similarly to early fire insurance requirements, spreading the potential cost of vulnerability and creating a safety net for risk-taking. However, flood insurance not only creates a safe-development paradox but also exacerbates New York's environmental and material contradictions by maintaining material geographies that increase risks to human and environmental health.

Shifts in lumber properties, resource availability, and local environmental and material properties call for a material logic more attuned to resources, species, and environments.[13] The United States must learn from the precautionary principles of European and Australian regulators, exercising caution with technologies that have unproven and potentially profound negative environmental impacts. In this context, such caution might involve aligning environmental risk zones with material and species selection, rather than depending on the chemical treatments and biocides that currently dominate American codes.

SOCIALLY GENERATIVE POTENTIAL

Cities can more proactively support affordability, health, and urban vitality by defining a material infrastructure aimed at generative opportunity. Historically, building construction served as a means of economic stabilization, but contemporary regulators often default to lower-investment materials as the only means to achieve affordability. Philadelphia's labor unions exerted decades of influence over building codes and construction job accessibility. Today's efforts to diversify the construction labor force are often limited to business owners rather than targeting the demographics of skilled laborers, leaving a narrow demographic workforce primarily residing outside of the city.

Building with durable materials that enhance longevity demands higher initial investment. However, this approach can yield long-lasting economic benefits if it involves employing local residents, leveraging synergistic design and regulatory incentives.

The lack of reliable labor data presents a formidable obstacle to diversification efforts in the construction workforce. As cities and communities seek further information disclosure from contractors and unions, advocates and architects can already utilize public census microdata and apprenticeship data to understand material specification as a mechanism for equitable building.

In Tampa's Central Avenue, building materials and occupancy codes controlled opportunities for sociospatial neighborhood vibrancy. Tampa's story demonstrates that material and corresponding occupancy opportunities are particularly relevant to populations displaced during twentieth-century urban renewal. As redevelopment progresses for public and subsidized housing nationwide, designing opportunities for live-work and small business occupancies is essential. This approach may foster entrepreneurship, creating more accessible opportunities for social interaction and cohesion.

Cities have the potential to redefine their material infrastructures to foster more inclusive and sustainable urban environments. By prioritizing durable materials and local labor, cities can create a virtuous cycle of economic and social benefits. This approach not only enhances the longevity and resilience of the built environment but also provides meaningful employment opportunities for residents, thereby strengthening the local economy.

Moreover, the integration of live-work spaces and small business occupancies into redevelopment plans can revitalize neighborhoods and support diverse economic activities. These spaces offer flexibility and affordability, making them accessible to a broader range of residents and entrepreneurs. By aligning material choices with the needs and aspirations of local communities, cities can promote a more equitable distribution of resources and opportunities.

A shift toward generative building material objectives can help cities address the intertwined challenges of affordability and vitality. By embracing durable materials, supporting local labor, and fostering flexible occupancies, cities can create environments that are not only resilient and sustainable but also vibrant and inclusive. This holistic vision of material performance, inspired by the lessons of the past and the needs of the present, can guide cities toward a more equitable and prosperous future.

LEGIBLE MATERIAL FUTURES

Communities and governments entrust building codes to protect "health, safety, and welfare," but their intricacy and resulting exclusivity make it difficult to analyze outcomes, debate priorities, or recognize the disconnect with their initial rationale. Building codes reflect and project the ideals that shape the American city, yet their nuance lulls the general population into indifference.

Construction types illustrate the effect of complexity and disaggregation, shifting codes away from public debate toward exclusive, "expert-driven" regulation. Scholars agree that regulatory opacity leads to inadequate public attention, underestimation of impact, and lack of access to standard-making, particularly for marginalized groups.[14]

The intricacy of building codes and construction types often obscures their true impact on urban environments and communities. Yet armed with spatial outcomes dictated by these codes, the public can participate in vital discussions about the cumulative impacts and potential social benefits of the built environment. Transparent aims and outcomes can lead to more informed decision-making, ensuring that building practices align with the broader goals of sustainability, equity, and resilience.

Information is a powerful leverage point in systems change. Building codes and resulting material data offer both a mirror and a mechanism, reflecting the relationships between building infrastructures and other urban systems over space and time. Though current codes remain opaque and their intentions unclear to the public, contemporary material, spatial, and social data offers new opportunities.

Throughout the twentieth century, insurers and economists employed mapping analysis to assign property risk and value to urban material landscapes. However, this critical information and perspective remained the exclusive domain of private industry until the latter part of the century. Historical maps, including HOLC residential security maps and fire insurance Sanborn maps were made broadly and publicly available by the Library of Congress late in the twentieth century.[15]

Aggregate material data was also once more accessible—and evidently demanded higher levels of public attention—through the US Census of Housing. The Census of Housing recorded construction material trends across urban housing stock through 1940, but it no longer includes building structural or exterior wall materials in its published data.[16] Only the census's Survey of Construction, within their business and industry data, includes regional and national construction characteristics such as exterior wall and framing types.[17]

Detailed, statistically sampled demographic census and labor data, such as the American Community Survey, has been tabulated and publicly available since 2008.[18] Additional statistical reports, like the Current Population Survey, have been incrementally added since 2014 and include labor demographic data. Graphic Information Systems software and more comprehensive urban, regional, and national spatial data became widespread starting in the 1980s.[19] Finally, in the last decade, city assessment data—typically managed by individual cities for property valuation and taxes—has become more readily accessible through open data portals.

The proliferation of data and visualization tools offers powerful opportunities for policymakers and public advocates. These tools can facilitate analysis of material, social, and spatial dynamics across American cities. As cities consider new building initiatives, investments, and regulations, effectively communicating regulation outcomes and interactions can foster a deeper understanding of overlapping economies, labor, environments, occupancies, and opportunities. Moreover, the integration of historical and contemporary data can reveal patterns and trends that inform future urban priority-setting. By understanding how past decisions have shaped present conditions, cities can avoid repeating mistakes and instead build on successful strategies. Ultimately, this approach can facilitate the creation of urban building infrastructures that function according to spatial, temporal, and social shared priorities.

What if Chicago's economic investments had supported material durability over risk segregation? What if its building code evolution had continued to invite the public input that once fueled protest marches? What if New York had applied precaution and protection to its material landscapes, safeguarding both ecological and human health? What if Philadelphia had incentivized labor-inclusive robust construction? What if Tampa had protected social and material value, resourcing rather than razing Central Avenue? Or, more recently, what if Tampa had not only rebuilt the dense housing of Central Avenue but also its material infrastructures for social interaction, live-work opportunities, and spatial vitality? And what if Seattle harnessed its capacity for material and building code innovation to champion spatial adaptation and flexible occupancy, creating a cityscape that evolves with its inhabitants?

In an era where urban landscapes are swiftly reshaped by emerging risks, it becomes imperative for city-builders to illuminate the impact of cumulative material infrastructures, their governing mechanisms, and their inherent tradeoffs.

Building codes—their intentions, limitations, failures, and opportunities—are, at the very least, social narratives etched into urban landscapes. They reveal the inherent uncertainties of risk, the paradox between desired stability and necessary change, and the power and priorities embedded in material progress.

ACKNOWLEDGMENTS

This book and the ideas that ground it developed in an atmosphere of intellectual generosity and mutual support at the University of Virginia. I am deeply grateful to my colleagues at the School of Architecture for fostering such an environment. In particular, Anselmo Canfora consistently shared his talent and insights, translating his optimism into unwavering encouragement.

I owe special gratitude to Bill Sherman for planting the seed for my initial inquiries and to Barbara Brown Wilson for her counsel, collaboration, and debates as we covered many miles. Several colleagues provided crucial advice, edits, and methodological guidance, including Sheila Crane, Nana Last, and Andrew Mondschein. Dean Malo Hutson and Dean Ila Berman furnished the time and resources for this project to flourish.

Thank you to all my colleagues in the Department of Architecture and those from adjacent disciplines and perspectives. Your insights over the years have pushed me to view the built environment from new vantage points. Special thanks to Brad Cantrell, Elgin Cleckley, Alissa Diamond, Robin Dripps, Beth Meyer, Liz Ogbu, Moira O'Neill, and Lucia Phinney.

I had the privilege of working with many talented students, thanks to support for research assistance from the UVA School of Architecture and UVA Office of the Vice Provost for Research. Jessica Smith and Zazu Swistel dedicated their talent and time to the project, serving as meticulous investigative partners. Joshua Aronson laid the groundwork in the earliest stages of data inquiries and visualizations. Alissa Diamond, Kevan Klosterwill, and Barbara B. Wilson collaborated on work in Charlottesville that served as the foundation for my investigation of Tampa. Others who made significant contributions include Sida Dai, Megan Friedman, Lydia Fulton, Anna Hickman, Kate Lipkowitz, Veronica Merril, Charlotte Pitts, Zimo Ren, Andrew Shae, Ben Small, Ed Taylor, and Julia Triman.

I am indebted to many individuals and institutions who provided invaluable archival resources. Special thanks to Jennifer Bibb from the University of North Florida Special Collections and University Archive, Jennifer Dietz and Alison Smith from the Archives and Records Division of the City of Tampa, Heather Hill at the Hillsborough Planning Commission Data Library, Joshua Blay at the City of Philadelphia Department of Records, the Philadelphia Historical Society, the Chicago History Museum, the Temple University Special Collections Library, the Tampa Bay History Center, the Tampa-Hillsborough Public Library, the Seattle Museum of

History and Industry, the Niewe Instituut, and to Rebecca Coleman Cooper at the University of Virginia Libraries.

This work draws insights from my architectural practice. My collaborators, Kara Boyd, Todd Zima, and Ellen Anderson, have shared their creative partnership and commitment to pushing architecture toward positive social and environmental impacts across scales and territories.

Thank you to my editor, Robert Devens, the advice of generous readers, and the team at University of Texas Press in Austin.

Finally, it is my family who made this book truly possible. My parents, Ann and Tony D'Agostino, gave me a foundation in algorithmic thinking as well as their perpetual interest and encouragement. My sister, Kristin D'Agostino, and brother, T. J. D'Agostino, share parallel passions and pursuits even from half a world away. Eden, Leo, and Paul, your inquisitiveness and joy give me endless inspiration and pride. And Chris, there won't be sufficient words to describe my gratitude for unwavering support and enriching life with your generosity, wit, and wisdom.

NOTES

Introduction

1. The transition from language referring only to fire control through geographic limits to regulation with categories of building classes and categories of fireproofing can be seen in Chicago's ordinances from 1866 and 1894. See "Laws and Ordinances Governing the City of Chicago, January 1, 1866," 46–58.

2. The term "five-over-one" is most often used to describe the general approach and increasingly loosened regulation of five to six stories of wood-frame construction over a concrete podium. Cities loosened the maximum height restrictions for wood-frame construction to varying degrees over the last several decades. In 2015, the IBC increased the number of allowable residential stories for Types III and V, both of which can be constructed from wood frame (see table 504.4). Type III can be built up to five stories, wood frame Type V up to four stories. See ICC, *2015 IBC Code and Commentary* (ICC Publications, 2015).

3. Linda R. Rowan et al., "Congressional Research Report R47665, Building Codes, Standards, and Regulations: Frequently Asked Questions," Congressional Research Service, November 22, 2023, https://crsreports.congress.gov/product/details?prodcode=R47665.

4. "AIA Public Comment to ICC Proposal," American Institute of Architects, https://content.aia.org/sites/default/files/2021-01/AIA_Public_Comments_to_ICC_Proposal_New_Energy_Standard.pdf; Tom DiChristopher, "Overhaul of Building Energy Code Deals Setback to Gas Ban Backers," *S&P Global Market Intelligence*, March 8, 2021, https://www.spglobal.com/marketintelligence.

5. The recent Inflation Reduction Act dedicated $225 million to "Cost-Effective Codes Implementation for Efficiency and Resilience" geared toward energy efficiency code adoption and compliance. This does not address embodied energy related to building material. Rep. John A. Yarmuth (D-KY-3), "H.R. 5376—Inflation Reduction Act of 2022," 117th Congress (2021–2022), https://www.congress.gov/bill/117th-congress/house-bill/5376/text.

6. See averages from 2009–2020 in "Number of Multifamily Buildings Completed by Framing" and "Type of Framing in New Single-Family Houses Completed," US Census Bureau, M.C.D. "Characteristics of New Housing," https://www.census.gov/construction/chars/current.html.

7. ICC, *2021 International Building Code* (ICC Publications, 2020).

8. Steven A. Moore and Barbara B. Wilson, *Questioning Architectural Judgment: The Problem of Codes in the United States* (Routledge, 2013), 126.

9. Ties between income and experience with urban heat islands are described by T. Chakraborty, A. Hsu, D. Manya, and G. Sheriff, "Disproportionately Higher Exposure to Urban Heat in Lower-Income Neighborhoods: A Multi-City Perspective," *Environmental Research Letters* 14, no. 10 (September 2019). A study of elevated lead levels in blood by racial category was conducted by Robert Jones et al., "Trends in Blood Lead Levels and Blood Lead Testing Among US Children Aged 1 to 5 Years, 1988–2004," National Library of Medicine, DOI: 10.1542/peds.2007-3608. A publication from the Center for Social Solutions at the University of Michigan describes the increased impact of flooding on communities of color: "Case Study: Floods and Socioeconomic Inequality," October 30, 2020, https://lsa.umich.edu/social-solutions/news-events.

10. Residential property characteristics data accessed from the Cook County Assessor (2020), https://www.cookcountyassessor.com; Property Valuation and Assessment data, NYC Department of Finance (2017), https://www.nyc.gov/site/finance/property

/property.page; Assessments Data, King County Department of Assessments, https://info.kingcounty.gov/assessor/; US Census Bureau, *American Housing Survey* (2019), average year built, https://www.census.gov/programs-surveys/ahs.html.

11. Rowan et al., "Congressional Research Report R47665."

12. Eran Ben-Joseph, *The Code of the City: Standards and the Hidden Language of Place Making* (MIT Press, 2005), xiv.

13. "Understanding Building Codes," National Institute of Standards and Technology (NIST), June 16, 2022, https://www.nist.gov/buildings-construction/understanding-building-codes; and Rowan et al., "Congressional Research Report R47665."

14. The IBC resulted from the consolidation of three previous regional codes: the Building Officials and Code Administration (BOCA), primarily adopted in the northeastern United States; the Uniform Building Code (UBC), primarily used in the West and Midwest; and the Standard Building Code (SBC), primarily used in the South. In 2000, these groups formed the ICC to consolidate the regional codes into the IBC, a national model code. In 2021, the ICC reported that IBC has been adopted in all fifty states, the District of Columbia, the US Virgin Islands, Guam, and the Northern Marianas Islands.

15. See discussion of public accountability and ANSI history in Moore and Wilson, *Questioning Architectural Judgment*, 47–48.

16. ICC, *2021 International Residential Code.*

17. "Understanding Building Codes," *NIST*, June 16, 2022, https://www.nist.gov/buildings-construction/understanding-building-codes.

18. Dominic Sims, "Bylaws for the International Code Council, Inc.," February 2013, https://www.iccsafe.org/wp-content/uploads/bylaws.pdf.

19. Christopher Flavelle, "Secret Deal Helped Housing Industry Stop Tougher Rules on Climate Change," *New York Times*, October 26, 2019.

20. Justin Gillis, "Opinion: What Will Happen to Your Next Home If Builders Get Their Way?," *New York Times*, January 21, 2021.

21. DiChristopher, "Overhaul of Building Energy Code Deals Setback."

22. Lawrence Busch, *Standards: Recipes for Reality* (MIT Press, 2011), 285.

23. "History of the California Green Building Standards Code CALGreen" (2018), Building Standards Commission, Historical Information, https://www.dgs.ca.gov/en/BSC/About/History-of-the-California-Green-Building-Standards-Code-CALGreen.

24. Aleksandra Jaeschke, *The Greening of America's Building Codes: Promises and Paradoxes* (Princeton Architectural Press, 2022).

25. Prominent private industry sources for ESG reporting and data verification in the real estate industry now include some methods for community impact reporting, yet they also acknowledge a lack of clearly defined methods to measure social impacts within the construction industry. See 2023 *GRESB Real Estate Standard and Reference Guide*, Global Real Estate Sustainability Benchmark, https://documents.gresb.com/generated_files/real_estate/2023/real_estate/reference_guide/complete.html; Miguel Ferreira, "Social Risk and Resilience," GRESB, March 22, 2021, https://www.gresb.com/nl-en/social-risk-and-resilience. See also Spenser Robinson and Michael G. McIntosh, "A Literature Review of Environmental, Social, and Governance (ESG) in Commercial Real Estate," *Journal of Real Estate Literature* 30, nos. 1–2 (July 2022): 54–67.

26. Addisu Lashitew, "The Coming of Age of Sustainability Disclosure: How Do Rules Differ Between the US and the EU?," Brookings, June 6, 2022, https://www.brookings.edu; "First Set of Draft European Sustainability Reporting Standards—EFRAG," https://www.efrag.org.

27. Robert C. Ellickson, Vicki Been, Roderick M. Hills, and Christopher Serkin, *Land Use Controls: Cases and Materials*, 5th ed. (Aspen Publishing, 2020), 74.

28. Ellickson, Been, Hills, and Serkin, *Land Use Controls*, 74.

29. The following recent texts discuss the history of zoning and its impact on various aspects of urban form, occupation, and social equity: Ben-Joseph, *Code of the City*; Emily Talen, *City Rules: How Regulations Affect Urban Form*, illus. ed. (Island Press, 2011); Sonia A. Hirt, *Zoned in the USA: The Origins and Implications of American Land-Use Regulation*, illus. ed. (Cornell University Press, 2014).

Type V Chicago

1. See "The Outrage at the City Hall," *Chicago Tribune*, January 16, 1872; and Karen Sawislak, *Smoldering City: Chicagoans and the Great Fire, 1871–1874* (University of Chicago Press, 1995), 149.

2. *Chicago Evening Post*, January 16, 1872, quoted in Christine Rosen, *The Limits of Power: Great Fires and the Process of City Growth in America* (Cambridge University Press, 2003), 103.

3. By 1894, the city of Chicago categorized classes of construction within the fire limits. In addition, groups of components were described as "fireproof," "skeleton," "ordinary," and "slow-burning" construction, precursors to the construction types discussed here. City of Chicago and Henry Binmore, *Laws and Ordinances Governing the City of Chicago: From April 2, 1890, to July 10, 1894; With Notes and Cross References to All Amended and Repealed Sections* (E. B. Myers and Co., 1894), 46–58.

4. For further discussion of industry appropriation of standard-making, see Moore and Wilson, *Questioning Architectural Judgment*, 53–54.

5. D. W. Meinig, *The Shaping of America: A Geographical Perspective on Five Hundred Years of History*, vol. 1: *Atlantic America, 1492–1800* (Yale University Press, 1986), 440. Meinig describes the impressions of European visitors to the United States in 1800, stating, "There was also the middle-class character of society and economy that had been so apparent for more than half a century. And vivifying all these differences were American traits that visitors found so striking: the informality and egalitarianism in manners, the assertive individualism and independence, the pervasive materialism and commercialism, the restlessness and lack of commitment to place or profession. Such features . . . shaped the general concept of an American national character. The staple of America at present consists of land, and the immediate products of land." Meinig also describes how American values resulted in distinct architectural geographies. "If we could map architecture classified into these three types, we would find that which was consciously designed to proclaim national distinctiveness on display. . . . Had we maps of these and other diagnostic features we might bring into clearer view the geographical dynamics of American cultural independence" (437).

6. Daniel E. Turbeville, "Cities of Kindling: Geographical Implications of the Urban Fire Hazard on the Pacific Northwest Coast Frontier, 1851–1920" (PhD diss., Simon Fraser University, 1985).

7. Thomas Jefferson, *Notes on the State of Virginia* (1825 ed.), 211.

8. "On the Architecture of America" (1790), reprinted in *Building the Nation: Americans Write About Their Architecture, Their Cities, and Their Landscape*, ed. Steven Conn and Max Page (University of Pennsylvania Press, 2003), 9–10.

9. William Cronon, *Nature's Metropolis: Chicago and the Great West*, rev. ed. (W. W. Norton, 1992), 169–180.

10. Cronon, *Nature's Metropolis*, 180.

11. Daniel J. Boorstin, *The Americans: The National Experience* (Vintage, 1967), 149.

12. D. H. Jacques, *The House: A Pocket Manual of Rural Architecture; Or, How to Build Country Houses and Out-Buildings . . . With Numerous Original Plans, Designed by F. E. Graef . . . and Others*, Rural Manuals No. 1 (Fowler and Wells, 1859), 34.

13. Jacques, *The House: Manual of Rural Architecture*, 29.

14. Carole Shammas, "The Housing Stock of the Early United States: Refinement Meets Migration," *William and Mary Quarterly* 64, no. 3 (2007): 554.

15. "Eighteen Thousand Buildings Destroyed," *Chicago Tribune*, October 11, 1871.

16. "Eighteen Thousand Buildings Destroyed," *Chicago Tribune*, October 11, 1871.

17. "The Fire Limits: How the Better Class of North Siders Feel on the Subject," *Chicago Tribune*, January 21, 1872.

18. W. B. Ogden, "The Honorable W. B. Ogden's Views: On the Questions of Fire Limits," *Chicago Tribune*, December 3, 1871.

19. Rosen, *Limits of Power*, 165.

20. N. Reeve, "Homes for Workingmen: The Improvement of Chicago by Building Associations," *Chicago Tribune*, August 4, 1872.

21. Bessie Louise Pierce, *History of Chicago*, vol. 3: *The Rise of a Modern City, 1871–1893* (1937; reprint, University of Chicago Press, 2007).

22. "The Fire . . . Fire Limits Made Coexistive with Those of the City," *Chicago Tribune*, July 21, 1874.

23. Rosen, *Limits of Power*, 109.

24. Rosen, *Limits of Power*, 165.

25. Rule-of-thumb rather than precisely measured performance was in keeping with building engineering at the time. In his history of the Chicago skyscraper, architect Tom Leslie points out that the predictable performance of masonry was very much limited due to mortar-mixing imprecision and susceptibility to freeze-and-thaw cycles. Leslie states that "it was impossible to calculate precisely the strength of a masonry pier or wall given these variables, and masonry design and calculation remained entrenched in rule-of-thumb methods." *Chicago Skyscrapers, 1871–1934* (University of Illinois Press, 2013), 5.

26. Murray Tuley, *Laws and Ordinances Governing the City of Chicago* (Bulletin Printing Co., 1873), 18.

27. Francis Adams Egbert, *The Municipal Code of Chicago* (1881), 299.

28. Master Car Builders' Association, *The Car-Builder's Dictionary* (Car Builders' Dictionary and Cyclopedia, 1879).

29. George V. Thompson, "Intercompany Technical Standardization in the Early American Automobile Industry," *Journal of Economic History* 14, no. 1 (1954): 1–20.

30. Susan Tunick and Peter Mauss, *Terra-Cotta Skyline: New York's Architectural Ornament* (Princeton Architectural Press, 1997), 7.

31. "Terra-cotta, Building Blocks of the Past Gain New Life," *Chicago Tribune*, June 11, 1983.

32. Claims of industry influence on building code changes can be seen in *Chicago Tribune* archive articles, including: "Heald Assails Council Unit on Building Code," October 24, 1949.

33. Chicago and Binmore, *Laws and Ordinances, 1890–1894*, 46–58.

34. Chicago and Binmore, *Laws and Ordinances, 1890–1894.*

35. Jeana Ripple, "Building Codes Don't Measure Up: A Case for Urban Material Performance Standards," in *Examining the Environmental Impacts of Materials and Buildings*, ed. Blaine Erickson Brownell (IGI Global, 2020).

36. "According to ASTM E 136, the combustibility of a material is determined by lowering it into a vertical tube furnace at 750 degrees Fahrenheit for periodic measurement of temperature and weight fluctuations. A passing grade launches a material up to international building code (IBC) construction Types I through III depending on its placement in a building. A failing grade relegates it to IBC type IV or more likely type V." Jeana Ripple, "The Type V City: Encoding Material Inequity," *Journal of Architectural Education* 70, no. 1 (2016): 13–16.

37. Sara E. Wermiel, *The Fireproof Building: Technology and Public Safety in the Nineteenth-Century American City* (Johns Hopkins University Press, 2000), 4.

38. Wermiel, *Fireproof Building*, 106.

39. Lynne Mueller, "Sanborn Fire Insurance Maps: History, Use, Availability," *Primary Source* 26, no. 2 (2004): article 2.

40. "Library Announces Digital Map Project," Library of Congress Information Bulletin (December 1997), https://www.loc.gov/loc/lcib/9712/map.html.

41. Hoyt's dissertation was published in book form as *One Hundred Years of Land Values in Chicago: The Relationship of the Growth of Chicago to the Rise in Its Land Values, 1830–1933* (University of Chicago Press, 1933), 107, http://archive.org/details/onehundredyearso00hoytrich.

42. Hoyt, *One Hundred Years of Land Values*, 440.

43. Shammas, "Housing Stock of the Early United States." Shammas also notes that these housing characteristics correlate closely with the rebuilding agenda observed in England and elsewhere in western Europe during the early modern period.

44. Hoyt, *One Hundred Years of Land Values in Chicago*.

45. Homer Hoyt used eight factors to analyze each block in his analytical maps, including average rental rate, total number of residential structures, percentage of residential structures less than fifteen years old, percentage of owner-occupied structures, percentage of structures in need of major repairs, percentage of structures used for commercial purposes, percentage of dwelling units with no private bath, and percentage of nonwhite residents. Hoyt, *The Structure and Growth of Residential Neighborhoods in American Cities* (reprint, Scholarly Press, 1972), 28.

46. Notably, in design education the popularization of overlay mapping is attributed to Ian McHarg, a landscape architect who employed the technique decades later in preservation and landscape design practice. Although McHarg and Hoyt used the same technique, the two men applied overlay mapping quite differently, highlighting the distinct priorities in New Deal–era versus environmental movement–era practices. McHarg used map overlays in 1968, primarily applying cultural and environmental values to development decisions. He measured and mapped historic, water, forest, wildlife, scenic, recreation, residential, institutional, and land values and protected ecological and cultural systems as long-lasting social assets. Hoyt protected investment risk, even at social and ecological cost.

47. Hoyt, *Structure and Growth of Residential Neighborhoods*, 48.

48. Hoyt, *Structure and Growth of Residential Neighborhoods*, 27, 62.

49. Scott N. Markley, Taylor J. Hafley, Coleman A. Allums, Steven R. Holloway, and Hee Cheol Chung, "The Limits of Homeownership: Racial Capitalism, Black Wealth, and the Appreciation Gap in Atlanta," *International Journal of Urban and Regional Research* 44, no. 2 (2020): 310–328.

50. "End of HOLC," *Time* magazine, June 4, 1951.

51. Kenneth T. Jackson, *Crabgrass Frontier: The Suburbanization of the United States* (Oxford University Press, 1987), 198.

52. Hoyt, *One Hundred Years of Land Values*; Robert K. Nelson et al., "Mapping Inequality: Redlining in New Deal America," American Panorama: An Atlas of United States History, https://dsl.richmond.edu/panorama.

53. Jackson, *Crabgrass Frontier*, 198.

54. FHA, *Fifth Annual Report of the Federal Housing Administration* (Government Printing Office, 1939), 42, https://www.huduser.gov/portal.

55. Hoyt, *Structure and Growth of Residential Neighborhoods*.

56. See the Chicago Residential Security Map and Descriptions, at "Mapping Inequality," American Panorama, https://dsl.richmond.edu/panorama. For example, see areas surrounding today's Hyde Park and Woodlawn neighborhoods. Area "D74" is listed as having all brick housing in fair to good condition, but the area is labeled "hazardous" due to (using the racist language of the time) "100% Negro Infiltration." Similarly, "D78," the "Washington Park sub-division of Woodlawn" is described as "blighted." The description goes to great lengths to note a racial restriction for the neighborhood, citing a *Chicago Tribune* article and stating, "The Supreme Court of Illinois on October 10 handed down an opinion which sustains the restrictions in force against Negro occupancy and ownership in

the old Washington Park sub-division, between 60th and 63rd Streets and Cottage Grove and South Park Avenue." The assessment cites "infiltration of Negroes, Jews, and Swedes." This area is marked hazardous despite all brick and stone dwellings in fair condition.

57. US Census Bureau, *American Housing Survey 2019;* Census Bureau, *1940 Census of Housing*, vol. 2: *General Characteristics*; Census Bureau, *1950 Census of Housing*, vol. 1: *General Characteristics*.

58. "Mapping Inequality," American Panorama, https://dsl.richmond.edu/panorama.

59. Renee Y. Chow, *Suburban Space: The Fabric of Dwelling* (University of California Press, 2002), 22.

60. "Minimum Property Standards for One- and Two-Family Dwellings: Part 1," National Institute of Building Sciences, March 2003.

61. "MPS for One- and Two- Family Dwellings: Part 1."

62. Following World War II, the US government created the Veterans' Mortgage Guarantee program to allow the roughly ten million returning veterans to obtain a mortgage loan with no down payment, but the program offered this benefit only to white veterans. For further documentation of racial bias in FHA and HOLC lending practices, see George Lipsitz, *The Possessive Investment in Whiteness: How White People Profit from Identity Politics* (Temple University Press, 2018); and Richard Rothstein, *The Color of Law: A Forgotten History of How Our Government Segregated America* (Liveright, 2017).

63. Amy E. Hillier, "Redlining and the Home Owners' Loan Corporation," *Journal of Urban History* 29, no. 4 (2003), https://doi.org/10.1177/0096144203029004002. More recent scholarship points out that the FHA also produced lending-risk maps that were allegedly destroyed by the agency in the 1970s. Price V. Fishback, Jessica LaVoice, Allison Shertzer, and Randall Walsh, "The HOLC Maps: How Race and Poverty Influenced Real Estate Professionals' Evaluation of Lending Risk in the 1930s," *Journal of Economic History* 83, no. 4 (2023): 1019–1056, doi:10.1017/S0022050723000475. See also "Mapping Inequality," American Panorama, https://dsl.richmond.edu/panorama.

64. Rothstein, *Color of Law*; David Imbroscio, "Race Matters (Even More than You Already Think): Racism, Housing, and the Limits of *The Color of Law*," *Journal of Race, Ethnicity and the City* 2, no. 1 (January 2, 2021): 29–53.

65. Cassie Owens, "Why a Chicago Artist Is Connecting Blight to Gold Bricks," Next City, August 22, 2017, https://nextcity.org/urbanist-news/chicago-artist-exhibit-blight-gold-bricks-amanda-williams.

66. Ben Austen, "The Death and Life of Chicago," *New York Times Magazine*, May 29, 2013.

67. Brian T. Melzer, "Mortgage Debt Overhang: Reduced Investment by Homeowners at Risk of Default," *Journal of Finance*, no. 2 (April 2017): 575–612.

68. John P. Harding, Eric Rosenblatt, and Vincent Yao, "The Contagion Effect of Foreclosed Properties," *Journal of Urban Economics* 66, no. 3 (July 2008): 164–178.

69. Centers for Disease Control, Agency for Toxic Substances and Disease Registry, defines and indexes social vulnerability using its Social Vulnerability Index (SVI). This study used the CDC SVI index as a data point in testing Chicago neighborhoods and also tested the individual factors included within the SVI to discover which social vulnerabilities are most predictive of abandonment and foreclosure rates. The social vulnerability factors included in the model are: percent below poverty line, percent renter occupied homes, percent unemployed, percent high school diploma, percent over age sixty-five, percent under age eighteen, percent disabled, percent minority, percent multiunit housing, percent "crowded" housing units, percent home without vehicle. Regression analysis revealed that the percent of Type V construction statistically explains 8.7 percent of abandonment and 6.9 percent of foreclosure in Chicago neighborhoods. Type V construction had a stronger correlation coefficient (stronger correlative relationship with foreclosure and abandonment) than each of the social vulnerabilities listed above. Data sources

include Chicago Residential Property Characteristics data accessed from the Cook County Assessor (2020), Chicago 311 service requests reporting vacant and abandoned building (2010–2019); Cook County Recorder—Foreclosures, Mortgages, and Quit Claim Deeds (2013–2015); Centers for Disease Control, Agency for Toxic Substances and Disease Registry Social Vulnerability Index (SVI) (2018); and HOLC Residential Security Maps (1935–1940). See also "Mapping Inequality," American Panorama, https://dsl.richmond.edu/panorama.

70. Viktor Mayer-Schönberger and Kenneth Cukier, "Big Data in the Big Apple," *Slate*, March 6, 2013.

71. R. S. Means Company's annual publication of construction industry costs is the source of material and labor cost estimates for each construction element. See Robert Mewis, ed., *Building Construction Costs with R. S. Means Data 2019*, annual ed. (Gordian, 2018). Service life averages across construction elements are provided by the International Association of Certified Home Inspectors, *InterNACHI's Standard Estimated Life Expectancy Chart for Homes*, https://www.nachi.org/life-expectancy.htm.

72. Ripple, "Building Codes Don't Measure Up."

73. Dana Anderson, "The Typical U.S. Home Changes Hands Every 13.2 Years," Redfin Real Estate News, March 2, 2022, https://www.redfin.com/news/2021-homeowner-tenure.

74. Ripple, "Building Codes Don't Measure Up."

75. Based on analysis of Chicago Residential Property Characteristics data accessed from the Cook County Assessor (2020).

76. Data source: Chicago Residential Property Characteristics data accessed from the Cook County Assessor (2020).

77. For further discussion, see J. Lovell, *Building Envelopes: An Integrated Approach* (Princeton Architectural Press, 2010); and S. Moghtadernejad, Luc E. Chouinard, and M. S. Mirza, "Multi-Criteria Decision-Making Methods for Preliminary Design of Sustainable Facades," *Journal of Building Engineering* 19 (2018): 181–190.

78. C. Thormark, "The Effect of Material Choice on the Total Energy Need and Recycling Potential of a Building," *Building and Environment* 41, no. 8 (2006): 1019–1026.

79. Scholarship focused on abandonment risks and impacts tends to ignore building material, while reports on building material maintenance does not connect the potential social and urban impacts. For example, see Zoé Lejeune, Guillaume Xhignesse, Marko Kryvobokov, and Jacques Teller, "Housing Quality as Environmental Inequality: The Case of Wallonia, Belgium," *Journal of Housing and the Built Environment* 31, no. 3 (September 2016): 495–512, which includes household size, occupant density, and the number of bathrooms but fails to test material as a potential risk factor.

Type V New York

1. Samuel Miles Hopkins, *Letters Concerning the General Health: With Notes and Considerable Additions to the Numbers, as They Lately Appeared in the New York Gazette* (Hopkins and Seymour, for Lang and Turner, 1805), 23, 4, 2.

2. See historical documentation of the impacts of building construction on health in Citizens' Association of New York, Council of Hygiene and Public Health, *Report upon the Sanitary Condition of the City* (D. Appleton, 1865); and John Duffy, *History of Public Health in New York City, 1625–1866*, vol. 1 (Russell Sage Foundation, 1968). A more recent publication describing the impact of the built environment is Richard Plunz, *A History of Housing in New York City* (Columbia University Press, 2016).

3. Several prominent contemporary texts describe the city's evolving coastal ecology and public health struggles as they influenced the expansion of the broader metropolis. Matthew Gandy's *Concrete and Clay: Reworking Nature in New York City* (MIT Press, 2003) traces the transition from water resources to urban infrastructures, highlighting health and water access challenges during the city's growth and industrialization. Kara Murphy Schlichting's

New York Recentered: Building the Metropolis from the Shore (University of Chicago Press, 2019) and Carl Zimring and Steven H. Corey's *Coastal Metropolis: Environmental Histories of Modern New York City* (University of Pittsburgh Press, 2021) examine the expansion of New York—the "greater New York metropolitan region"—relative to its coastal economies. In particular, Zimring and Corey highlight the transition in the outer boroughs from a community based on natural ecosystems toward the "reclaiming" of wetlands for residential and business development.

4. New York (Colony), William Walton, and Peter Van Schaack, *Laws of New-York: From the Year 1691, to 1773 Inclusive* (Printed by Hugh Gaine, 1774), 465.

5. New York, *Laws and Ordinances, Ordained and Established by the Mayor, Aldermen, and Commonality of the City of New-York, in Common Council Convened for the Good* (Printed by Goerge F. Hopkins, 1803), 25, 47.

6. Edwin G. Burrows and Mike Wallace, *Gotham: A History of New York City to 1898* (Oxford University Press, 2000), 359.

7. Lloyd G. Steenson, "Putting Disease on the Map: The Early Use of Spot Maps in the Study of Yellow Fever," *Journal of the History of Medicine and Allied Sciences* 20, no. 3 (1965): 235.

8. Burrows and Wallace, *Gotham*, 359.

9. Burrows and Wallace, *Gotham*, 359.

10. Philip Ashton Rollins and Samuel L. Mitchill, "The Medical Repository," in *Medical Repository of Original Essays and Intelligence Relative to Physic, Surgery, Chemistry, and Natural History*, ser. 1, vol. 1, 3rd ed., 1797–1824, 124.

11. Rollins and Mitchill, "The Medical Repository," 130.

12. See further details of disease outbreak and water infrastructural development in Gandy, *Concrete and Clay*, 24–32.

13. Lionel Pincus and Princess Firyal Map Division, New York Public Library, *The Firemen's Guide: A Map of the City of New-York, Showing the Fire Districts, Fire Limits, Hydrants . . .* (1834), New York Public Library Digital Collections, https://digitalcollections.nypl.org/items/510d47df-e52f-a3d9-e040-e00a18064a99.

14. John H. Griscom, *The Sanitary Condition of the Laboring Population of New York: With Suggestions for Its Improvement* (Harper & Brothers, 1845), 9.

15. See Duffy, *History of Public Health in New York City*, 302–308; and Alexander von Hoffman, *The Origins of American Housing Reform* (Joint Center for Housing, Harvard University, 1998), 8.

16. Health Department, City of New York, Tenement House Acts, Chapter 908, Laws of 1867, 4–5.

17. William J. Fryer, *The Tenement House Law of the City of New York* (Record and Guide, 1901).

18. "Tuberculosis window" is a nickname given to interior windows separating the first interior room and the front parlor or kitchen, which typically faced the street, as required by the 1901 Tenement House Law of New York. The resulting improved interior ventilation was a strategy to fight the prevalence of disease in the tenements, particularly tuberculosis. The regulation states: "No room in a new existing tenement house shall here-after be occupied for living purposes unless it shall have a window upon the street, or on a yard not less than five feet deep, or upon a court or shaft of not less than twenty-five square feet in area, open to the sky without roof or skylight, or unless such a room has a sash window opening into an adjoining room in the same apartment which itself has a window opening onto the street, or on a yard not less than five feet deep" (§79: Rooms, Lighting, and Ventilation of," in Fryer, *Tenement House Law*. The tenement housing acts demonstrated some measures of material adaptation to moisture, even while they neglected to tune the building infrastructure to an urban topographic logic.

19. Steven Kurutz, "When There Was Water, Water Everywhere," *New York Times*, June 11, 2006.

20. Egbert L. Viele, "Principles and Practice of Drainage and Sewerage, in Connection with Water-Supplies," *Public Health Papers and Reports* 2 (1875): 335–336.

21. NYC, W. Ash, and Mark Ash, *The Building Code of the City of New York as Constituted by the Greater New York Charter, Enacted in 1899* . . . (Baker & Voorhis & Co., 1899), 26.

22. William J. Broad, "How the Ice Age Shaped New York," *New York Times*, June 5, 2018.

23. Broad, "How the Ice Age Shaped New York."

24. Jasper Danckaerts, *Journal of Jasper Danckaerts, 1679–1680*, in *Original Narratives of Early American History*, ed. J. Franklin Jameson (Charles Scribner's Sons, 1913), 60, https://www.loc.gov/item/13013556.

25. Henry R. Stiles, ed., *History of King's County, Including Brooklyn* (W. W. Munsell & Co., 1884), 38.

26. See Frederick Black, *Jamaica Bay: A History* (Department of the Interior, 1981); and Henry Reed Stiles, L. B. Proctor, and L. P. Brockett, *The Civil, Political, Professional and Ecclesiastical History, and Commercial and Industrial Record of the County of Kings and the City of Brooklyn, N.Y., from 1683 to 1884* (Munsell and Co., 1884), https://archive.org/details/cu31924088998061.

27. Gertrude Lefferts Vanderbilt, *The Social History of Flatbush, and Manners and Customs of the Dutch Settlers in Kings County* (D. Appleton & Co., 1881), 175.

28. Frederick J. H. [James Hamilton] Merrill, *New York City Folio: Paterson, Harlem, Staten Island, and Brooklyn Quadrangles, New York–New Jersey* (US Geological Survey, 1902), 13–14.

29. The 1914 building codes set fire limits in Brooklyn just north of the glacial ridgeline parks, with no construction requirements beyond this limit in the outwash plains. By 1916, the fire limits expanded to the southern side of the same parks and "suburban limits," allowing wood-frame construction in the outwash plain areas. NYC, "An Ordinance Adopting the Building Code of the City of New York" (1914), in *Building Code: City of New York, Borough of Manhattan . . . Bureau of Buildings . . .* (1916).

30. New York Public Library. "Use District Map" [1916], New York Public Library Digital Collections, https://digitalcollections.nypl.org/items/1496eff0-c605-012f-d01e-58d385a7bc34.

31. NYC, *Building Code: City of New York, Borough of Manhattan* . . . (1916), 29–30.

32. Raphael Fischler, "The Metropolitan Dimension of Early Zoning: Revisiting the 1916 New York City Ordinance," *Journal of the American Planning Association* (November 2007): 171.

33. See §BC D105, "Exceptions to Restrictions in Fire District," in "2022 Construction Codes—Buildings," https://www.nyc.gov/site/buildings/codes/2022-construction-codes.page#bldgs. In appendix D: "One- or two-family detached or semidetached dwellings of two stories or less in height and 2,500 square feet (232 m^2) or less in area per story located within Zoning Districts R-2 through R-5 may be constructed or reconstructed of construction Type VA, or if damaged for any cause only the damaged portions shall be required to be reconstructed to conform to Type VA construction. In addition, one-family dwellings located within Zoning District R-1 anywhere in the city, may be constructed of Type VB construction in conformance with the area and height limits established by Tables 504.3, 504.4 and 506.2 of this code."

34. NYC, *Building Code of the City of New York: With Amendments to April 12, 1906* (M. B. Brown Press, 1906), 39; NYC, *Building Code City of New York, Borough of Manhattan* . . . (1916), 50; City of Chicago, *Laws and Ordinances Governing the City of Chicago: April 1890 to July 1894* (1894), 46–58.

35. NYC, *Building Code of the City of New York: With Amendments to April 12, 1906*, 39; NYC, *Building Code City of New York, Borough of Manhattan* (1916), 50.

36. New York (Colony), Walton, and Van Schaack, *Laws of New-York: 1691 to 1773* (1774), 465; David W. Chen, "In New York, Drawing Flood Maps Is a 'Game of Inches,'" *New York Times*, January 8, 2018.

37. Zimring and Corey, *Coastal Metropolis*, 40.

38. Zimring and Corey, *Coastal Metropolis*, 42.

39. Black, *Jamaica Bay*, 84.

40. "Jamaica Bay, Foul with Sewage, Closed to Oyster Beds," *New York Times*, January 30, 1921.

41. "Jamaica Bay, Foul with Sewage," *New York Times*, January 30, 1921.

42. "Brooklyn's Flooded Districts," *New York Times*, December 29, 1888.

43. "Flood in Brooklyn Cuts Water Supply," *New York Times*, August 22, 1928; "Flood Damage Here from 36-Hour Rain; Sidewalks Cave In," *New York Times*, February 8, 1929; "Storm Sweeps City: High Wind Fells Fifty Trees in Brooklyn . . . Many Cellars Flooded," *New York Times*, November 20, 1932.

44. Black, *Jamaica Bay*, 76.

45. Dorothy M. Peteet et al., "Sediment Starvation Destroys New York City Marshes' Resistance to Sea Level Rise," *Proceedings of the National Academy of Sciences* 115, no. 41 (October 2018): 10, 281, 286; "An Update on the Disappearing Salt Marshes," Gateway National Recreation Area, National Park Service, US Department of the Interior, Jamaica Bay Watershed Protection Plan Advisory Committee, August 2, 2007.

46. "Fund Appeal Renewed" *New York Times*, August 22, 1951.

47. Timothy W. Kneeland, "The Risky Business of Flood Control: When Dams and Levees Put People at Risk," in *Playing Politics with Natural Disaster: Hurricane Agnes, the 1972 Election, and the Origins of FEMA*, ed. Timothy W. Kneeland (Cornell University Press, 2020).

48. Raymond J. Burby, "Hurricane Katrina and the Paradoxes of Government Disaster Policy: Bringing About Wise Governmental Decisions for Hazardous Areas," *Annals of the American Academy of Political and Social Science* 604, no. 1 (March 2006): 171–191.

49. Kneeland, *Playing Politics with Natural Disaster*, 18; Jeroen C. J. H. Aerts and W. J. Wouter Botzen, "Flood-Resilient Waterfront Development in New York City: Bridging Flood Insurance, Building Codes, and Flood Zoning," *Annals of the New York Academy of Sciences* 1227, no. 1 (June 2011): 27.

50. Burby, "Hurricane Katrina and Government Disaster Policy."

51. NYC, "Local Laws of the City of New York for the Year 1983," no. 58, December 13, 1983.

52. Testimony of W. Craig Fugate, Administrator, Federal Emergency Management Agency, Before the House Appropriations Committee, Subcommittee on Homeland Security, March 13, 2013.

53. Barry Yanowitz, "A Stronger, More Resilient New York," *PlanNYC* (NYC Economic Development Corp., 2013).

54. S. Narayan et al., "Coastal Wetlands and Flood Damage Reduction: Using Risk Industry–Based Models to Assess Natural Defenses in the Northeastern USA" (October 2016), The Nature Conservancy, https://www.nature.org/en-us.

55. Sarah Maslin Nir, "Questions Emerge About the Mold That Hurricane Sandy Left Behind," *New York Times*, March 2, 2013.

56. Hurricane Sandy Rebuilding Task Force, "Hurricane Sandy Rebuilding Strategy: Stronger Communities, a Resilient Region" (August 2013), https://www.hud.gov/sites/documents/HSREBUILDINGSTRATEGY.PDF.

57. FEMA, "Building Science Support and Code: Changes Aiding Sandy Recovery Hurricane Sandy Recovery, Fact Sheet No. 3" (November 2014), https://www.fema.gov/sites/default/files/documents/fema_building-science-support-code-changes-sandy.pdf.

58. Office of NYC Comptroller Brad Lander, "Ten Years After Sandy" (October 13, 2022), https://comptroller.nyc.gov/reports/ten-years-after-sandy.

59. Christie Thompson, Theodoric Meyer, and Al Shaw, "Fed Flood Maps Left NY Unprepared for Sandy—and FEMA Knew It," Podcast (December 6, 2013), WNYC, https://www.wnyc.org.

60. Corinne Ramey, "New York Disputes FEMA on Flood Risk," *Wall Street Journal*, August 18, 2015. New Yorkers are "federally required to have flood insurance if they live in a high-risk flood zone and have a federally backed mortgage; they previously received federal disaster assistance for flood damage." https://access.nyc.gov/programs/national-flood-insurance-program.

61. Daniel Zarilli, "Appeal of FEMA's Preliminary Flood Insurance Rate Maps for New York City," NYC Office of Recovery and Resiliency, 2015.

62. Ramey, "New York Disputes FEMA on Flood Risk," *Wall Street Journal*, August 18, 2015.

63. The buildings in the "flux zone" (area between the expanded 2015 and reduced 2018 FEMA flood zone maps) include 15,761 Types I–IV structures and 24,948 Type V structures (i.e., 60 percent single-family Type V construction). Results based on FEMA maps retrieved from FEMA map service center (2019) and property assessment data retrieved from NYC Department of Information Technology & Telecommunications [NYDOITT], NYC Open Data (2017), Property Valuation and Assessment Data, NYC Department of Finance.

64. Chen, "Drawing Flood Maps," *New York Times*, January 8, 2018.

65. Jaclyn Jeffrey-Wilensky, "The Legacy of 'Sandy Cough' and Why Mold Is Still a Major Problem After Storms," *Gothamist*, October 20, 2022, https://gothamist.com/news.

66. Greg B. Smith, "Mold Plagues Homes Flooded During Hurricane Sandy: Deadly Spores Cause Breathing and Other Health-Related Problems," *New York Daily News*, February 10, 2013.

67. Lisa M. Gargano, Sean Locke, Hannah T. Jordan, and Robert M. Brackbill, "Lower Respiratory Symptoms Associated with Environmental and Reconstruction Exposures After Hurricane Sandy," *Disaster Medicine and Public Health Preparedness* 12, no. 6 (December 2018): 697–702.

68. Regression analysis based on mold violation reports and property assessment material data. Sources: "311 Service Requests from 2010 to Present," NYC Open Data (2019), NYDOITT website; NYC Open Data (2017), Property Valuation and Assessment data, NYC Department of Finance: "Census tracts with more than 50% Type V construction within the inundation zone show a rate of 121% of mold violation reports compared to the city's median rate. Communities with less than 50% Type V construction tracts show a rate of 72% compared to the city's median." See also Ripple, "Building Codes Don't Measure Up."

69. In the city overall, poverty is a more significant risk factor for predicting mold violation reports: high-poverty areas show an additional 30 percent increase in average violations for the dense Type V neighborhoods within the inundation zone. It is also important to note that this analysis relies on mold-violation reports made to the city via 311 self-reporting. These reports are almost exclusively made within renter-occupied units to trigger city inspections. Therefore, the poverty and mold violation correlation may appear more prominent in part because higher-poverty neighborhoods are also higher in rental occupancies.

70. Marcus Vitruvius Pollio, "The Architecture of Vitruvius, Book I," in *The Architecture of Marcus Vitruvius Pollio: In Ten Books*, translated by Joseph Gwilt (Cambridge University Press, 2015), 17.

71. Vitruvius, "Building Materials," in *Vitruvius: Ten Books on Architecture*, ed. Ingrid D. Rowland and Thomas Noble Howe (Cambridge University Press, 1999), 43.

72. HUD, "Review of Structural Materials and Methods for Home Building in the United States: 1900 to 2000" (January 25, 2001), https://www.huduser.gov/portal/Publications/PDF/review.pdf.

73. *The Building Code of the City of New York* (Department of Buildings, 1909), 118.

74. HUD, "Review of Structural Materials: 1900 to 2000."

75. HUD, "Review of Structural Materials: 1900 to 2000," 12.

76. Michael A. Dunn, Richard P. Vlosky, and Todd F. Shupe, "What Homebuilders Think of Southern Yellow Pine Lumber," Louisiana State University AgCenter, October 12, 2015, https://www.lsuagcenter.com.

77. Robinson Meyer, "Lumber Prices Are off the Rails Again: Blame Climate Change," *The Atlantic*, January 19, 2022; Clarisa Diaz, "North American Lumber Is Moving South," *Quartz*, October 28, 2022, https://qz.com/north-american-lumber-is-moving-south-1849699339.

78. Sini Metsä-Kortelainen and Hannu Viitanen, "Decay Resistance of Sapwood and Heartwood of Untreated and Thermally Modified Scots Pine and Norway Spruce Compared with Some Other Wood Species," *Wood Material Science and Engineering* 4, nos. 3–4 (September 2009): 105–114.

79. Ripple, "Type V City."

80. American Wood Council, *Wood Structural Design Data*, 1986.

81. See Ripple, "Type V City," 13–16; see also W. Simpson and A. TenWolde, "Physical Properties and Moisture Relations of Wood," in *Wood Handbook—Wood as an Engineering Material* (Forest Products Laboratory, 1999), 463.

82. "History of APA, Plywood, and Engineered Wood" (n.d.), APA, https://www.apawood.org/apas-history.

83. W. J. Fisk, Q. Lei-Gomez, and M. Mendell, "Meta-Analyses of the Associations of Respiratory Health Effects with Dampness and Mold in Homes," *Indoor Air* 17, no. 4 (2007): 284–296.

84. J. W. Lstiburek, "BSI-027: Material View of Mold" (November 11, 2009), Building Science Corporation, https://buildingscience.com.

85. W. B. Rose, *Water in Buildings: An Architect's Guide to Moisture and Mold* (Wiley, 2005).

86. J. W. Lstiburek, "BSI-084: Forty Years of Air Barriers—The Evolution of the Residential Air Barrier" (February 15, 2015), Building Science Corporation, https://buildingscience.com.

87. *New York City Building Code* (2008). See also *Building Code of the City of New York* (1968), Local Law No. 76, Effective December 6, 1968; and *Building Code of the City of New York* (1938).

88. For example, Sears, Roebuck and Co. produced two types of precut structural framing systems: one using the "honor-built" system and the other using the "standard-built" system, both of which used one-by-six exterior wood siding. See HUD, "Review of Structural Materials: 1900 to 2000," 12.

89. Vitruvius is one of the first authors to mention lead poisoning in reference to lead pipes. See "Commentary," in Rowland and Howe, *Vitruvius: Ten Books on Architecture*, 135–318.

90. In 1897, A. J. Turner published a comprehensive review of seventy-six cases of lead poisoning treated at the Brisbane Children's Hospital, Australia, seven of which ended fatally. He covered paralytic cases characterized by footdrop and wristdrop, abdominal pain, pain in limbs, and epileptic convulsions. See Herbert L. Needleman, *Human Lead Exposure* (CRC Press, 1991).

91. M. A. Smith, "Lead in History," in *The Lead Debate: The Environmental Toxicology and Child Health* (Croom Helm, 1984), 24.

92. Gerald Markowitz and David Rosner, *Lead Wars: The Politics of Science and the Fate of America's Children* (University of California Press, 2013), 27.

93. Jacqueline M. Chiofalo, Maxine Golub, Casey Crump, and Neil Calman, "Pediatric Blood Lead Levels Within New York City Public Versus Private Housing, 2003–2017,"

American Journal of Public Health 109, no. 6 (June 2019): 907; Matthew L. Wald, "Lead Paint: New Rules, Old Questions," *New York Times*, February 12, 1995.

94. Lisa M. Nicholson, Kent P. Schwirian, and Patricia M. Schwirian, "Childhood Lead Poisoning Laws in New York City: Environment, Politics and Social Action," *Children, Youth and Environments* 20, no. 1 (2010): 179.

95. Wald, "Lead Paint," *New York Times*, February 12, 1995.

96. HUD, "National Survey of Lead-Based Paint in Housing" (June 1995), HUD Contract Number HC-5848 and EPA Contract Numbers 68-D9-0174, 68-D2-0139, and 68-D3-0011, 2–2.

97. "Blood Lead Reference Value" (December 2, 2022), CDC, https://www.cdc.gov.

98. Joseph R. Downes, "Lead Hazards in U.S. Housing: The American Healthy Homes Survey II," *PDR Edge*, March 2022, https://www.huduser.gov/Portal/pdredge/pdr-edge-trending-030822.html.

99. Katherine A. Ahrens, Barbara A. Haley, Lauren M. Rossen, Patricia C. Lloyd, and Yutaka Aoki, "Housing Assistance and Blood Lead Levels: Children in the United States, 2005–2012," *American Journal of Public Health* 106, no. 11 (November 2016): 2049–2056.

100. Elise Gould, "Childhood Lead Poisoning: Conservative Estimates of the Social and Economic Benefits of Lead Hazard Control," *Environmental Health Perspectives* 117 (July 2009): 1162–1167.

101. "The Precautionary Principle: Definitions, Applications and Governance" (December 9, 2015), Think Tank, European Parliament, https://www.europarl.europa.eu/thinktank/en/document/EPRS_IDA(2015)573876.

102. American Academy of Pediatrics Committee on Environmental Hazards and Committee on Accident and Poison Prevention, "Statement on Childhood Lead Poisoning," *Pediatrics* 79, no. 3 (March 1987).

103. Eric Lipton, and Rachel Abrams, "The Uphill Battle to Better Regulate Formaldehyde," *New York Times*, May 4, 2015.

104. New York City reporting is based on an 84 percent test rate for children below three years of age and includes more than 400,000 new tests per year. In a multivariable regression analysis explaining 56 percent of the variation in BLL elevation across census tracts, Type V housing had a stronger correlation to BLL than rates of renter occupancy. The regression analysis is based on a BLL report ("Lead Poisoning in New York City: Continued Decline in 2012," NYC Department of Health and Mental Hygiene, March 2014) and Property Assessment Material Data, NYC Open Data, Property Valuation and Assessment data, NYC Department of Finance, 2017. The numeric results are as follows: R-squared = 56 percent; 3 variables include percent Type V construction, percent renter occupied homes, and percent population over 65. Coefficients for the three statistically significant variables are 1.16, 0.42, and 0.01, respectively. Census tracts with more than 50 percent Type V construction correspond to an average elevated BLL rate of 3.73 percent per 1,000 children tested. Census tracts with less than 50 percent Type V construction correspond to an average elevated BLL rate of 2.59 percent per 1,000 children tested. The average city rate overall was 2.99 percent per 1,000, and high-poverty neighborhoods correspond to a rate of 2.8 percent per 1,000. In this study, a neighborhood is considered "high poverty" if 12 percent or more of the population was living below the poverty line according to 2019 census data.

105. See patent: Sheila M. Tinetti, Paul Foley, Li Wang, Michael V. Enzien, and Sanjay B. Bishnoi, Mold-resistant wallboard, World Intellectual Property Organization WO2008091794A2, filed January 18, 2008, and issued July 31, 2008, https://patents.google.com/patent/WO2008091794A2/en.

106. PCP was one of the most used biocides from 1950 to 1987, and CCA's common use spanned from 1970 to 2003. See further information, including current allowable uses, at US EPA, OCSPP, "Overview of Wood Preservative Chemicals" (June 3, 2024), https://www.epa.gov/ingredients-used-pesticide-products.

107. L. Coudert, J.-F. Blais, G. Mercier, P. Cooper, and A. Janin, "Remediation Processes for Wood Treated with Organic and/or Inorganic Preservatives," in *Handbook of Recycled Concrete and Demolition Waste*, ed. F. Pacheco-Torgal, V. W. Y. Tam, J. A. Labrincha, Y. Ding, and J. de Brito (Woodhead Publishing, 2013), 527; Athena S. Jones et al., "Arsenic, Copper, and Chromium from Treated Wood Products in the U.S. Disposal Sector," *Waste Management* 87 (March 2019): 731–740.

108. US EPA, OCSPP, "Chromated Arsenicals (CCA)" (January 16, 2014), https://www.epa.gov/ingredients-used-pesticide-products.

109. Dennis Jones and Christian Brischke, eds., "Performance of the Bio-Based Materials," in *Performance of Bio-Based Building Materials* (Woodhead Publishing, 2017), 249–333.

110. Australian Standard AS 5604-2005, Table A1. See also Colin MacKenzie, *Timber Service Life and Durability* (Forest and Wood Products Australia, 2012), 20.

111. European Committee for Standardization, tables 2 and 3 in European Standard EN 350-2:1994, "Durability of Wood and Wood-Based Products—Natural Durability of Solid Wood—Part 2: Guide to Natural Durability and Treatability of Selected Wood Species of Importance in Europe" (1994).

112. NYC, *New York City Building Code* (2008), §2304.12.1.

113. FEMA, "Flood Damage–Resistant Materials Requirements for Buildings Located in Special Flood Hazard Areas in Accordance with the National Flood Insurance Program," *Technical Bulletin 2* (August 2008), 7.

114. See AWPA, "Sponsor List" and "Standards," https://awpa.com/sponsors/list and https://awpa.com/standards.

115. Paul Morris, Peter Laks, and Stan Lebow, "Standardization of Naturally Durable Wood Species" in *Proceedings: 107th Annual Meeting of the American Wood Protection Association*, Marriot Harbor Beach Hotel, Fort Lauderdale, May 15–17, 2011, 154–164.

116. Morris, Laks, and Lebow, "Standardization of Naturally Durable Wood Species," 155.

117. Morris, Laks, and Lebow, "Standardization of Naturally Durable Wood Species," 155.

118. State of California, "DTSC Requirements for Generators of Treated Wood Waste (TWW) Fact Sheet" (September 2021), Department of Toxic Substances Control, https://dtsc.ca.gov/requirements-for-generators-of-treated-wood-waste-tww-fact-sheet.

119. Fernando Pacheco-Torgal, Yining Ding, Joao Labrincha, Vivian Tam, and Jorge de Brito, *Handbook of Recycled Concrete and Demolition Waste* (Elsevier Science & Technology, 2013), 527–528.

120. Jones, "Arsenic, Copper, and Chromium from Treated Wood Products," 731–740.

121. P. A. Cooper, "Disposal of Treated Wood Removed from Service: The Issues," in *Proceedings: Environmental Considerations in the Manufacture, Use, and Disposal of Preservative-Treated Wood* (Carolinas-Chesapeake Section of the Forest Products Society, May 13, 1993); C. C. Felton and R. C. De Groot, "The Recycling Potential of Preservative-Treated Wood," *Forest Products Journal* 46, nos. 7–8 (1996): 37.

122. Cooper, "Disposal of Treated Wood"; Felton and De Groot, "Recycling Potential of Preservative-Treated Wood."

123. EPA, Office of Inspector General, "EPA Has Developed Guidelines for Disaster Debris but Has Limited Knowledge of State Preparedness," Report No. 16-P-0219 (June 29, 2016), https://www.epa.gov/sites/default/files/2016-06/documents/20160629-16-p-0219.pdf.

124. Vince Elias, "Recovery Field Office Completes Mammoth New York Debris Removal Mission," US Army Corps of Engineers, New York District (June 26, 2013), https://www.nad.usace.army.mil/Media; Philip T. McCreanor, "Disaster Debris Management–Planning Tools," *US Environmental Protection Agency Region IV* (1999).

125. Brajesh Dubey, Helena M. Solo-Gabriele, and Timothy G. Townsend, "Quantities of Arsenic-Treated Wood in Demolition Debris Generated by Hurricane Katrina," *Environmental Science and Technology* 41, no. 5 (March 2007): 1533–1536.

126. Anemona Hartocollis and Julie Turkewitz, "Storm Victims, in Cleanup, Face Rise in Injuries and Illness," *New York Times*, November 20, 2012.

127. "Finding High Lead Levels in Residents' Blood After Hurricane Sandy," NJ Spotlight News.org, April 22, 2015.

128. New York City's flood-resistant requirements reference FEMA federal flood-resistant mandates: "Flood Damage–Resistant Materials Requirements for Buildings Located in Special Flood Hazard Areas in Accordance with the National Flood Insurance Program," *FEMA Technical Bulletin 2* (August 2008), 7.

129. Hopkins, *Letters Concerning the General Health*, 23.

Type V Philadelphia

1. Juliana Feliciano Reyes, "Broken Rung: The Building Trades First Organized in Philadelphia: Black People Never Got a Fair Shot at Their Jobs," *Philadelphia Inquirer*, August 30, 2022.

2. Statistics cited in the text were generated by Jeana Ripple using data.census.gov, March 16, 2021; see US Census Bureau, Current Population Survey: Annual Social and Economic (March) Supplement: 2014–2020 (hereafter ASEC), https://www.census.gov/data/datasets/time-series/demo/cps/cps-asec.html.

3. Reyes, "Broken Rung," *Philadelphia Inquirer*, August 30, 2022.

4. Matthew Countryman, *Up South: Civil Rights and Black Power in Philadelphia* (University of Pennsylvania Press, 2007), 64.

5. "Bricklayer Balks at Crossing Picketers: Defies Union Order for Benefit of Kids' Future," *Philadelphia Tribune*, June 1, 1963.

6. Thomas J. Sugrue, "Affirmative Action from Below: Civil Rights, the Building Trades, and the Politics of Racial Equality in the Urban North, 1945–1969," *Journal of American History* 91, no. 1 (2004): 219.

7. See Justin Gammage, "Black Power and the Power of Protest: Re-Examining Approaches for Radical Economic Development," *Review of Black Political Economy* 44, nos. 1–2 (January 2017): 23–36. See also Countryman, *Up South*; and Sugrue, "Affirmative Action from Below."

8. Sugrue, "Affirmative Action from Below," 146.

9. National Urban League, *Negro Membership in American Labor Unions* (Negro Universities Press, 1969), 41.

10. Timothy J. Lombardo, *Blue-Collar Conservatism: Frank Rizzo's Philadelphia and Populist Politics* (University of Pennsylvania Press, 2018), 104. The *1940 Census of Housing* reports 92 percent brick buildings in Philadelphia (with frame buildings constituting 3 percent and stucco 2 percent). Contemporary data brings the brick masonry total up to 94.3 percent brick masonry, 2.6 percent stone, and 2.3 percent frame buildings. See US Census Bureau, *1940 Census of Housing*, Vol. 2: *General Characteristics*; Philadelphia Open Data, Philadelphia Properties and Assessment (2022).

11. *US Congressional Record, 115, Part 30 (December 19, 1969, to December 23, 1969)* (Government Printing Office, 1969). The Philadelphia Plan focused on the "mechanical trades": e.g., electricians, plumbers. See US Department of Labor, "Public Hearing for the Purpose of Providing Information to Be Used by the Department of Labor in Devising Definite Standards and Goals of Minority Manpower Utilization Pursuant to the Revised Philadelphia Plan" (Atlas Reporting Service, 1969), 329.

12. Roger William Moss Jr., "Master Builders: A History of the Colonial Philadelphia Building Trades" (PhD diss., University of Delaware, 1972), 2.

13. Heinrich Ries and Henry Leighton, *History of the Clay-Working Industry in the United States* (J. Wiley & Sons, 1909), 196–197.

14. The 1841 ordinances outline funding sources "to pull down and remove all wooden buildings, as well [as] those made of wood and other combustible materials

as those called brick-paned, or frame buildings, filled in with bricks, that are erected within the limits of the city of Philadelphia; and also to prohibit the erection of any such building within the said city's limits at any future time." Authority of Councils, "Ordinances of the Corporation of the City of Philadelphia, and Acts of Assembly" (1841), 94. By 1851, Philadelphia ordinances described both the authority to remove wood buildings and penalties for erecting any wood or combustible building within the city limits. "Ordinances of the Corporation of the City of Philadelphia, and Acts of Assembly" (1851), 51, 433.

15. *Encyclopedia of Greater Philadelphia*, "Brickmaking and Brickmakers," by Tamara Gaskell and Sara K. Filik, 2017, philadelphiaencyclopedia.org.

16. David Montgomery, *The Fall of the House of Labor: The Workplace, the State, and American Labor Activism, 1865–1925* (Cambridge University Press, 1989).

17. Department of Labor, *Public Hearing . . . Pursuant to the Revised Philadelphia Plan*, 329.

18. W. E. B. Du Bois and Isabel Eaton, *The Philadelphia Negro: A Social Study* (University of Pennsylvania, 1899), 130.

19. Du Bois and Eaton, *The Philadelphia Negro*, 128.

20. Philadelphia, *Ordinances of the City of Philadelphia from January 1 to December 31, 1905, and Opinions of the City Solicitor* (Dunlap Printing Co., 1906), 303.

21. For example, ordinances in the city of Philadelphia in 1905 spend over two hundred pages (beginning at p. 142) describing various salaries for public work, including specifying companies to receive contracts (pp. 258, 262) and union wages to be paid for specific trades (p. 303). See *Ordinances, January 1 to December 31, 1905*. By contrast, Boston's 1908 statutes describe the city's material regulations, salaries of public officials, teachers, and prison workers, and certification required for some skilled labor. It does not describe building labor appropriations or salaries. See *The Consolidated Statutes Relating to the City of Boston* (Municipal Printing Office, 1908.)

22. Population figures from US census data from 1910, 1920, 1930, 1940, 1970, and 2019, accessed through Social Explorer (based on data digitally transcribed by Inter-university Consortium for Political and Social Research, edited and verified by Michael Haines), https://www.socialexplorer.com.

23. Du Bois and Eaton, *Philadelphia Negro*, 100, 128, 295.

24. In 1950, Black Americans comprised 10 percent of the total population; see NAACP, *The Negro Wage-Earner and Apprenticeship Training Programs: A Critical Analysis, with Recommendations* (Labor Dept., NAACP, 1960), 8; Campbell Gibson and Kay Jung, *Historical Census Statistics on Population Totals by Race, 1790 to 1990, and by Hispanic Origin, 1970 to 1990, for the United States, Regions, Divisions, and States*, US Census Bureau Working Paper Series No. 56, September 2002.

25. Lombardo, *Blue-Collar Conservatism*, 104, 118.

26. Mark Bricklin, "Protest Links Pickets with Common Bond: School Kids Show Up Bringing Dogs, Each Outburst Unites Spectators with Cause," *Philadelphia Tribune*, June 1, 1963. The expression, "We're tired of carrying bricks" likely refers to the common relegation of Black laborers to strenuous manual labor such as hod-carrier positions.

27. Countryman, *Up South*, 140.

28. Juliana Feliciano Reyes, "How Black Workers Got Locked Out of Construction's Best Jobs," *Philadelphia Inquirer*, August 8, 2022.

29. "City Urged to Hit Biased Labor Unions in Wallets: Halt Construction on All Buildings Until Agreement," *Philadelphia Tribune*, May 4, 1963.

30. City of Philadelphia Commission on Human Relations, "Re: Investigation into Alleged Discrimination by Employers, Labor Unions and Others on Public Works Contracts in the City of Philadelphia, Further Public Hearing" (May 8, 1963), Philadelphia Department of Records, City Archives, 403.

31. Philadelphia Commission on Human Relations, "Conclusions and Recommendations Pertaining to Employment Discrimination on Certain City Work Contracts and in the Construction Trades" (May 20, 1963), Philadelphia Department of Records, City Archives.

32. Philadelphia Commission on Human Relations, "Conclusions and Recommendations" (May 20, 1963).

33. Department of Labor, *Public Hearing . . . Pursuant to the Revised Philadelphia Plan*, 315.

34. Arthur A. Fletcher, "Statement by Arthur A. Fletcher, Assistant Secretary for Wage and Labor Standards, US Department of Labor," 60th Annual NAACP Convention, Jackson, MS, July 2, 1969 (Remarks at the Signing of the Philadelphia Plan), Library of Congress, 1969.

35. NAACP, *The Negro Wage-Earner*, 8.

36. *Congressional Record, 115, Part 30 (December 19, 1969, to December 23, 1969)*, H: 40920.

37. *Congressional Record, 115, Part 30 (December 19, 1969, to December 23, 1969)*, H: 40920.

38. US Census Bureau, "PHC(2)-40, Pennsylvania, General Demographic Trends in Metropolitan Areas, 1960 to 1970," in *1970 Census of Population and Housing*.

39. Lombardo, *Blue-Collar Conservatism*, 120.

40. US Department of Labor, Bureau of Labor Statistics, "Bulletin No. 1590, Union Wages and Hours: Building Trades," July 1, 1967, https://fraser.stlouisfed.org/files/docs/publications/bls/bls_1590_1968.pdf.

41. Thomas C. Mobley, "Union Wage Scales in Building Trades, 1960," *Monthly Labor Review* 84, no. 5 (1961): 513–516.

42. Richard O'Keefe, "Housing Costs Boosted by Multiplicity of Codes," *Philadelphia Inquirer*, January 9, 1948.

43. O'Keefe, "Housing Costs Boosted by Codes," *Philadelphia Inquirer*, January 9, 1948.

44. Jenny Hohenstein, "Historical Philadelphia Building Code Research," Jenkins Law Library, March 3, 2020, https://www.jenkinslaw.org/blog/2020/03/03/historical-philadelphia-building-code-research.

45. City of Philadelphia, *Code of General Ordinances of the City of Philadelphia* (February 29, 1956), 88–89.

46. Hohenstein, "Historical Philadelphia Building Code Research," Jenkins Law Library, March 3, 2020.

47. O'Keefe, "Housing Costs Boosted by Codes," *Philadelphia Inquirer*, January 9, 1948.

48. Comptroller General of the US, *Problems in the Program for Rehabilitating Housing to Provide Homes for Low-Income Families in Philadelphia* (HUD, March 19, 1971), 40.

49. Alastair McFarlane, Janet Li, and Michael Hollar, "Building Codes: What Are They Good For?," *CityScape* 21, no. 1 (2021): 101–132.

50. Chris Benner and Alex Karner, "Low-Wage Jobs-Housing Fit: Identifying Locations of Affordable Housing Shortages," *Urban Geography* 37, no. 6 (August 2016): 883–903.

51. City of Philadelphia, Mayor's Advisory Commission on Construction Industry Diversity, *Report and Recommendations*, (March 2009), https://www.econsult.com/wp-content/uploads/2014/09/031609_MACCID_Full_Report-1.pdf.

52. City of Philadelphia, Mayor's Advisory Commission on Construction Industry, *Report and Recommendations* (March 2009), 3.

53. An estimated 80 percent of Philadelphia-area construction jobs are held by residents outside of the city. (Philadelphia data from the 2000 US census was compiled by the Mayor's Advisory Commission on Construction Industry Diversity; see *Report and Recommendations* [March 2009], 37.) Of the remaining 20 percent, 15 percent of the jobs are held by Black workers for an aggregated 3 percent of the total and 2 percent are held by women for an aggregated .4 percent of the total. (Data generated by Jeana Ripple using data.census.gov [January 17, 2022], Bureau of Labor Statistics data, ASEC.)

54. In Philadelphia, 46 percent of Black households and 50 percent of Hispanic households are cost burdened by rent or mortgages. See Pew Charitable Trust, Philadelphia Research and Policy Project, "The State of Housing Affordability in Philadelphia" (September 10, 2020), https://pew.org/3bGxHkO; Stacy Elliott, Stacia M. West, and Amy B. Castro, "Rent Burden and Depression Among Mothers: An Analysis of Primary Caregiver Outcomes," *Journal of Policy Practice and Research* 2, no. 4 (2021): 1–16.

55. Ira Goldstein and William L. Yancey, "Public Housing Projects, Blacks, and Public Policy: The Historical Ecology of Public Housing in Philadelphia," in *Housing Desegregation and Federal Policy*, ed. John M. Goering (University of North Carolina Press, 1986), 266.

56. National Association of Home Builders, "The Economic Impact of Home Building in a Typical Local Area: Income, Jobs, and Taxes Generated," 2015.

57. Booker T. Washington, "The Negro and the Labor Unions," *The Atlantic*, June 1, 1913.

58. National Urban League, *Negro Membership in American Labor Unions* (Negro Universities Press, 1969), 19.

59. W. E. B. Du Bois, *The Black Man and the Unions*, ca. February 1918, Du Bois Papers (MS 312, p. 7), Special Collections and University Archives, University of Massachusetts Amherst Libraries.

60. Herbert Hill, *Black Labor and the American Legal System: Race, Work, and the Law* (University of Wisconsin Press, 1985), 96.

61. Hill, *Black Labor*, 97. Hill also references Robert C. Weaver and the federal government's attempts through the Public Works Administration to require racial diversity quotas on federal construction sites; see Robert C. Weaver, *Negro Labor: A National Problem* (Harcourt, Brace & Co, 1946). The PWA's trial-and-error approach was not effective in changing union practices or providing significant government employment opportunities, but it was likely important to the development of legal frameworks for the enforcement of nondiscrimination attempted through the Philadelphia Plan.

62. Hill, *Black Labor*, 255.

63. NAACP, *The Negro Wage-Earner*, 9.

64. Sugrue, "Affirmative Action from Below," 169.

65. National Urban League, *Negro Membership in American Labor Unions.*

66. Sylvia A. Law, "'Girls Can't Be Plumbers'—Affirmative Action for Women in Construction: Beyond Goals and Quotas" *Harvard Civil Rights–Civil Liberties Law Review* 24, no. 1 (1989): 45–78.

67. Claire McAnaw Gallagher, "The Construction Industry: Characteristics of the Employed, 2003–2020; Spotlight on Statistics," https://www.bls.gov/spotlight/2022/the-construction-industry-labor-force-2003-to-2020/home.htm.

68. Mayor's Advisory Commission on Construction Industry Diversity, *Report and Recommendations* (March 2009).

69. City of Philadelphia, Office of Economic Opportunity, https://www.phila.gov/departments/office-of-economic-opportunity.

70. Philip Shabecoff, "Blacks Making Few Gains in the Construction Trades," *New York Times*, June 27, 1971.

71. Philadelphia Commission on Human Relations, "Conclusions and Recommendations" (May 20, 1963).

72. *Building Barriers: A Report on Discrimination Against Women and People of Color in New York City's Construction Trades* (NYC Commission on Human Rights, 1993), 23.

73. "As Nation Fights Systemic Racism," *Chicago Sun-Times*, September 8, 2020.

74. Quoted in Whet Moser, "Rahm Emanuel, Trade-Union Racism, and the Burden of History," *Chicago Magazine*, October 4, 2012.

75. See Mayor's Advisory Commission on Construction Industry Diversity, *Report and Recommendations* (March 2009); "Annual Disparity Study: Fiscal Year 2018," City of

Philadelphia Office of Economic Opportunity, Department of Commerce; US Census Bureau QuickFacts: Philadelphia County, Pennsylvania.

76. See US Census Bureau, "About the Current Population Survey," census.gov; and Lawrence Mishel, "Diversity in the New York City Union and Nonunion Construction Sectors," Economic Policy Institute, 2017.

77. According to a recent Urban Institute survey report, even though the Supreme Court ruled that citizenship questions could not be included in the census, many non-citizens were reluctant to comply: "Nearly one-third of adults (31.6 percent) think it is extremely or very likely that answers to the census will be used to find people living in the US without documentation, and another third think it is somewhat likely, despite federal laws preventing this from occurring." See Michael Karpman, Stephen Zuckerman, and Dulce Gonzalez, "On Eve of 2020 Census, Many People in Hard-to-Count Groups Remain Concerned about Participating," Urban Institute (February 20, 2020), https://www.urban.org/research.

78. Center for American Progress, "Millions of Undocumented Immigrants Are Essential to America's Recovery, New Report Shows" (December 2, 2020), https://www.americanprogress.org.

79. Data cited in text from the ASEC, generated by Jeana Ripple using data.census.gov, March 16, 2021.

80. US Census Bureau QuickFacts: Philadelphia County, Pennsylvania, retrieved from census.gov (January 3, 2022).

81. Based on contemporary census demographic data (US Census Bureau, 2020), historical accounts of labor exclusion (Countryman, *Up South*, 64), and contemporary material data (Philadelphia Open Data, Philadelphia Properties and Assessment 2022), the demographics of construction labor can be extrapolated spatially across Philadelphia.

82. Sources include ASEC averages from 2014–2021, census demographic data for each city, and Bureau of Labor Statistics data. Data generated by Jeana Ripple using data.census.gov (January 17, 2022); US Census Bureau Quickfacts, 2021, retrieved from census.gov. Wage averages by trade and by city, Bureau of Labor Statistics, 2020–2030 Employment Projections, retrieved from bls.gov (January 17, 2022); EEO-1 data from the EEOC, retrieved from https://www.eeoc.gov/data/eeo-data-collections (January 17, 2022).

83. EEOC data report EEO-1 is "collected annually from private firms with 100 or more employees, firms with a federal contract with 50 or more employees, and those holding a contract with the federal government worth $50,000 or more," https://www.eeocdata.org.

84. Philadelphia data from the 2000 census was compiled by the Mayor's Advisory Commission on Construction Industry Diversity, *Report and Recommendations* (March 2009), 37.

85. Du Bois, "The Black Man and the Unions," February 1918, at Teaching American History, https://teachingamericanhistory.org.

86. Mimi Zeigler, "Remembering Whitney M. Young Jr.'s Landmark Speech," *Architect* magazine, May 8, 2018.

87. Philadelphia Commission on Human Relations, "Conclusions and Recommendations" (May 20, 1963).

88. Julian Gross, "CBAs: Definitions, Values, and Legal Enforceability," Partnership for Working Families, https://www.forworkingfamilies.org/resources/publications.

89. City of Detroit, "Community Benefits Ordinance," https://detroitmi.gov/departments/planning-and-development-department/design-and-development-innovation/community-benefits-ordinance.

90. Philanthropy Network Greater Philadelphia, "Rebuild Philadelphia" (January 16, 2018), https://philanthropynetwork.org/rebuild-philadelphia.

91. Mark Dent, "Philly's Union Diversity Problem," *Philadelphia Citizen*, May 31, 2018.

92. Dent, "Philly's Union Diversity Problem," *Philadelphia Citizen*, May 31, 2018.

93. Mayor's Advisory Commission on Construction Industry Diversity, *Report and Recommendations* (March 2009).

94. Max Bond and Paul Broches, "Social Content in Teaching and Design," *Journal of Architectural Education* 35, no. 1 (September 1981): 51–56.

95. Lance Hosey, "The Ethics of Brick," *Metropolis* magazine, June 1, 2005.

96. See US Census Bureau, "About the Current Population Survey," Census.gov; and Mishel, "Diversity in the New York City Construction Sectors," 2017.

97. *City of Richmond v. J. A. Croson Co., 488 U.S. 469*, 1988.

98. See the Philadelphia Office of Economic Opportunity Annual Disparity Studies, 2015–2020, https://www.phila.gov/documents/office-of-economic-opportunity-disparity-studies. Many cities, including Philadelphia, regulate, track, and report the participation of woman- and minority-owned businesses on public projects. However, very few track the diversity of the workers. This data remains difficult to find in most locations. Even Philadelphia's data is inconsistent in levels of detail across mayoral administrations, making progress comparisons or targeting of diverse contractors difficult.

Type V Tampa

1. *Central Avenue Remembered*, WEDU PBS, 2024, https://video.wedu.org/video/wedu-documentaries-central-avenue-remembered.

2. D. B. McKay, "Some Tampa 'Firsts' as Old Timers See Great Growth Here," *Tampa Tribune*, July 7, 1946.

3. Historians refer to the neighborhood surrounding Central Avenue as "Central Avenue," "The Central Avenue District," "The Scrub," or "The Scrubbs." For the sake of consistency, I will refer to the business and residential district bound by Central Avenue as Central Avenue or the Central Avenue neighborhood.

4. City Commission, *Charter and Ordinances of the City of Tampa Together with the Rules and Important Resolutions of the City Council* (1918), 98–100, 171.

5. Canter Brown and Larry Rivers, "'The Negroes Are There to Stay': The Development of Tampa's African-American Community, 1891–1916," *Sunland Tribune* 29, no. 1 (April 2018): article 6.

6. Brown and Rivers "Negroes Are There to Stay," 63.

7. Sanborn Map Co., *Insurance Maps of Florida* (1915) *Insurance Maps of Florida* (1931).

8. For the epigraph above, see Cheryl Rodriguez, "Recapturing Lost Images: Narratives of a Black Business Enclave," *Practicing Anthropology* 20, no. 1 (January 2010): 9; Brown and Rivers, "'Negroes Are There to Stay."

9. Brown and Rivers, "Negroes Are There to Stay."

10. David R. Goldfield, "Black Life in Old South Cities," in *Before Freedom Came: African-American Life in the Antebellum South*, ed. E. D. C. Campbell (University Press of Virginia, 1991), 138.

11. Goldfield describes the prevalence of free Black communities in wood-frame neighborhoods on the outskirts of the fire limits in southern cities: see "Black Life in Old South Cities," 138. In addition, see a discussion of the association between racial demographics, racialized imagery, and building material in Charlottesville, Virginia, during urban renewal in Kevan J. Klosterwill, Alissa Ujie Diamond, Barbara Brown Wilson, and Jeana Ripple, "Constructing Health: Representations of Health and Housing in Charlottesville's Urban Renewals," *Journal of Architectural Education* 74, no. 2 (July 2020): 222–236.

12. Brown and Rivers, "Negroes Arc There to Stay," 71.

13. Minnie Pearl Moore, "Personal Mention and Items of Interest," *Afro-American Monthly* 1 (November 1916): 14, quoted in Otis R. Anthony, "Black Tampa: The Roots of a People," Hillsborough County Museum, 1979, reprinted by the City of Tampa in 1989, 4.

14. Brown and Rivers, "Negroes Are There to Stay," 71.

15. Brown and Rivers, "Negroes Are There to Stay," 71.

16. Susan Greenbaum, "Central Avenue Legacies: African American Heritage in Tampa Florida," *Practicing Anthropology* 20, no. 1 (January 2010): 6.

17. Greenbaum, "Central Avenue Legacies," 67.

18. Hillsborough County Planning Commission, "The History of Discriminatory Planning in Hillsborough County: A Brief Summary of Some Key Political Parties, Policies, and Displacement Patterns from 1900–1964," https://planhillsborough.org/wp-content/uploads/2021/02/History-of-Racist-Planning.pdf.

19. Tampa City Commission, *Charter and Ordinances* (1918), 98–100, 171.

20. Committee on Fire Prevention and Engineering Standards, National Board of Fire Underwriters, *Report on the City of Tampa, Florida* (1927), 25–26, George W. Simons Jr. Planning Collection, Thomas G. Carpenter Library Special Collections, University of North Florida, Jacksonville (hereafter cited as Simmons Planning Collection, Carpenter Library, UNF).

21. See the first essay in this work for a discussion of redlining and racially limited lending patterns.

22. Arthur Franklin Raper, *A Study of Negro Life in Tampa: Made at the Request of the Tampa Welfare League, the Tampa Urban League and the Tampa Young Men's Christian Association* (1927), https://digitalcommons.usf.edu/regional_ebooks/38. Also referred to as the Raper Report or the Mays Report.

23. Raper Report (1927).

24. Raper Report (1927).

25. The changes in material and business occupancy can be seen by comparing Sanborn Map Co., *Insurance Maps of Florida* (1915) and *Insurance Maps of Florida* (1931).

26. Sanborn Map Co., *Insurance Maps of Florida* (1915 and 1931).

27. Sanborn Map Co., *Insurance Maps of Florida* (1915 and 1931).

28. Sanborn Map Co., *Insurance Maps of Florida* (1915 and 1931).

29. Brown and Rivers, "Negroes Are There to Stay," 63.

30. Brown and Rivers, "Negroes Are There to Stay," 63.

31. Translated from Sanborn Map Co., *Insurance Maps of Florida* (1915), with further detail derived from Burgert Brothers Photographic Collection of the Hillsborough County Public Library, https://hcplc.org/research/burgert.

32. See Sanborn Map Co., *Insurance Maps of Florida* (1915 and 1931).

33. Building codes preceded zoning ordinances in the early days of American urban construction. Edward Bassett, the author of New York City's 1916 zoning ordinances, argued for adopting early zoning policies to apply different rules in different districts. Bassett stated, "Uniform building laws do not bring about the orderly condition desired. They do not recognize that the heights of buildings which may be permitted in the intensively used parts of the city should not prevail in the suburbs. They do not recognize that stores which may be built on car-lined streets should not be built promiscuously among homes. . . . In other words, they apply uniformly over the entire city. The usefulness of zoning regulations consists in their being different in different districts." See Edward Murray Bassett, *Zoning* (National Municipal League, 1922), 318. Planning scholar Sonia Hirt claims American oversight of zoning regulation leads to the association between zoning and a particular view of social and economic spatial values. Hirt claims that "by regulating what gets built and where [zoning] sets the basic spatial parameters of where and thus *how* we live, work, play, socialize, and exercise our rights to citizenship." She argues that these rules define and perpetuate consensus on social and spatial relationships. See Sonia A. Hirt, *Zoned in the USA: The Origins and Implications of American Land-Use Regulation* (Cornell University Press, 2014), 3.

34. In 1961, Jane Jacobs famously described the necessary ingredients for urban diversity and vitality in her canonical book *The Death and Life of Great American Cities*.

She recognized that building variety was impactful, describing "the mingling of building ages and condition" as one of four critical ingredients, along with a dense concentration of people, short blocks, and multiple functions. Jacobs emphasized that buildings of various ages would "vary the economic yield [the buildings] must produce" and therefore encourage business variety. See *The Death and Life of Great American Cities* (Vintage, 1961), 194.

35. Much of the older fabric of New York that Jacobs examined was built of brick masonry by virtue of historical fire limit regulations. Additionally, the city had controlled the diversity and mix of building functions according to building materials for decades preceding Jacobs's work. By 1932, New York's building codes restricted occupancy based on the size and material of a building. For example, a civic, political, educational, religious, or recreational assembly space must be within a brick masonry building if it exceeded 5,000 square feet. Likewise, a business space larger than 7,500 square feet with no sprinklers that faced a single street must be within a brick masonry building.[1] New York's 1968 building codes continued to regulate occupancy classifications (residential, mercantile, assembly, etc.) based on size and material categories (combustible versus noncombustible).

36. ICC, "Occupancy Classification and Use," in *2021 IBC Code* (International Code Council, 2022).

37. There are fewer restrictions on live-work residential buildings with an "office" than on any other type of live-work occupancy mix. "Dwelling or sleeping units that include an office that is less than 10 percent of the area of the dwelling unit are permitted to be classified as dwelling units with accessory occupancies in accordance with 508.2." See §508.5, "Live-Work Units," *2021 IBC Code.*

38. Tampa City Commission, *Charter and Ordinances* (1918), 98–100, 171.

39. Raper Report (1927).

40. US Census Bureau, *Sixteenth Census of the United States: Housing* (Dept. of Commerce, Bureau of the Census, 1942), 463.

41. Committee on Fire Prevention and Engineering Standards, National Board of Fire Underwriters, *Report on the City of Tampa, Florida* (1927), 13, Simmons Planning Collection, Carpenter Library, UNF.

42. Raper Report (1927).

43. George D. Strayer, *Report of the Survey of the Schools of Tampa, Florida*, Made by the Institute of Educational Research Division of Field Studies Teacher's College, Columbia University (1926). Table 9 (p. 82) lists $35,428.17 dedicated to Black school buildings of a total $601,451 dedicated to school buildings across all schools. Table 10 (p. 123) lists expenditures per pupil, and table 11 (p. 125) lists teacher salaries. Simmons Planning Collection, Carpenter Library, UNF.

44. Strayer, *Report of the Survey of the Schools of Tampa*, 89.

45. Simons-Sheldrick Co., *Final Report of Comprehensive Plan City of Tampa, Florida* (1945), 93, Simmons Planning Collection, Carpenter Library, UNF.

46. Simons-Sheldrick, *Final Report of Comprehensive Plan City of Tampa*, 93.

47. George W. Simons, *Report on the City Plan of Tampa, Florida* (1951), 57, Simmons Planning Collection, Carpenter Library, UNF.

48. Housing Authority of City of Tampa, "Good and Bad Housing" (1951), 10, Simmons Planning Collection, Carpenter Library, UNF.

49. See Klosterwill, Diamond, Wilson, and Ripple, "Constructing Health," 222–236.

50. Tampa Housing Authority, "Good and Bad Housing," 1–10.

51. Tampa Housing Authority, "Good and Bad Housing," 7.

52. Rodriguez, "Recapturing Lost Images," 6.

53. US Census Bureau, *Sixteenth Census of the United States: Housing*, 120. The table lists 22,558 wood-frame homes out of 24,029 total; see "Residential Structures by Type and

by Exterior Material, and Dwelling Units by Conversion of Structure for Cities of 50,000 Inhabitants or More Housing."

54. *Grubstein v. Urban Renewal Agency of the City of Tampa*, 115 So.2d 745 (Fla. 1959).

55. Paul Guzzo, "Tampa Housing Authority Is Rebuilding a Historic Black Neighborhood," *Tampa Bay Times*, May 10, 2022.

56. A. R. Ragsdale to Mayor Nick Nuccio, 1958, Nick Nuccio Papers, Archives and Records Division, City of Tampa.

57. Travis R. Bell, "Documenting an Imperfect Past: Examining Tampa's Racial Integration Through Community, Film, and Remembrance of Central Avenue" (PhD diss., University of South Florida, 2017).

58. Robert W. Saunders to Mayor Nick Nuccio, April 15, 1958, Nick Nuccio Papers, Archives and Records Division, City of Tampa.

59. "ENCORE! Fact Sheet" (2019), https://encoretampa.com.

60. Jodi Pushkin and Sue Bedry, "50+ Years of Fair Housing: Past, Present and Future in the City of Tampa," *Tampa Bay Times*, 2019, 14.

61. As of 2024, Tampa's new Encore district is zoned as a Planned Development (PD) district, which allows office, residential, and zoning uses. See chapter 27, "Zoning and Land Development," *Code of Ordinances, Tampa* (2024), https://library.municode.com/fl/tampa/codes/code_of_ordinances?nodeId=10132.

62. Author interview with Brian Winterhalter on housing pressures and development influences in Northern Virginia, February 29, 2024; author interview with Mitch Crispell on low-income housing development in Virginia, February 13, 2024.

63. Marina Khoury, "Lean Urbanism Brief: Leaning Toward Live-Work Units," Working Paper, Project for Lean Urbanism, www.leanurbanism.org/research/; ICC, *2021 IBC Code*, §508.5, "Live-Work Units."

64. Sue Carlton, "Once Tampa Public Housing, Encore Is Fully Occupied. Where Are the Shops?," *Tampa Bay Times*, March 27, 2024.

65. "Encore Tampa Building Momentum," *Tampa Magazine*, March 23, 2023, https://tampamagazines.com/encore-tampa-building-momentum.

66. Calos Moreno, "Black Wall Street's Second Destruction," *Next City*, May 31, 2021, https://nextcity.org/features/black-wall-streets-second-destruction.

67. Klosterwill, Diamond, Wilson, and Ripple, "Constructing Health," 222–236.

Type V Seattle

1. Bill Yenne, "Boeing Wonderland: The Fake Cities on America's West Coast," *Warfare History Network* (Summer 2013), https://warfarehistory.com.

2. Yenne, "Boeing Wonderland."

3. Library of Congress, "Today in History—December 7, 1941," https://www.loc.gov/collections/today-in-history.

4. Jeffrey Karl Ochsner, *Shaping Seattle Architecture: A Historical Guide to the Architects*, 2nd ed. (University of Washington Press, 2017).

5. Donna Blankinship, "Architect Detlie Helped 'Hide' Boeing Plant," *Seattle Times*, December 5, 2005.

6. E. M. Gibson, *The Urbanization of the Strait of Georgia Region* (Environment Canada 1976), 5, quoted in Daniel E. Turbeville, "Cities of Kindling: Geographical Implications of the Urban Fire Hazard on the Pacific Northwest Coast Frontier, 1851–1920" (PhD diss., Simon Fraser University, 1985), 68.

7. King County Assessor, https://kingcounty.gov/en/dept/assessor. Single-family residential property designated as 80 percent or more brick or stone was considered masonry. Multifamily housing is classified according to construction type, referred to as building class within municipal data.

8. John Brinckerhoff Jackson, *Discovering the Vernacular Landscape* (Yale University Press, 1984), 67.

9. Mark Hinshaw describes a range of industry booms and busts over the last century and a half, beginning with logging, transitioning to the Boeing Corporation in the early twentieth century. Boeing's "bust" occurred in 1969, creating a regional recession after tens of thousands of layoffs. The 1980s brought the introduction of the technology economy that continues today, first with Microsoft and now Amazon headquarters. Several other corporate headquarters (e.g., Nordstrom, Starbucks, REI) are also located in today's Seattle. Mark L. Hinshaw, *Citistate Seattle: Shaping a Modern Metropolis* (American Planning Association, 1999).

10. Charles W. Smith et al., "Asa Shinn Mercer, Pioneer in Western Publicity," *Pacific Northwest Quarterly* 27, no. 4 (1936): 347–366.

11. Asa Shinn Mercer, *Washington Territory: The Great North-West; Her Material Resources and Claims to Emigration; A Plain Statement of Things as They Exist* (L. C. Childs, printer, 1865), 17.

12. Mercer, *Washington Territory*, 18.

13. Thomas Walter Pohl, "Seattle 1851–1861: A Frontier Community" (PhD diss., University of Washington, 1970).

14. Daniel J. Boorstin, *The Americans: The National Experience* (Knopf, 2010), 150.

15. Earl Pomeroy, "The Urban Frontier of the Far West," in *The Frontier Challenge: Responses to the Trans-Mississippi West*, ed. John Garretson Clark and George L. Anderson (University Press of Kansas, 1971).

16. Turbeville, "Cities of Kindling," 83.

17. Turbeville, "Cities of Kindling," 103.

18. Flora P. Engle, "The Story of the Mercer Expeditions," *Washington Historical Quarterly* 6, no. 4 (October 1915).

19. The women who traveled with Mercer are referred to as "Mercer Girls" or "Mercer Maids" in historical accounts. See Clarence B. Bagley, "The Mercer Immigration: Two Cargoes of Maidens for the Sound Country," *Quarterly of the Oregon Historical Society* 5, no. 1 (March 1904).

20. Jeffrey Karl Ochsner and Dennis Alan Andersen, *Distant Corner: Seattle Architects and the Legacy of H. H. Richardson* (University of Washington Press, 2003), 19.

21. 1884 Sanborn Fire Insurance Map from Seattle, King County, Washington, Sanborn Maps, Geography and Map Division, Library of Congress, https://www.loc.gov/item/sanborn09315_001.

22. Ochsner and Andersen, *Distant Corner*, 28–30.

23. Documentation of the Methodist Church can be found in the *Seattle Daily Post-Intelligencer*, August 19, 1882. Documentation of the Squire Building can be found in the same publication, issue dated September 27, 1883.

24. Ochsner and Andersen, *Distant Corner*, 19.

25. *Seattle Post-Intelligencer*, July 5, 1889.

26. "All buildings hereafter erected within the fire limits of the City of Seattle shall be made and constructed of brick or stone, and every building of brick or stone or of both that shall be newly roofed or covered, shall be constructed with side walls or party walls of brick or stone, or of both, and such side walls or party walls shall extend from the foundation to the top of and through the roof of the building, and said roof shall be covered with such material as will afford protection against fire, and said walls shall be so constructed as to separate all woodwork thoroughly and completely of the interior and exterior of such building from all and every part of the interior and exterior of any adjoining building; and every such side wall or party wall shall pass through the roof of the building to which it may pertain in each manner as to break entirely any communication of wood whatever between such roof and any

other building. And all partition walls shall also extend from the foundation, and through the roof, the same as side walls or party walls." *Seattle Post-Intelligencer*, July 5, 1889.

27. *Lawrence J. Gutter Collection of Chicagoana* (University of Illinois at Chicago); *Fire Ordinances of the City of Chicago: Laws, Etc.* (Published by the order of the Board of Public Works, 1872), https://archive.org/details/fireordinancesof00chic.

28. See Ochsner and Andersen, *Distant Corner*, 19, for a description of the "particular enmity between Seattle and Tacoma."

29. *Seattle Post-Intelligencer*, July 5, 1889.

30. Relatively tall buildings following the fire included Elmer H. Fisher's Burke Building at Front and Marion, built in 1889, and Stephen Meany's Occidental Hotel, built in 1889. "Report of Fire Commissioners," in *Seattle Municipal Reports for the Fiscal Year Ending December 31, 1891*, 187, cited in Ochsner and Andersen, *Distant Corner*, 68.

31. Turbeville, "Cities of Kindling," 109.

32. Turbeville, "Cities of Kindling," 125.

33. Arthur Armstrong Denny, *Pioneer Days on Puget Sound* (C. B. Bagley, 1888), 43.

34. Turbeville, "Cities of Kindling," 69.

35. J. B. Jackson, "The Westward-Moving House," *Landscape* 2, no. 3 (1953): 8–21.

36. Jackson, "Westward-Moving House."

37. Jacob A. Riis, *The Battle with the Slum* (Macmillan, 1902), 152.

38. John R. Stilgoe, *Common Landscape of America, 1580 to 1845* (Yale University Press, 1982), 160.

39. Solon Robinson, *Solon Robinson, Pioneer and Agriculturist: Selected Writings* (Indiana Historical Bureau, 1936), 555.

40. Earl Pomeroy, *The Pacific Slope* (University of Washington Press, 1965), 3, quoted in Turbeville, "Cities of Kindling," 67.

41. Earl Pomeroy, "The Urban Frontier of the Far West," in Clark and Anderson, *The Frontier Challenge*.

42. *Seattle Post-Intelligencer*, July 5, 1889.

43. Ochsner and Andersen, *Distant Corner*, 70.

44. The study was sponsored by Forintek Canada Corp., a publicly funded research and development corporation focused on forestry. Athena Institute, *Minnesota Demolition Survey: Phase Two Report* (2004), https://briscoman.com/sites/default/files/Athena_Demolition_Survey.pdf.

45. Examples include the American Society of Heating, Refrigerating, and Air-Conditioning Engineers, "ASHREA 90–1975 Energy Conservation in New Building Design" (1975), https://ashrae.iwrapper.com/ASHRAE_PREVIEW_ONLY_STANDARDS/STD_90_1975; Energy Policy Conservation Act, Public Law (United States) 94–163, 89 Stat. 871, enacted December 22, 1975, https://www.congress.gov/bill/94th-congress/senate-bill/622.

46. John Hogan, "Energy Codes and the Evolution of Fenestration: Twenty Years of NFRC Ratings in Seattle," *ASHRAE Transactions* 120, no. 2 (July 2014): 118–133.

47. Rep. John A. Yarmuth (D-KY-3), "H.R.5376–117th Congress (2021–2022): Inflation Reduction Act of 2022," Legislation, August 16, 2022, 2021-09-27, https://www.congress.gov/bill/117th-congress/house-bill/5376/text.

48. For example, building code scholar Aleksandra Jaeschke points out that terms such as "sustainable development" demonstrated an early stage of the capital market laying claim to the "greening" of architectural standards. See *The Greening of America's Building Codes: Promises and Paradoxes* (Princeton Architectural Press, 2022).

49. Stewart Brand, *How Buildings Learn: What Happens After They're Built* (Penguin, 1995), 23.

50. See John Habraken, *Supports: An Alternative to Mass Housing* (Architectural Press, 1972). See also Stichting Architecten Research (SAR), Next 21, in Osaka, or "the work

developed by Kenneth Frampton, Christopher Alexander or even (later) Avi Friedman point[ing] toward a similar or at least rival direction." H. Ferreira, L. da Silva, and V. Murtinho, "The Maison Dom-ino of Le Corbusier and the Supports of John Habraken: Differences and Similarities," in *Structures and Architecture: Beyond Their Limits*, ed. Paulo J. Cruz (CRC Press, 2016).

51. See Council on Open Buildings, https://councilonopenbuilding.org; see also Open-Building, https://www.openbuilding.co/network.

52. *Dezeen*, "Mies van Der Rohe Award 2017 Goes to NL Architects and XVW Architectuur," May 12, 2017, https://www.dezeen.com/awards.

53. *The Independent*, "Could 'Naked' Homes Solve the Housing Crisis?," December 17, 2017.

54. D. M. Abramson, *Obsolescence: An Architectural History* (University of Chicago Press, 2016), 152.

55. Ji Si Yoon, "Global Monitoring of Policies for Decarbonising Buildings: Multi-level Approach," https://www.wto.org/search.

56. Athena Institute, *Minnesota Demolition Survey: Phase Two Report*.

57. Athena Institute, *Minnesota Demolition Survey: Phase Two Report*.

58. Athena Institute, *Minnesota Demolition Survey: Phase Two Report*. It is notable that the study does not clarify the age of wood buildings in disrepair relative to the age of concrete or steel buildings in disrepair.

59. For discussion of depreciation rates, see Brand, *How Buildings Learn*, 84. Building-age statistics per city retrieved from each city's assessment data (see references in each chapter); national averages per United States, average year-built source: US Census Bureau, *American Housing Survey 2019*.

60. Type V average building age is 51 years. Types I–III average building age is 79 years, based on King County Department of Assessments: Assessments Data Download, March 2020, from https://info.kingcounty.gov/assessor/DataDownload/default.aspx; City of Seattle Open Data Portal, Demolition Permits (March 2020), https://data.seattle.gov/Permitting/Demolition-Permits/8tzw-eq3m.

61. K. Simonen, *Life Cycle Assessment* (Routledge, 2014).

62. While data collection from manufacturers is improving, today's databases still draw from varying sources and often lack sufficient location specificity (K. Simonen, B. X. Rodriguez, and C. D. Wolf, "Benchmarking the Embodied Carbon of Buildings," *Technology|Architecture + Design*, 1, no. 2 [2017]: 208–218.)

63. These calculations use a six-story building for each type, sized for an urban lot (25 ft. by 60 ft.) and standard selections for each construction type (based on IBC table 721.1) for material measurement and proportions of roofs, walls, and floors per square foot of occupiable floor area. ASHRAE standard 90.1 is used to normalize assemblies by required insulation averages. ICC, *2018 IBC Code and Commentary* (ICC Publications, 2018); Quartz: Open Data for a Healthier, More Sustainable Future (2015), http://quartzproject.org; ANSI/ASHRAE/IES Standard 90.1-2019—Energy Standard for Buildings Except Low-Rise Residential Buildings.

64. Because engineered timber is constructed from laminated layers and is often cross-laminated, it does not expand and contract like solid wood cross sections.

65. Alexandra Kleeman, "Use of Cross-laminated Timber May Rise in the U.S.," Reuters, August 25, 2022.

66. Mark Hinshaw, "The New 5 over 1 Seattle, Where 'Everything Looks the Same,'" *Archinect News*, April 28, 2015. Additional detail in follow-up emails, January 30, 2019.

67. Mark Hinshaw, "Re: Seattle's Code," email message to Edward Taylor and Jeana Ripple, April 13, 2019.

68. Seattle City Council Bills and Ordinances, Ordinance 108508, September 10, 1979, 64. Referenced in 1980 Seattle Municipal Codes, Title 22, Building and Construction Codes.

69. Hinshaw, "New 5 over 1 Seattle," *Archinect News*, and follow-up emails, January 30, 2019.

70. See Seattle City Council Bills and Ordinances, Ordinance 116012, December 20, 1991, 84, for an example of modified height limits for Type V residential construction.

71. In 2015, table 504.4 increased the number of allowable residential stories for Types III and Type V, both of which can be constructed from wood frame. Type III can be built up to five stories, wood-frame Type V up to four stories. ICC, *2015 IBC Code and Commentary* (ICC Publications, 2015).

72. US Census Bureau, MCD, "Characteristics of New Housing," https://www.census.gov/construction/chars/current.html.

73. On average, since data became available in 2009 and through 2022, 89 percent of rental multifamily buildings are wood-frame, while only 70 percent of buildings intended for unit purchases are wood-frame. US Census Bureau, MCD, "Characteristics of New Housing," https://www.census.gov/construction/chars/current.html.

74. Justin Fox, "Why America's New Apartment Buildings All Look the Same," *Bloomberg*, February 13, 2019.

75. See Mike Rosenberg, "Pace of Downtown Seattle Construction Back on the Rise," *Seattle Times*, September 6, 2018; Marco Santarelli, "Seattle Housing Market Forecast 2020: Rise in Demand," Norada Real Estate Investments, March 8, 2020.

76. See Mike Rosenberg and Angel Gonzalez, "Thanks to Amazon, Seattle Is Now America's Biggest Company Town," *Seattle Times*, August 23, 2017; and Monica Nichelsburg, "Amazon Surpasses Microsoft in Number of Seattle Region Employees amid Big Growth Plans Across US," *GeekWire*, September 9, 2019.

77. Estimates indicate that Amazon hired four men to every one woman in Seattle. See Kristen Clark, "Shocker: It's Mostly Men Moving to Seattle for Tech Jobs," *Crosscut*, January 16, 2018.

78. Jacobs, *Death and Life of Great American Cities*, quoted in Brand, *How Buildings Learn*, 85.

79. Jacobs, *Death and Life of Great American Cities*, quoted in Brand, *How Buildings Learn*, 85.

80. Interview with Stephen Karcha, developers' representative, on March 19, 2024.

81. Jacobs, *Death and Life of Great American Cities*, 260.

Conclusion

1. Table 504.3 specifies a sixty-foot height limit for Type V residential constructions equipped with sprinkler systems. This datum increases when the multistory wood frame is above a concrete podium. ICC, *2021 IBC Code and Commentary* (ICC Publications,).

2. Ji Si Yoon, "Global Monitoring of Policies for Decarbonising Buildings," https://www.wto.org/search.

3. Pomeroy, "Urban Frontier of the Far West," in Clark and Anderson, *The Frontier Challenge*.

4. Jacobs, *Death and Life of Great American Cities*, quoted in Brand, *How Buildings Learn*, 85.

5. Brand, *How Buildings Learn*.

6. Residential property characteristics data accessed from the Cook County Assessor (2020); NYC Open Data, Property Valuation and Assessment Data (2017), NYC Dept. of Finance; King County Department of Assessments: Assessments data download (March 2020), https://info.kingcounty.gov/assessor/DataDownload/default.aspx; US Census Bureau, *American Housing Survey 2019*, average year-built source.

7. Robinson Meyer, "Lumber Prices Are off the Rails Again: Blame Climate Change," *The Atlantic*, January 19, 2022.

8. See Clarisa Diaz, "North American Lumber Is Moving South," Quartz, October 28, 2022, https://qz.com/north-american-lumber-is-moving-south-1849699339. See also Meyer, "Lumber Prices," *The Atlantic*, January 19, 2022.

9. Diaz, "North American Lumber Moving South," Quartz, October 28, 2022; Nature Conservancy, "Tree-Killing Pests Across the United States Are Increasing the Threats of Climate Change," October 19, 2021, https://www.nature.org/en-us/newsroom/pests-pathogens-threats-forests-climate.

10. Diaz, "North American Lumber Moving South," Quartz, October 28, 2022.

11. David N. Bilow and Mahmoud E. Kamara, "Fire and Concrete Structures," in *Structures Congress 2008* (American Society of Civil Engineers, 2008), 1–10.

12. William Langer, "Aggregate Resource Availability in the Conterminous United States, Including Suggestions for Addressing Shortages, Quality, and Environmental Concerns," US Geological Survey, 2011.

13. The sources for plate 20 include W. H. Langer, "Natural Aggregates of the Conterminous United States," US Geological Survey, 2003; "Forest Resources of the United States," National Atlas of the United States of America; "The U.S. Has Been Warming Fast Since the First Earth Day," Climate Central, http://csi.climatecentral.org/, based on data from NOAA, "Climate at a Glance" report.

14. Ben-Joseph, *Code of the City*, xvi; Lawrence Busch, *Standards: Recipes for Reality* (MIT Press, 2011), 285; Moore and Wilson, *Questioning Architectural Judgment*, 49.

15. "Library Announces Digital Map Project" (December 1997), Library of Congress Information Bulletin, https://www.loc.gov/loc/lcib/9712/map.html.

16. US Census Bureau, American Housing Survey 2019; *Sixteenth Census of the United States, 1940, Housing:* Vol. 2, *General Characteristics* (Government Printing Office, 1943); *Census of Housing, 1950,* Vol. 1: *General Characteristics* (Government Printing Office, 1953).

17. US Census Bureau, Survey of Construction, 2020.

18. US Census Bureau, Census History Staff, "History—U.S. Census Bureau," https://www.census.gov/history.

19. Paul A. Longley, *Geographic Information Science and Systems*, 4th ed. (Wiley, 2015).

INDEX

Note: Page numbers in *italics* denote images and associated captions.